Why Can't Johnny Just Quit?

A Common Sense Guide to Understanding Addiction
(And how to finally win the war on drugs!)

By

Kyle Oh, M.D.

D1280370

Cover designed by Mya Emad

Dedication

∞

To all the patients
I have lost to this disease
And to their families

∞

And to all the lost souls out there
looking for a way
to end their enslavement
to this affliction

∞

And to all the children in the world
that they may learn
how not to fall victim
to this disease.

Acknowledgments

∞

To my patients
who have taught me over the years,
not only about addiction,
but also how to be a better physician.

∞

When it comes to addiction,
only by parsing together
the commonality of their stories,
was I able to see the forest for the trees.

∞

To all my mentors and colleagues
who have taught me
the art and science of medicine
over the years.

∞

To my editor,
Julia Denton,
whose insights and guidance helped me
bring this book together.

Table of Content

Introduction

SO WHY CAN'T JOHNNY JUST quit? This is a question family members often ask about their loved ones whom I have treated for addiction. To answer this question, one must understand what addiction is, why some people get hooked while most don't, and what happens in the brain as addiction sets in that makes those who are addicted follow such self-destructive behaviors that often baffle common sense. In this book, I will try to answer these questions about addiction and shed new light on this age-old problem that has haunted so many.

I wrote this book for three reasons:
- to redefine addiction in a way that finally makes sense of this often misunderstood subject
- by making sense of addiction, help those who suffer from this disease learn how to get it under control
- and by understanding addiction and why it happens to some, help prevent many others from getting hooked in the first place.

A mother of a patient I was treating for addiction once told me, with tears in her eyes, that her 18-year-old son had cost her everything, including her husband's wedding ring, which her son had sold to buy drugs. She just couldn't understand how he could do these things. She had paid for his inpatient and outpatient drug rehabilitations on multiple occasions, only to see him relapse back into his addiction time after time.

I could see the pain in her son's face as she told me this. He was deeply ashamed of the things he had done and

1

the pain he had caused his family. But even after all he had done, his mother didn't hate him; she just wanted him to stop, to get help, and become the man he once was before he got hooked. Too often, this is the story that I hear.

I am a doctor specializing in Physical Medicine and Rehabilitation. As part of my practice, I have seen my share of pain patients. I started out as a pain specialist, but over time, I became an addiction specialist as well—not by choice, but out of necessity. It may seem strange to some that a pain specialist would be interested in treating addiction. Unfortunately, as I have learned the hard way, if you are treating pain, you better understand addiction, because some of your patients will become addicted (if they are not already).

I finally came to understand addiction and ultimately started treating it in large part because of what happened to one of my patients early in my career.

In 1997, I lost a patient. It wasn't the first time someone had died under my care, nor would it be the last. But this was the first time I felt responsible. This was a patient I had been treating for about a year for his low back pain. For me, treating pain would never be the same.

Andy (all names have been changed to protect the patient's privacy) was a patient I first saw for an acute low back pain. His family doctor referred him to me. It turned out that he had a herniated disc. An MRI confirmed this. I did an epidural steroid injection (ESI), and his pain improved. He went through physical therapy and home exercise programs. The pain improved, but it never went away. Andy was eventually put on a low-dose, chronic opiate pain medication to help manage his pain. He was put on OxyContin 20 mg twice a day.

OxyContin was a fairly new drug at the time. It was first introduced in 1996 as a wonder drug. The danger of OxyContin and its addictive nature and abuse potential (for some) did not become public knowledge until much later. Had I known then what I know now about this drug, I would have never put patients on it.

One morning, I got a call from Andy's wife. Andy had apparently overdosed on OxyContin and died. I had no idea he had gotten hooked; he had shown no signs of addiction. He had never lost his prescriptions or asked for an early refill. He wasn't escalating his pain medications. To my knowledge, he wasn't getting any pain medication from any other doctor. He seemed like an ideal patient.

Andy's wife told me that he had been smoking the OxyContin for a while. Apparently, he would save up his OxyContin so he could get high on weekends. I would later learn that this meant he was in the early stage of his addiction. On that particular weekend, he did one too many, and it killed him. She told me she had known about his problem, but had felt helpless to stop him. She wasn't blaming me—she just wanted me to know what had happened.

After I gave Andy's wife my deepest condolences and hung up the phone, I felt sick to my stomach. I felt like someone had punched me in my gut. I felt guilty that I had somehow contributed to his death, and at the same time I felt angry that he would betray my trust and do this to himself (yes, I felt angry at Andy!).

Everything I thought I knew about addiction flew out the window that day. Guilt can be a powerful motivator—so can anger. At an appropriate level, both guilt and anger can motivate you to act, to learn from your mistakes, and help you make a change for the better. However, at other times, these emotions can make you lash out. They can make you feel defensive. Instead of learning from your mistakes, you may become more entrenched in your own belief system and feel forced to defend them tooth and nail, even when there is evidence to the contrary.

For me, my guilt and anger made me want to learn as much as I could about this disease. I admitted that I had failed Andy, but I would be damned if I was about to let this happen again. By admitting that I had no idea what had happened or why, I let myself open my mind to try to understand what was going on around me, and this helped me ask the right question. The right question was, "How did the drug make you feel?"

Over the years, the more I learned about addiction, the more I realized how much misinformation is out there, both in the public as well as within the medical community. Even among those who have gotten hooked on one drug or another, these misconceptions are prevalent. I read many books on addiction. The more I read, the more I realized the story was incomplete. However, when I finally started understanding addiction, everything started to make sense. Like most things, once you understand something, the answer is rather simple.

Everything I have learned about addiction over the years came from talking to my patients (from asking the right questions and listening to them without judging them) and from reading as much as I could about addiction. By parsing together the commonalities of their stories, I was able to make out the forest for the trees.

It still amazes me that many who suffer from this affliction don't understand this beast themselves. They know of the drug's allure and the powerful grip it has on them, but they often fail to understand how they got there. Over the years, I came to understand their struggles and their deep desire to free themselves from this deadly choke-hold around their souls. Over time, I came to understand why they fell victim to its allure and the reasons behind (what at times seems to be) an insurmountable difficulty in climbing out of the depth of their addiction, and why it is a lifelong struggle not to fall victim to it again.

Until now, when it comes to addiction, all the focus has been on treatment. Alcoholics Anonymous (AA) and Narcotics Anonymous (NA) focus on the path to recovery and stopping relapses. The same is true with drug rehab programs. However, they do not address prevention. Our only national attempt at prevention has been the "Say No to

Drugs" campaign, which has been a dismal failure. This campaign's focus is fear. It says anyone who tries these drugs will get hooked, which is not true, and that everyone's response to drugs is the same, which is also not true.

It is my belief that the only way we can help prevent others from getting hooked is by educating them about why some people get hooked and what the early warning signs are that one may be susceptible to getting hooked. It is my experience that, when a person understands these points, he can often prevent himself from getting hooked in the first place. I have had a number of patients tell me that they should stop their pain pills as their pain started to subside because the pills were starting to make them "feel too good." Yes, once one understands why addiction happens and knows the early warning signs that he is susceptible to getting hooked, he can prevent himself from getting hooked.

Unlike the "Say No to Drugs" campaign, we need to educate the public about this new way of looking at addiction, and armed with this knowledge we can help many from falling victim to this disease in the first place. So far, our focus has been on treatment rather than prevention. But we know that "an ounce of prevention is worth a pound of cure." Yes, knowledge is power, and it can change the world. With a true understanding of addiction, we can finally win the war on drugs.

Why Can't Johnny Just Quit?

Chapter 1 Addiction

THERE ARE MANY REASONS WHY addiction is so misunderstood. There are many myths and misconceptions about addiction. There is a saying in medicine, "The more there is written about something, the less we really understand it." There are volumes written about addiction, with many contradicting each other, but once you understand something, the truth is quite simple.

The Current Definition of Addiction

Before we can have an intelligent conversation about addiction, we must first define it. Although there are many ways addiction is defined, the best current definition of addiction is probably the following one. Addiction is defined as "a continued behavior in spite of knowing that such continued behavior will harm oneself." It is characterized by "the lack of self-control and feeling of helplessness in spite of such knowledge." Unfortunately, this describes addiction once it takes hold, but it does not explain why addiction happens. Once we finally understand addiction, we will have a better definition of addiction at the conclusion of this book.

The Current Theory on Addiction

The most commonly accepted theory on addiction is that addiction is a maladjusted coping mechanism for dealing with underlying psychological ills in one's life; the feeling of helplessness or hopelessness and depression/anxiety leads some to seek solace from a drug and thus they become addicted. The current treatment of addiction is based on this premise. If you treat the person's underlying psychological problem(s), then you can treat the addiction. They ask an addict what led him to become addicted. By this, they are asking whether the person was sexually abused as a child, neglected, had a bad childhood, or came from a broken home that made him feel the need to turn to drugs.

The above theory may seem to offer hope; an addict can be treated for his psychological ills and be cured of his addiction. However, this theory misses the mark because it confuses abuse with addiction. Not everyone who abuses drugs to find solace for their depression or anxiety becomes addicted, and not everyone who becomes addicted is trying to find solace from a drug. The above theory gives rise to many misconceptions about addiction, and complicates this topic. If the current approach to addiction worked, we wouldn't have an addiction epidemic, and I wouldn't be proposing a new way of looking at this age-old problem.

The Current Model of Addiction as a Set of Behaviors

Currently, the medical community diagnoses addiction as a set of behaviors, such as forging prescriptions, doctor shopping, escalation of drug use, or multiple DUIs. Because only the behavior is used to diagnose and explain addiction, it is as if four blind men are describing an elephant from the parts they feel. Using behaviors to explain addiction is like using a circular argument to prove a point. Those who "drink too much and suffer the consequences of too much drinking must be addicted, and because they are addicted, they drink too much"—so goes this logic.

Without understanding why such behaviors develop, you can only diagnose addiction as a set of behaviors. The current treatment of addiction believes that depression and other mental illnesses are the reasons behind any addiction, and once the patient figures this out, he can be cured of his addiction. However, there is a problem with this approach. Although for some, when the depression is dealt with or a psychological wound heals, their behaviors may change, for others, they don't.

Ten Common Myths and Misconceptions about Addiction

The literature is full of instances where addiction is equated with physical dependence and tolerance. It insists that physical dependence is a necessary part of addiction. Abuse is often equated with addiction itself. The reason someone abuses drugs, such as depression or anxiety, is often confused with the cause of addiction. Behaviors are used to define this disease rather than trying to understand the true reason behind such behaviors. Let me debunk some of these myths and misconceptions.

1. Addiction is a myth

As incredulous as it may sound to those who got hooked, there are many who have written that heroin and cocaine are not addictive. They cite their own experiences as well as those of others who have used these drugs recreationally but did not get hooked. Sigmund Freud used cocaine recreationally and wrote about its wondrous benefits.[1] He wrote how cocaine helped him concentrate and be more productive. He insisted that cocaine is not addictive. What he failed to realize is that although it was not addictive for him, it is addictive for others.

Those who became addicted to these drugs will strongly disagree. Such differences of opinion exist because each group fails to see that others may experience these drugs differently. The truth is most people are not susceptible to most drugs, but a percentage of people are susceptible to different drugs, and for them, these drugs are quite addictive. And once they are addicted, the grip of their addiction can be quite strong.

On the opposite end of the spectrum, there are those who argue that anyone can get hooked, and that everyone gets extremely euphoric on these drugs. Therefore, they see addiction not as a disease, but rather a personal choice and failing. Once again, such misconceptions arise from the failure to understand that most people do not find these drugs highly euphoric. They ask, "How can this be true?" They fail to see that other people's experiences can be quite different from their own. Only when they ask others about their experiences with these drugs and hear how others had quite different experiences from their own will they begin to understand.

2. *High is anything that alters your mind*

One of the reasons why addiction is so misunderstood is because of how the high has always been portrayed on TV and the movie screen. The person who is high looks inebriated, intoxicated, and half falling asleep, with a silly grin on his face. Unfortunately, this image is wrong! The emotion of happiness and sedation are mutually exclusive. Because the media don't understand what the true high is, they juxtapose these two emotions together. The high that produced the happy grin can be followed by the aftermath of the high that produces the sedation, but they do not occur at the same time.

The reason why we call illicit drugs *dope* is because most people think that's what these drugs do—make you dopey. Most people associate any altered state of mind as being high. They think that becoming intoxicated or sedated from a drug or feeling mild euphoria is getting high, but this is not what those who got hooked on these drugs are talking about. Those who got hooked often describe their high as a heightened sense of awareness, increased energy, like being ten feet tall, feeling invincible, and most people often describe it as an intense orgasmic experience. This is true, at least at first.

Many patients who got addicted to their drugs describe their initial reaction to their drugs as an incredibly enjoyable experience that was stimulating and energizing rather than sedating. While for most people, sedation is the predominant sensation from opiates, alcohol, and pot, for those who got hooked, their initial response was that of

10

stimulation, and the sedation set in at a much higher dose and only as the high faded.

Someone who becomes highly excited and talkative and becomes the life of the party after a drink or two is the one who is experiencing the true high from the alcohol. Someone who is getting high on opiates or pot will tell you that they share this common experience.

The true high is anything that artificially makes you happy. The true high produces the same chemical reaction in your brain as sex! It releases dopamine, the feel-good neurotransmitter. Drugs just do it much more quickly and powerfully than sex, at least for those who are susceptible. Just like during sex, when someone is getting high, there is no sedation or calming effect, only excitement and euphoria. For the rest of us, there is only sedation (from downers) or stimulation (from uppers) at first, without any euphoria.

3. *Pot is a gateway drug*

Pot is not an opiate. Its active ingredient is tetrahydrocannabinol (THC); it's a central nervous system (CNS) depressant derived from the cannabis plant. More than 40% of Americans have admitted to having tried pot.[2] If pot is a gateway drug, the incidence of addiction would be close to 40%, and we know that's not true. Most people who smoke pot think that they get high, but in fact most people just get intoxicated—not high. Once again, the high is not a dopey feeling, but intense euphoria. I will show in my Addiction Overlap chapter that even among my addiction patients, only about 15% of them could get high on pot. However, the argument that pot is not addictive is also wrong. Those who do get a *true* high from pot can get addicted.

4. *Some drugs are so addictive that anyone would get hooked*

Even drugs like heroin or crystal meth are not addictive to most people. Heroin belongs in the same class as most opiate pain medications. If you can get hooked on heroin, you can get hooked on most pain medications. Some opiate pain medications are stronger than heroin. Morphine is the same strength as heroin. On the other hand, oxycodone is twice as strong, and Dilaudid is four times stronger. If everyone were susceptible to heroin, then everyone would be susceptible to getting hooked on opiate pain medications. If this were true, we wouldn't be using opiates to treat pain; it would be too dangerous.

Even crystal meth is not addictive to everyone. Once again, in my Addiction Overlap chapter, I will show that even among my opiate addiction patients, only about a third could get high on crystal meth. The rest could not, and hated their experience with it. My Addiction Overlap chapter will also show that every drug has a different genetic basis.

5. *Some drugs are so addictive that you are hooked the first time you try them*

In order to understand why you can't get hooked on any drug after just one try or even a few tries, you must understand how addiction happens. Addiction only happens when a pleasure spot in the brain (of those who are susceptible to that drug) is overstimulated repeatedly that, over time, the drug rewires the brain.[3] It is only with repeated overstimulation of the pleasure center that such rewiring occurs.

6. *Physical dependence is addiction*

Most people confuse physical dependence with addiction. Most people think that anyone who smokes cigarettes on a daily basis for years must be addicted to cigarettes. However, physical dependence is not addiction! Going through physical withdrawal does not necessarily mean that you got addicted! Physical dependence is defined by the physical withdrawal symptoms one experiences when the drug is taken away too quickly. It happens with any chronic opiate or alcohol use. Other drugs, such as benzodiazepines

(Valium, Xanax, etc.) and barbiturates, also cause physical withdrawal symptoms. So do nicotine and caffeine. Everyone who is exposed to these drugs for a prolonged period will become physically dependent on them. However, only an unlucky few will become addicted to them. Addiction is much more than just physical dependence, and just being physically dependent on something does not make you addicted to it.

A person who is not addicted will go through physical withdrawal, but will not suffer from the craving that makes those who are addicted feel like they have to go right back to using it again. For those who are truly addicted, physical withdrawal is only the beginning of their hell and not the end, and ultimately the least of their problems (although most do not understand this at the time that they are going through the withdrawal). Addiction is psychological and happens when the drug rewires the brain after repeated overstimulation of the pleasure spot.

7. *Physical dependence is necessary for addiction*

Unfortunately, most physicians and even some addiction specialists believe that physical dependence is always present in addiction. I beg to differ. Some addictions do not have any discernible physical withdrawal symptoms. Yet, they elicit overpowering cravings. Prior to the 1980s, some argued that because cocaine does not cause any physical withdrawal symptoms, it can't be addictive. However, the crack cocaine epidemic of the 1980s changed how we view cocaine. Yes, it is addictive (for some).

Because there is no physical withdrawal from pot either, many people still insist that pot is not addictive. However, I have many patients who did get addicted to pot who would vehemently argue against this notion. The argument that we should legalize pot for general consumption is based in part on the misconception that pot is not addictive.

We consider sex addiction and gambling addiction to be true addictions, yet there are no physical withdrawal symptoms associated with these addictions either. However, the powerful grip of their addictive potential for some is not disputed. Some seem to experience extreme euphoria from their stimuli. They also seem to have overwhelming cravings for them.

If we define sex addiction and gambling addiction as true addictions, then we must acknowledge that the physical dependence and withdrawal symptoms that come with it are not necessary components of all addictions. A common denominator to all addictions is not physical dependence, but rather powerful euphoria and the subsequent cravings the euphoria generates.

8. *Abuse is addiction*

Abuse is not addiction, at least not all of the time. Because only the behavior has been used to diagnose addiction, we have confused abuse with addiction. No one ever asks an addict, "How did the drug make you feel?" I have read many books on addiction and have attended many seminars on addiction, and this question never comes up. However, abuse is just a behavior and does not explain the reason behind the behavior. Because we have failed to ask the right question, so many misconceptions about addiction exist, and why addiction has become such a difficult subject to understand. Throughout this book, I will show the true reason behind any addiction and a better way of understanding addiction, and will explain the difference between abuse and addiction.

9. *Myths about the addictive personality*

The theory behind the addictive personality is that there are personality or psychological traits that make a person more susceptible to addiction. Such traits include attention deficit disorder/attention deficit hyperactivity disorder (ADD/ADHD), obsessive-compulsive disorder (OCD), impulsivity, low self-esteem, depression, anxiety, perfectionism, and poor coping skills.[4] Once again, such misunderstanding exists because we confuse abuse with addiction and because we have always looked only at behavior to diagnose addiction.

Another myth about addiction that goes along with the addictive personality theory is that "a drug is a drug is a drug." If you can abuse a drug to self-medicate yourself to treat an underlying emotional problem, then you can abuse any drug to do the same, according to this theory. Unfortunately, once again, such misconception exists because only the behavior is being used to diagnose addiction.

As my data in the Addiction Overlap chapter will show, although some people may be vulnerable to multiple drugs, most are not vulnerable to all drugs. Yes, once someone gets addicted to one drug, he may try to recapture that initial high by experimenting with other (often more powerful) drugs, but it does not necessarily mean that he will become addicted to all of them. You are only vulnerable to those drugs that make you highly euphoric.

The term "addictive personality" implies that there is a personality trait that makes a person more likely to become addicted. It blames the victim; they got hooked because of a defect in their personality. In my opinion, there is no such thing. I have had parents tell me that one child was a good child, a smart one, and they thought that he would never get hooked, whereas another one was always a sort of troublemaker and they were worried that he may get hooked. However, in the end, it was the "good" child who got hooked.

Unfortunately, there is no litmus test when it comes to who is susceptible or not. There is no personality trait that predicts who may get hooked. The only thing that predicts whether a person is susceptible to a drug or not is one's genetics. The only way you will know whether you are susceptible to a drug is by the way the drug makes you feel.

I see all types of patients fall victim to one addiction or another. Addiction does not discriminate. It crosses all ages, sexes, races, and socioeconomic classes. Most addicts have no common personality trait that may have predicted that they may be susceptible to a given drug. The only common denominator is their family history of addiction to that drug.

10. *Mental illness leads to addiction*

Many studies show that there is a higher incidence of alcoholism and drug abuse among the mentally ill. Many cite such studies to say that mental illness, including bipolar disorder and ADD/ADHD, increase someone's risk of becoming addicted. In fact, most clinical tools designed to help clinicians predict which patients are at a high risk of becoming addicted use both the family as well as the patient's history of mental illness to put such patients in the high-risk category. I must disagree.

Without understanding the true reason behind any addiction, such misconceptions are easy to make. Such coincidences just point out that more people with mental illnesses are likely to have tried these drugs, and thus a higher number of them got addicted. However, this does not prove a cause and effect.

The medical community still classifies all addictions under the psychiatric DSM-IV (Diagnostic and Statistical Manual of Mental Disorders) classification. Yes, the medical community classifies all addictions as a mental disorder. This needs to change.

Studies show that once addiction takes hold, depression and other mental illnesses often set in. A Duke University study showed that the incidence of mental illness in a given population does not change over time unless addiction or post-traumatic stress disorder (PTSD) take hold.[5] Most people who got hooked were as well-adjusted as anyone else before they became addicted. However, after their addiction takes root, their lives fall apart and they become poster children for the mentally ill.

Some will use depression or stresses in their lives to explain why they got addicted. However, since not everyone who abuses drugs to deal with his underlying psychological ills gets hooked, one must understand that such circumstances do not explain why addiction takes place. The common denominator is not their circumstances, but how they reacted to their drug in the first place.

I am not saying that those with a history of sexual abuse or some deep psychological trauma, or those who suffer from anxiety and depression, are not more likely to suffer from addiction (or pain, for that matter). Of course they are. The mind cannot be separated from the body. For those who are dealing with deep emotional scars or anxiety and depression, turning to drugs may have offered them temporary solace. Many may abuse drugs, but not all will get addicted.

For those who do become addicted while trying to find solace for their emotional trauma or pain, dealing with their addiction is doubly difficult because you must first help them deal with their emotional problems before the addiction can be brought under control. Sometimes, the drug may seem like the only escape that they have. Until you help them address the underlying emotional issue and teach them a way to heal that wound or break the grip of anxiety/depression, it is often difficult to treat their addiction. But, sometimes, just helping patients realize that the root of their addiction (or pain in some cases) is their deep emotional pain or anxiety can be a step in the right direction.

What One Fails to Understand, One Tends to Ignore

Because most people, including physicians and family members, do not understand addiction, when they are confronted with someone who is addicted, they tend to choose not to see the problem or to try to ignore it at first, hoping that it will just go away. Like most problems in life, pretending it does not exist usually makes the matter worse over time. Many people may even find it easier just to enable the victim rather than confront them. After all, when it comes to opiate addiction, in many instances, we are dealing with addiction to prescription medications.

Many physicians choose not to see the signs of addiction in their patients, or if they see the signs, most will rush to discharge the patient. For most physicians, I believe it is easier to give in to the patient's demands and give him what he wants rather than trying to delve too deep beneath the surface. Unfortunately, most physicians lack the training to deal with this issue. In turn, many patients as well as their families may think, "Hey, how bad can it be if it's being prescribed by a doctor?"

With better understanding, we can recognize the problem earlier and treat it before it causes irreparable damage. By that, I do not mean financial ruin or imprisonment. As bad as they may be, the ultimate price many addicts pay is with their lives.

Withdrawal Symptoms

We have always looked at withdrawal symptoms only as physical ones. The literature and the mass media have portrayed this aspect of withdrawal well. Who has not read or seen depictions of an addict going through physical withdrawal, having the shakes, delirium, nausea, sweating, and shivering? However, withdrawal for those who are truly addicted is more than just physical. This is less well written about and even less well understood. It is my opinion that, for those who are addicted, physical withdrawal symptoms are often followed by psychological ones.

Withdrawal symptoms should be divided into the physical and the psychological stages. The physical stage happens to everyone who has been using the drug for a while, whereas the psychological stage only happens to those who become addicted to it.

Physical

For opiates, physical withdrawal consists of agitation, shakes, profuse sweating, nausea and vomiting, elevated blood pressure, increased pulse, feelings of doom, dilated pupils, flu-like symptoms, diarrhea, runny nose, goose bumps, and pain (the degree to which may vary depending on whether the patient is addicted or not).

Delirium tremens (DTs), a term used to describe withdrawal from alcohol, benzodiazepines (commonly called benzos), and barbiturates, have all of the above withdrawal symptoms, but, in severe cases, they also have other unique features, such as visual, tactile, and auditory hallucinations, and they can also result in seizures, which makes them potentially fatal. Patients will not only complain of spiders crawling on their skin, but they will also have visual hallucinations of the spiders. The joke about the pink elephant is no joke!

Physical withdrawal usually happens about 24 hours after the active ingredient of the drug has stopped working, and it lasts about seven to ten days. Physical withdrawal symptoms happen to anyone who has been on opiates or alcohol for a long time.

Psychological

For those who are hooked on opiates or alcohol, physical withdrawal is often followed by psychological withdrawal. This consists of lethargy and somnolence. One has no energy, is constantly yawning, feels tired, and can't get up in the morning. The person is not depressed; it is as if these drugs had given them the kick they needed to get up and get going (remember that alcoholics often need a drink in the morning as an eye-opener). This stage lasts much longer than the physical one—usually weeks, if not months.

Unfortunately, the literature is full of instances in which both physical and psychological withdrawal symptoms are lumped together. Thus, we see agitation and anxiety listed with yawning and lethargy as part of the physical withdrawal symptoms. These two groups of symptoms are mutually exclusive. Such misconceptions give the public the impression that we don't really know what we are talking about. It only makes sense when you understand that they are different stages of withdrawal and that one follows the other. Of course, one must remember that only those who get addicted go through the psychological phase of the withdrawal.

The True High

The true high is never dopey, intoxicating, or mind-altering (at first). The true high is anything that artificially makes you happy. All highs produce the same chemical reaction in your brain as sex! It releases dopamine, the feel-good neurotransmitter. The drugs just do it much more quickly and intensely. Just like sex, when someone is getting high, there is no sedation or calming effect, only excitement and euphoria. Someone who is getting high on his drug becomes more excited and stimulated at first.

The Aftermath of the High

A reason why most people confuse getting high with the state of intoxication that can follow (for downers) is because one can see the aftermath of their high, but they can't see the initial ecstasy they were experiencing. Because no one asks them, "How did the drug make you feel?" we do not hear about the euphoria they were chasing. But because we can see the aftermath of their high, we confuse it with the high. An alcoholic will eventually get drunk and slur his speech, with a half-awake look on his face. An opiate addict will also become intoxicated by his drug, and sedation will eventually follow at a high enough dose.

Unfortunately, the state of intoxication that follows is often portrayed by the mass media as being "stoned." Who hasn't seen Cheech and Chong or Harold and Kumar acting foolish and intoxicated while being doped on pot? They were just acting the part, without truly understanding the role.

For those who are truly getting high on their drug, the aftermath of intoxication that follows is usually much stronger than what the average person experiences. The higher the high, the more likely it is that the person will chase the euphoric feeling. The dose he uses will be greater, and the subsequent intoxication that follows will be much stronger. For those for whom there is no extreme euphoria, but only sedation, there is no reason to chase that feeling. For those who are truly getting high, the higher the high, the lower the subsequent lows.

If you have ever seen a heroin addict shoot up (online), you will see his eyelids flutter and his eyes roll backward. This is the orgasmic experience that he is chasing. However, this can be quickly followed by extreme sedation as the power of the drug overwhelms him. One minute he could be on top of the world, and the next he can hardly keep his eyes open as the drug shuts down his brain. At a high enough dose, an addict can stop breathing, overdose, and die. Because the central nervous system (CNS) depression can happen fairly quickly and because the media has done a good job portraying this aspect of addiction, many confuse this as the high and not the initial ecstasy that he was chasing.

How Did the Drug Make You Feel (at First)?

As physicians, we wouldn't ask our patients whether they think they are addicted or not, because the question carries negative connotations and is pejorative. Instead, what we should be asking our patients is, "How did the drug make you feel?"

Because we are not taught to understand that differences may exist in how one person responds to an opiate pain medication versus another, this is not an intuitive line of thinking. Most people are taught to believe that everyone must experience the same thing they do. Most of the time, this is correct. However, when you ask this simple question about how a person reacted to opiate pain medications, the answers you get are profoundly different from those who got hooked versus those who did not.

This simple question is not offensive and is non-judgmental. It allows patients to share their own experiences with us. This simple question can allow us to see if the patient may be at risk of becoming addicted. Only by asking people how the drug made them feel at first can we understand that there is a fundamental difference in how some respond to the drug versus what most others feel. For most physicians as well as most patients, this important insight is lost. However, when we understand that there is a profound difference in how one reacts to these drugs (namely the extreme euphoria), and that this difference is the reason why some get hooked on these drugs while most do not, it makes all the sense in the world. For some, this concept may seem too simplistic, and thus, they think it can't be true.

This simple question should also be asked when it comes to other addictions. As my data will later show, every drug has a different genetic basis. Only when we understand that different people can have night-and-day different reactions to different drugs can we truly understand the real reason behind any addiction.

Most people will readily acknowledge that some people seem to enjoy alcohol much more than they do (because they have seen it), but they fail to grasp that such differences may also exist with other drugs as well. In part, the fault lies with the mass media. The other half of the blame falls on the fact that most of us do see the world through the prism of our own experience.

When someone tells you that a drug, whether it is alcohol, pot, or opiates, makes him feel like a million bucks, while most others tell you that the same drug just makes them mellow or sedated, only then can you finally understand the appeal the drug has on that person. Only then can we truly understand addiction. Only then can we look at addiction as what is going on inside the person's brain and not just as a set of behaviors. Behaviors can be misinterpreted. When you understand what is going on inside the person's head, you can better interpret his actions.

I have been asking my patients this simple question. I have asked this of my pain patients as well as those whom I have treated for addiction. The answers I got surprised me at first. However, it helped shed light on why some got hooked while others didn't.

Unfortunately, when a person chases such a highly euphoric feeling, the trap is that eventually he becomes enslaved by it. Eventually, the desire becomes a need. A need becomes an all-consuming force that overpowers all other needs and reason. Then, the behavior we call addiction kicks in. In order to fully understand the final outcome of addiction, we must first understand this fundamental difference in how a drug affects the person's brain to understand why it happens.

Because the sense of euphoria fades over time, it is important to ask, "How did the drug make you feel early on?" rather than "How does the drug make you feel now?" Once truly hooked, most addicts are using their drugs just to feel "normal" or just to survive more often than to get high.

Addiction Is Psychological (Not Physical)

Addiction only happens when the pleasure center (the mesolimbic reward center) of the brain has been overstimulated to the point where one can't seem to live without the drug or that stimulation. We now understand that there is more than one pleasure pathway in the brain. However, all highs trigger one or more of these pleasure centers in the brain to a point of such euphoria that such experiences are sought after, and if this is repeated, after a while, the craving sets in. Without the craving, there is no addiction. Without the extreme euphoria and the subsequent overstimulation of the pleasure spot, there is no craving.

Over time, chasing such a pleasurable stimulus will change that person's brain and rewire it. There is scientific evidence that shows the number of dopamine receptors increases over time with the repeated overstimulation of these pleasure spots.[6] At the same time, one's ability to produce his own endorphins (the natural feel-good neurotransmitter) diminishes.[7] This double-whammy effect seems to be the reason for the craving as well as the ultimate reason for its own downfall. What made you extremely happy at first eventually takes away the happiness. The overwhelming craving, which is the true hallmark of any addiction, only happens to those who are addicted to it and not just physically dependent on it.

Think of this craving as that overwhelming desire for

something that cannot be reasoned with and must be quenched at all cost, regardless of the consequences. Think of it as a need greater than the desire for life itself. Those who are truly addicted exhibit such behavior.

Dopamine and the Mesolimbic Pathway

Dopamine is the feel-good-neurotransmitter.[8] It is one of the key neurotransmitters in the brain responsible for the reward system that produces feelings of well-being, contentment, and euphoria at different levels. It is an integral part of our life. It is the engine behind the reward system. What makes us happy and content makes us want to keep repeating such experiences. It is this reward system that makes us eat, engage in social activities, including sex, and it prompts us to seek out new pleasurable experiences. We would not survive as a species without it.

A lack of dopamine in the brain is associated with such diseases as Parkinson's, where one of the hallmarks of the disease is that it robs the person's ability to experience joy and creates a lack of emotional response to day-to-day stimuli. On the other hand, with schizophrenics, there is too much dopamine. For them, the excess dopamine is thought to be responsible for their feelings of paranoia and anxiety.

Even in a normal person, the administration of a high dose of dopamine can produce anxiety and paranoia. Dopamine is a vasopressor, a drug that elevates blood pressure by constricting blood vessels. Dopamine is used in medical emergencies to help bring blood pressure up when it is bottoming out. Its dysphoric side effects in medical settings have been well documented. It was once thought that patients coming out of a cardiac arrest became paranoid and anxious because of their traumatic experiences. For some, this may be true. However, with better research, we now understand that these reactions are side effects of dopamine.

All addictions involve the mesolimbic pathway and the release of dopamine. However, unlike the normal feeling of contentment or happiness, with addiction, there is a super-charged response that produces a huge surge of dopamine and a heightened sense of euphoria that can lead to chasing that burst of pleasurable feeling, which eventually leads to the trap that we call addiction. This biochemical reaction in the brain that produces such a high ecstasy is the basis for addiction.

The True Hallmark of Addiction

The true hallmark of addiction is the extreme euphoria (the true high). For addiction to take hold, first there has to be an extreme euphoria produced by a drug or the stimulus in the brain. Without it, there is no allure. It is only when such a highly pleasurable feeling is present that one is likely to want to repeat such an experience, and only with the repeated excitation of the pleasure center that addiction can set in over time. No one is truly hooked after just one exposure.

The Craving (The Other Component of Addiction)

The craving distinguishes addiction from abuse. Not everyone who abuses a drug develops cravings for the drug. Only those who are genetically susceptible to that drug and experienced that supercharged overstimulation of the pleasure spot eventually develop cravings.

For those who are addicted, the craving starts immediately after their last use, even before the onset of the physical withdrawal symptoms, and it does not stop, even after the psychological withdrawal symptoms go away. The literature also mistakes craving as a part of the physical withdrawal symptoms and mistakenly states that the physical withdrawal happens immediately after the last use. Most addicts think so, too. In reality, the physical withdrawal does not start until about 24 hours after the drug has stopped working. For long-acting drugs, the physical withdrawal does not start until 48–72 hours after the last use.

Most addicts think the reason they can't stop is because of the severe physical withdrawal associated with quitting. In reality, it is the craving, not the withdrawal that makes it difficult for them to quit. One only has to see an addict successfully go through an inpatient detoxification only to relapse as soon as he is released to understand this. Once you finish the detox, there is no physical withdrawal. Yet, many succumb to the power of cravings and relapse time after time.

I had a patient who was hooked on heroin who went through an inpatient detox and stayed clean and sober for about one and a half years. He told me that trying to stay clean and sober was a struggle every day. It was as if there was a monkey on his back telling him that he needed his drugs. He fought this demon for one and a half years until he succumbed. He was back on heroin for six months before I met him.

If you wake up every morning with cravings, it is a battle to overcome them—a battle you may lose one day. With sobriety, over time, cravings do fade. However, the memory of how good the drug made the person feel does not fade with time. We call these memories triggers— something that reminds an addict how good the drug once made him feel. The trigger is fleeting, whereas cravings are constant. Sobriety is a lifelong struggle, one which many addicts fail many times.

Normal versus Supercharged Euphoria

The average person gets a mild buzz from alcohol and pot, but this experience is not comparable to the high that someone who is genetically susceptible to these substances experiences. For most of us, alcohol gives us a normal feeling of contentment, not a heightened sense of extreme euphoria. For most of us, alcohol has a calming effect. For those who are susceptible to its allure, it acts as a stimulant at a low dose. The same is true with pot.

We can distinguish a normal experience to these drugs versus an abnormal one by determining how these drugs made the person feel at first. Did it stimulate the meso-limbic pleasure center in the brain so powerfully that it made that person want to keep chasing such a feeling? If the answer is yes, then he did get high. If not, he didn't.

We must start looking at addiction from the perspective of what is going on inside the person's brain rather than as a set of behaviors in order to fully understand it and correctly diagnose it. Most things we know are based on careful observations. This is the fundamental basis of good science. But sometimes, observations alone are not enough.

As long as the euphoric experience is not far above the normal euphoric experiences one may feel with normal day-to-day activities, you are not at risk. Only when the euphoric experience is supercharged and makes you feel like this is the best you have ever felt will you want to keep chasing it. However, most people do not feel such euphoria from opiate pain medications or from most drugs, for that matter. This, then, is the fundamental difference.

One only needs to examine one's own experiences with different drugs to know that this is true. How did alcohol make you feel? Did it make you feel like a million bucks or being on top of the world? Did opiate pain pills make you extremely euphoric? Did pot make you feel great? Those who got addicted to these drugs describe their experiences as such. You may answer "yes" to one, but "no" to others, or "no" to all. Then, you can understand that others may have profoundly different experiences with these drugs than you did.

Interestingly, most people who got hooked on one drug but not another don't seem to understand that others may find the other drug highly addictive. When I tell my opiate-addicted patients that some people find pot highly addictive, most of them find this difficult to believe. When I tell them that some of my patients found pot to be better than sex, they say "Really?" or "That can't be true!", usually with a chuckle. Only when I point out that most of us do not find their drug of choice to be extremely euphoric do they finally get it; when I ask them whether their drug was better than sex, and they gleefully admit that it was, they finally understand this concept.

Degree of Euphoria

Are there different degrees to which a person may find a drug euphoric? Of course. However, most people do not find most drugs highly euphoric. For those who find a mild form of a drug mildly euphoric, does it necessarily lead to addiction? Probably not. The mild euphoria most people experience from alcohol does not lead to alcoholism. The reward such an experience produces in most people is not enough for them to keep chasing that feeling. Chewing coca leaves does not produce enough euphoria for Inca Indians to become addicted to it. However, when a drug is purified or made more potent, its addictive potential increases for those who are susceptible.

There are studies that show anesthesiologists and nurse anesthetists have a higher rate of opiate addiction than other medical specialists. This is thought to be because they accidentally inhale vapors from powerful opiates as they administer them to their patients (an occupational hazard) and are thus more likely to fall victim themselves.[9] Of course, most do not become addicted, since only some are susceptible. However, for those who are susceptible to these drugs' highly euphoric allure, the stronger the drug, the quicker the onset of addiction. Because there is a higher percentage of people being exposed to these drugs, there is a higher number of those who get hooked. Fentanyl is a synthetic opiate that is often used during surgery; it is 80 times stronger than morphine.

"Birds of a Feather Flock Together"

Most patients who got hooked on a given drug seem to know many others who share their common experience. The opposite is also true; most people who are not vulnerable to these drugs often don't know anyone who got hooked. Often, young people who got hooked on opiates state that all of their friends are also hooked. Most patients who get high on pot also state that everyone they know also seems to get high on pot.

Do you remember your high school or college classmates? Most of us remember the party crowd who got drunk every weekend, or the "pot heads" who couldn't seem to stop smoking pot. Most of us who did not share their taste for alcohol or pot tended not to travel in their circles. It's no fun hanging around people with whom you do not share a common experience, especially if they seem to be having a lot more fun than you are, or vice versa.

These shared experiences probably tend to skew each group's perception of their own reality. When we understand that other people's experiences can be quite different from ours, we can begin to understand why other groups behave the way they do.

Abuse versus Addiction

Because this is probably one concept that most people will struggle with, let me explain it further. Abuse is defined as a set of aberrant behaviors, such as forging prescriptions, getting multiple DUIs, doctor shopping, etc. These are just behaviors and do not explain the true reason behind the behavior. Because we only look at the person's behavior rather than trying to understand what is going on inside the person's brain, we tend to lump all who abuse drugs as addicts. But fundamental differences exist.

For most people, abuse is synonymous with addiction. That's because most people judge others by their actions rather than their intent. For most people, a person's action is his intent. Unfortunately, the general public still believes that anyone who drinks excessively must be an alcoholic and anyone who uses an illicit drug is an addict.

However, people may misuse or abuse drugs, be it alcohol or opiates, to escape their life's ills or to drown out their sorrows. Just because someone drinks excessively does not necessarily mean that he is an alcoholic. Just because someone uses (or abuses) illicit drugs does not necessarily mean that he is an addict, either.

One may drink to cope with depression or stress, but that same person may not be hooked on alcohol if they did not experience the extreme joy from the alcohol early on. Those who did not experience the true euphoria from alcohol can often quit or decrease their use once their depression or stress lifts, while those who experienced such euphoria find it difficult to do so even when their circumstances change for the better.

Even some drug and alcohol treatment centers seem to confuse this point. There are many books written about why addiction is not a disease, but rather a maladjusted coping mechanism to deal with the stresses in one's life. Because of these misconceptions, they lump all who abuse drugs as addicts. Some drug and alcohol treatment centers operate on these premises. They point out that when someone is taught the errors of his ways, often such behavior can be changed. They believe that if a patient is made to understand the reason why he was abusing the drug was to cope with his emotional pain, he can be shown a way to cure himself of his addiction. Because they look at addiction only as a set of behaviors, they fail to distinguish abuse from addiction.

How can we distinguish those who are truly addicted to a drug versus others who may be abusing it to treat other ills in their lives? The answer, again, lies in understanding what true addiction is and asking the right question. Remember it as that "better than you should have a right to feel" type of feeling that a drug produced. Unless a person experienced such a highly euphoric feeling to that drug early on, he is not addicted to it. You will only know whether the person is truly addicted or not when you ask the right question.

This does not mean that abuse is not a problem. Nor does it mean that someone who started out abusing a drug to treat his emotional pain or anxiety may not get hooked as well. It is just that someone who is abusing a drug but is not truly hooked has a fundamentally different problem than someone who is truly hooked. Once their environment changes or they are shown a better way to cope with their emotional pain, often their behavior changes. Their problem is easier to treat. For those who are truly hooked, the answer to their problem is not so simple. Let me give you a few examples.

Jill was a lovely 43-year-old who had gotten addicted to opiate pain medications that her doctor was giving her. Because of her addiction, her marriage fell apart. While she was going through a divorce, she lost custody of her daughter because of her addiction. As she struggled to get her opiate addiction under control, Jill started drinking heavily. Although she managed to stop her opiates, she found herself drinking even more. She had multiple spells of blackouts and DTs. By most people's standards, she would be classified as an alcoholic as well. Both her ex-husband and her chemical dependency counselor thought so.

By the time I saw her, she had been clean for a few years. She had gone through an inpatient drug rehab program, but was still seeing a court-mandated chemical dependency counselor as a condition of getting back partial custody of her daughter. She was put on Suboxone by another physician and had done well.

As I do with all my patients, I asked her how different drugs made her feel. She told me about the incredible highs she got from opiates. However, when it came to alcohol, she told me that she did not experience any euphoria from it. She drank to drown out her sorrows and mask her depression and anxiety. Even on Suboxone, she admitted that at times she still thought about how good opiates used to make her feel. However, she had no such cravings for alcohol.

When I told her I did not believe that she got addicted to alcohol, but that she was just abusing it, she was shocked and did not believe me at first. She had been attending AA meetings for years. She chaired her meetings. She sponsored others to help them with their alcohol addiction. However, she had never asked anyone how alcohol had made them feel. I asked her to ask this question at her next AA meeting.

Over the course of the next few visits, I explained to her my ideas about what addiction is and why it happens. I explained to her the difference between abuse and addiction. She was bright. Once I explained these concepts to her, she got it. She did ask others at her meetings about how alcohol made them feel and learned that her experience with alcohol was nothing like what others were describing. She still attends AA meetings and finds that they help her stay clean from her opiate addiction. But now she understands that alcohol was never her drug of choice.

Jim was a 50-year-old businessman who came to see me because he thought he was hooked on heroin. He had been attending NA meetings to help him quit, but found himself relapsing time after time. Someone told him about Suboxone and introduced him to me.

On our first visit, I asked him what he was using. He told me, "heroin." Once again, I asked him how heroin made him feel. He told me that it was a powerful sedative, that it knocked his lights out, and made him forget about all his problems. I said, "Really? It didn't make you extremely happy before you passed out?" With a puzzled look, he said, "No." I told him that people who are truly hooked on heroin experience extreme joy before they pass out. He said, "Really?"

I asked Jim how he got started. He told me that in high school, his best friend got him hooked on it. But then, he pointed out, when he graduated and went away to college, he stopped using. He told me he had been clean until last year. I asked him what happened. He told me he was going through a divorce, and the stress of it all made him remember how heroin made him forget about his problems. I told him that he was not addicted, but was just abusing it. His jaw dropped, and he said, "No way!"

I told him that the reason why he was using it in high school was because of peer pressure, but since he was not hooked, he was able to stop when the peer pressure was gone. I told him the reason why he was using it now was because of the stress of the divorce. I told him when the divorce is finally over and the dust settles, he would be able to quit it again as well. I told him to go back to the meetings and ask others how their drugs made them feel. Only when he hears how others got extreme joy from their drugs would he understand that what he has is fundamentally different from what others were suffering from. His problem is much easier to "cure."

I told him that I would put him on Suboxone under one condition: he has to agree to see a counselor to help get his stress under control. I put him on Suboxone but was able to wean him off of it within weeks. Since he had no cravings for heroin, when he was given another way to deal with his stress, he had no problem getting off of it.

Last year on the radio I heard a British author talk about a book he wrote. It was about his past drug addiction. He had written a few works of fiction prior to this book. The moderator asked him, "So, how were you able to get your addiction under control?" The author told him that he started doing drugs when he was unemployed. He said the financial stress made him turn to drugs. After he had written a few books and gotten on a solid financial footing, he asked himself, "Why am I still using?" When he couldn't come up with a reason why, he said he quit. And then, he wrote a book about his past drug addiction. Someone who doesn't understand addiction will probably listen to his story and say, "Gee, that makes sense!"

Without asking this author how the drugs made him feel, I can't know with 100% certainty whether he was truly hooked or not. However, given the fact that he was able to just walk away from his drugs so easily makes it highly unlikely that he was truly hooked. However, because people like him think that they got hooked, it makes discussing addiction that much more difficult.

Dan Rather recently revealed that he used heroin in 1955 as an experiment for a story.[10] When asked what he experienced when he was high on heroin, he stated that he felt "otherworldly" and that heroin gave him a hell of a headache. When he was asked whether he ever wanted to do it again, he said, "Never!" This suggests that he did not get high, but I would bet that he thinks he did.

Too often, we judge the book by its cover without delving beneath it. Because we have always defined addiction as a set of behaviors, we have confused the two. No one had asked these people the right question. How did the drug make you feel?

Tobacco and Other Addictions

Unfortunately, because we misuse the term *addiction* when it comes to societal problems with drugs like cigarettes and other drugs, we confuse what addiction is. Most people think that anyone who smokes cigarettes on a daily basis must be addicted to cigarettes. Well, it turns out that they are not!

We found a genetic marker for tobacco addiction in 2008, and it turns out that most people who think they are addicted to cigarettes because they smoke are not actually addicted.[11] They are physically dependent on cigarettes, but most are not addicted. For most people, smoking is just a bad habit and not an addiction.

Once again, we must remember that addiction can only happen with a drug that makes a person extremely happy, at least at first. With any true high, there is stimulation, not sedation. It turns out that most people who smoke cigarettes got dizzy and lightheaded the first time they smoked. It always has a calming effect on them. For them, they are not addicted. Some, however, do find cigarettes quite enjoyable and stimulating. For these people, if they have been smoking for a while, they are hooked.

I remember the first time I smoked. I got dizzy and lightheaded. I got more of a buzz from the cigarette than I had from pot years earlier. I smoked for about a year in college because all of my friends at the time were smoking. However, when I went on to medical school, I quit and never looked back. I remember going through mild physical withdrawal, but it wasn't difficult to give up the habit. It turns out that I wasn't addicted.

I have patients who admit that they get highly euphoric on tobacco. When it comes to tobacco, even for those who get euphoric from it, the potency of the drug in its natural state may not be strong enough to cause the same type of addictive behaviors that we see with other drugs. However, these are questions that need further study.

We do know that a stronger form of tobacco has caused more people to become "hooked" on it. In countries where tobacco companies were unregulated and were allowed to increase the potency of the nicotine in cigarettes, there is a higher incidence of tobacco usage. Some will argue that societal attitudes about smoking probably play a more important role in the usage rate, and they are right. However, such a statement should not minimize the role that the level of nicotine has on usage as well.

However, when it comes to tobacco addiction, there are more questions than answers. Does nicotine produce such a high degree of euphoria in those who are genetically susceptible that it can cause true addiction? These and many other questions are what we do not fully understand yet. Tobacco addiction does not seem to produce those behaviors that we associate with other addictions, such as doing anything it takes to get it.

When was the last time you heard of someone breaking into a grocery store to get a pack of cigarettes or holding up a liquor store to get money to buy their drugs? Some of this has to do with the fact that a pack of cigarettes is still inexpensive, even at $7 a pack. When was the last time you heard of someone holding up a liquor store to steal liquor? Same argument. Yet, most of us understand how addictive alcohol can be for some.

The reason I bring up tobacco addiction is to point out that many public misconceptions about addiction exist because of misconceptions surrounding tobacco addiction. More specifically, because most people equate physical dependence on nicotine with addiction, it clouds the discussion about what true addiction is.

How about sex addiction? Since everyone experiences

euphoria from sex, how can we distinguish sex addicts from those with a normal sexual appetite? Once again, their euphoria is probably quite different from that of most people. Otherwise, why would they chase that feeling regardless of the cost or consequences?

Normies

The experience that addicts have with their drug is so profoundly different than that of the average person that some addicts have started calling those of us who do not share their experience "normies." This is usually said with envy. Those who got hooked on their drugs are envious of those of us who do not seem susceptible to the allure of their drugs. Only by understanding that such differences exist can we truly start to understand addiction.

I apologize if I seem to repeat myself. But I find that some concepts are so important to understanding this problem that they bear repeating.

References

[1] http://www.historyhouse.com/in_history/cocaine/

[2] http://www.golocalprov.com/news/New-Gallup-Poll-Shows-38-of-Americans-Have-Tried-Marijuana-/

[3] http://www.ncbi.nlm.nih.gov/pmc/articles/PMC281732/pdf/pnas00293-0337.pdf

[4] http://www.compasshealthgroup.com/addiction-blog/personality-traits-and-addictive-behavior/

[5] I.C. Siegler, A.B. Zonderman, J.C. Barefoot, R.B. Williams Jr., P.T. Costa Jr., and R.R. McCrae. Behavioral Medicine Research Center, Duke University Medical Center, Durham, North Carolina 22710. *Psychosomatic Medicine*, Vol 52, Issue 6 644-652, Copyright © 1990 American Psychosomatic Society.

[6] http://www.ncbi.nlm.nih.gov/pmc/articles/PMC281732/pdf/pnas00293-0337.pdf

[7] http://www.ncbi.nlm.nih.gov/pmc/articles/PMC3104618/

[8] http://en.wikipedia.org/wiki/Dopamine

[9] http://scienceblogs.com/ethicsandscience/2009/01/anesthesiology_and_addiction.php

[10] http://www.huffingtonpost.com/2014/01/09/dan-rather-heroin_n_4569319.html

[11] http://www.webmd.com/smoking-cessation/news/20080808/gene-linked-to-early-nicotine-addiction

Chapter 2 The Disease Model of Addiction

THE FIRST ADDICTION TO GAIN PUBLIC acceptance as a disease was alcoholism. However, the argument over whether it is nature versus nurture as to why someone becomes addicted to alcohol is age-old, and unfortunately, for many the debate still rages on. Even with mounds of scientific evidences supporting the disease model of addiction, for many their own personal bias and misunderstanding prevent them from accepting alcohol addiction as a disease.

Even for those who became addicted, the question as to whether addiction is truly a disease or not still haunts them. For those who got hooked, they often believe that they are just paying for their own mistakes. They believe that there is something fundamentally wrong with themselves that got them hooked. They see others not succumbing to the same drug and think that others must be stronger than they are. They often blame their childhood, other past failings, or traumas in their lives. Unfortunately, such feelings are reinforced by the public's misconceptions about addiction.

Some argue that unlike other diseases, such as diabetes or cancer, those who became addicted did it of their own free will. After all, they made the mistake of taking the drug in the first place. Had they been good and never touched the stuff in the first place, they wouldn't have gotten hooked.

Seneca, a Roman senator during the first century AD, was the first person in western civilization to describe the difference between someone who became drunk by choice and others who seemed unable to stop.[1] Without understanding the scientific basis for their differences, he understood that such differences do seem to exist. By pointing out such differences, he described what we would later understand to be the reason behind alcohol addiction.

In 1849, a Swedish physician, Dr. Magnus Huss, first coined the term alcoholism.[2] Instead of labeling someone as an alcoholic, alcoholism finally described a person's illness and placed the emphasis on the disease, not the person. It distinguished the disease from the act. After all, most of us recognize that a bad behavior does not necessarily mean that a person is inherently bad.

Not too long ago, public drunkenness was considered a crime (as it is still for opiate addiction, unfortunately). In colonial times, a town drunk was often put in a pillory stock (wooden blocks with openings for the head and hands) in the town square to make an example of the evils of the alcoholic's overindulgence. It is only with the general acceptance of alcoholism as a disease that such treatments gradually gave way to more humane treatments. Yet, this is a battle still being fought.

The general acceptance of alcoholism as a disease is a fairly recent one. Even more tragic is that most people say they accept alcoholism as a disease without understanding why. Many still view it as a personality flaw, a lack of morals, or just overindulgence. And because such views are commonplace, a deep-rooted bias against those with alcohol addiction persists. Many people are still apt to blame alcoholics for their own troubles.

In 1951, the World Health Organization (WHO) accepted alcoholism as a medical problem.[3] In 1956, the American Medical Association (AMA) declared it an illness, and then in 1966 further classified it as a disease.[4] In 1965, the American Psychiatric Association accepted alcoholism as a disease, and in 1969, the American Bar Association came on board as well.[5]

In 1960, E.M. Jellinick published "The Disease Concept of Alcoholism" and with it came an avalanche of criticism. Jellinick based his conclusion on a questionnaire that he sent to a group of AA members. Of the 158 questionnaires that were returned, 60 were rejected. From the remaining questionnaires, he classified alcoholics into five categories: Alpha, Beta, Gamma, Delta, and Epsilon (basically different types of alcoholics) and concluded that alcoholism was a disease.

The biggest criticism of Jellinick's conclusion, surprisingly, was not that it had a poor research design or a small number of subjects (even Jellinick himself admitted to these flaws in his study). The opponents of the disease concept felt that, by calling alcoholism a disease, it took the personal responsibility away, stigmatized people for life, set them up for failure, excused their behavior, and enabled them to remain victims. They pointed to the fact that there was no proof of a genetic marker (at least at the time), that alcoholism seemed to take a long time to take hold, and the fact that there were many who could control their "alcoholism."

As late as 1988, the US Supreme Court ruled that alcoholism is a personal choice and not a disease (Traynor v. Turnage).[6] It took an act of Congress to overturn the Supreme Court ruling later that year, declaring alcoholism not to be "a willful misconduct" of those who are addicted but rather a manifestation of a medical illness/disease.[7]

What is a Disease?

In order to understand the disease model, we must first define what a disease is. Unlike a poor choice or a character flaw, a disease must have commonalities and defining characteristics that all who suffer from it must have. There must be a cause and effect that can be linked.

The ultimate smoking gun when it comes to defining something as a disease is a genetic marker. For some, even when a genetic marker was found, it didn't always sway their deep-seated conviction that anyone who becomes addicted is just a "rotten bum who should just be locked up with the key thrown away." Although such views are becoming less and less frequently expressed out loud (with the exception of some talk radio hosts), many people still implicitly agree with such sentiments. Otherwise, the public outcry against such sentiments would be so overwhelmingly negative that they would not be repeated again. The fact that these sentiments still pollute our airways (on a not-so-seldom basis) suggests that there must be enough people who share these views.

When it comes to most addictions, we have not found genetic markers. However, even before the genetic marker for Type II diabetes was found, most people accepted it as a disease. Most people did not need a smoking gun to prove that it fit the model of a disease. By the way, we do not yet have a genetic marker for heart disease, (most) cancers, or Alzheimer's. For that matter, we do not have a genetic marker for most diseases. However, when it comes to illnesses that are not linked to one's behaviors (in this case, bad behaviors), most people don't seem to have any problem accepting them as diseases.

I don't mean to suggest that we should consider all ills related to bad behaviors as illnesses or diseases. Many self-destructive behaviors do lead to negative consequences. Yes, it would be hard to argue that all such negative outcomes mean that there is an underlying disease behind them. Should laziness be considered a disease? Is obesity a disease or the result of a bad diet or a bad nutritional habit? Are these negative traits learned or genetic? We do not have an answer to many of these questions. In most extreme cases, many of life's ills probably have a genetic basis. Most of us do accept deep clinical depression as a disease. On the other hand, can one's own negative attitudes or belief systems lead to clinical depression for some people? There is plenty of clinical evidence that says yes to this as well. Some will use such data to show why alcoholism is not a disease as well. So what makes something a disease?

Clinical Definition of a Disease

One commonly used definition of a disease is[8]:

- A disease can be described.
- The course of a disease is predictable and progressive.
- A disease is primary; it is not just a symptom of some other underlying disorder.
- It's permanent. It may be managed, but there is no cure for it.
- It's terminal. Left untreated, it results in insanity or premature death.

Another definition of a disease is that it is as an illness or sickness that causes an interruption, cessation, or disorder of bodily functions, systems, or organs. A disease is characterized by at least two of the three following criteria[9]:

- A recognizable etiologic agent (or agents).
- An identifiable group of signs and symptoms, OR
- Consistent anatomical alteration of known anatomical systems.

Does Alcoholism Pass the Definition of a Disease?

Today, the medical community as well as the majority of the public accepts alcoholism as a disease. However, most people say it is a disease but still blame alcoholics for their own ills and can't understand why they would do this to themselves or why they can't just stop.

In order to understand alcoholism as a disease, one must understand that, when exposed to alcohol, these people experience such a highly intense euphoric feeling that it made them chase such an experience. For the rest of us who can take or leave it, it is not fair for us to judge those who had such an enjoyable experience without first trying to understand what is going on inside their brains.

AA, from its beginning, asserted that alcoholism was a disease. This was probably based on its members' shared experience and knowledge that those who succumbed to this disease, unlike the rest of us, shared a common identifiable group of signs and symptoms that produced such an overwhelming, euphoric experience that led to their addiction.

However, even among AA members, there is a deep sense of guilt and shame associated with their own illness. Even for them, this is a true dichotomy. On one hand, they know that alcoholism is a disease. On the other hand, they still feel ashamed that they let this happen to themselves.

The pathology associated with a lifetime of heavy alcohol consumption has been well documented. The only thing that had been missing was the smoking gun, the genetic marker that separated these people and explained why they are susceptible to this disease. In 2004, the genetic marker for alcoholism was finally isolated.[10] Yet, the naysayers still exist in part because they confuse those who abuse alcohol with those who are truly addicted.

Passage of "Civil Rights" for Alcoholics

With the passage of the Hughes Act in 1970, US Congress finally accepted alcoholism as a disease and established the National Institute of Alcohol Abuse and Alcoholism (NIAAA).[11] As a society, our acceptance of alcoholism came after the passage of the Civil Rights Act. This may ultimately explain why, for some people, there is still much ambivalence and resistance about accepting alcoholism as a disease even today. The passage of a bill does not change people's attitudes or beliefs overnight. Some say that it takes a generation or more to change deeply held beliefs and biases.

Critics of Addiction as a Disease

One of the arguments against calling addiction a disease is that it labels people and subjects these people to a life-sentence and makes them helpless victims. Nonsense! I will argue that when we don't accept addiction as a disease, we still "label" those who become victims to it. We just label them as weak-willed, morally depraved, overindulgent, etc., even if we may not say so out loud.

When you believe that there is no fundamental difference between those who get hooked versus those who don't, those who don't get hooked have a sense of moral superiority and those who do have a sense of inferiority. It's the same as saying, "Hey, it's your own damn fault that you got hooked!" or "Just snap out of it!" Such sentiments resonate with many people. Even the question, "Why can't Johnny just quit?" is based on such misconceptions.

Of course, we do not want to victimize those who get hooked even further. But trying to understand their struggles and the fundamental reason why they get hooked doesn't add to their victimization. It helps us, as well as those who get hooked, understand their struggles. It helps them deal with their guilt and shame. Stating that an addict is like everyone else may seem non-judgmental and non-discriminatory, but the opposite is true; it minimizes their struggles. It's not any different than saying, "Oh, there is nothing wrong with you!" or "If you really wanted to, you could get better." Such statements show the true ignorance and biases we have against those who fall victim to addiction and fail to understand the true reason behind their ailment.

Unfortunately, addiction is a lifelong struggle, and for now, there is no cure. However, like any illness or disease, this doesn't mean that we cannot control it. It does not mean that an addict has to wallow in self-pity. Understanding the true reason why one becomes addicted while most people don't should give an addict a better understanding of his own problem. Knowledge gives us power to withstand or overcome adversity rather than stay victim to it. We can teach someone to treat and control their addiction even if we cannot cure them, and understanding addiction can prevent others from getting hooked in the first place!

The Importance of Defining Alcoholism as a Disease

The importance of defining alcoholism as a disease was not just an academic one; it carried huge social implications. Prior to the adoption of alcoholism as a disease, health insurance companies did not have to cover treatments for alcoholism or alcohol-related illnesses. The legal system tended to punish alcoholic behaviors rather than refer the person to medical treatment. It also opened the door to a more humane and compassionate discussion about how to treat those who are afflicted. It is only with the acceptance of alcoholism as a disease that an institution such as Alcoholics Anonymous could have become accepted into the mainstream. As a society, we are now less inclined to throw an alcoholic in jail than to offer him treatment. However, because we have not fully accepted opiate addiction as a disease, we are still more inclined to punish those who are addicted to opiates rather than treat their addiction as a medical illness.

Although Narcotics Anonymous does exist, the social acceptance of narcotic addiction as a true disease still lags behind that of alcoholism. One only needs to see the treatment of opiate addicts in our society to understand this. Because opiate addiction was in large part a problem of the inner city poor, we found it easier to just lock them up rather than try to understand their problem. However, now that the opiate epidemic has reached middle- and upper-class America, our attitude toward it is finally changing.

Understanding that all addictions are a disease does not mean that we need to abandon personal responsibility or stigmatize those who are addicted as those unable to help themselves. It is just a more humane way of understanding their struggle. Only when we realize that there are fundamental differences between the experiences of those who succumbed to addiction versus the majority of people who did not, can we finally accept addiction as a disease.

Accepting all addictions as a disease allows us to look at them more rationally and practically. For those who become addicted, it helps them address their problem rather than punish themselves (feeling that they deserve what they got) and seek help. Trust me, most addicts feel guilty and shameful enough. What they need is a little sympathy and understanding from us, not judgment and punishment, because punishing them does no one any good. It is much more costly to punish an addict and lock him away than it is to provide him with treatment for his addiction.

Once we truly understand the genetic difference in how drugs affect different groups of people, the acceptance of all addiction as a disease makes all the sense in the world. Knowing that such fundamental differences exist is not intuitive, but can come about when you ask the right question, "How did it make you feel?"

Only when one attempts to walk in another person's shoes rather than judge him can such awareness come about. Only then can we have a more intelligent discussion about how to treat those who are addicted and prevent addiction for others. In the end, preventing addiction is the only way we will ever truly win the war on drugs.

References

[1] Royce & Scratchley "Alcoholism and Other Drug Problems" 1996, page 124.

[2] Royce & Scratchley "Alcoholism and Other Drug Problems" 1996, page 124.

[3] www.alcohol-drug-treatment.net/disease_concept.html

[4] www.ama-assn.org/ama/pub/category/1926.html

[5] Royce & Scratchley "Alcoholism and Other Drug Problems" 1996, page 124.

[6] http://caselaw.lp.findlaw.com/scripts/getcase.pl?court=us&vol=485&invol=535

[7] http://www.encyclopedia.com/doc/1G1-7096689.html

[8] www.sosdallas.com/addiction.htm

[9] *Stedman's Medical Dictionary*, 24th Edition.

[10] www.medicinenet.com/script/main/art.asp?articlekey

[11] www.niaaa.nih.gov/AboutNIAAA/OrganizationalInformation/History.htm

Chapter 3 Why Does Anyone Get Addicted?

THE REASON WHY SOMEONE GETS addicted to a drug is because it made them feel good. I mean *really* good. If something makes you feel dopey, intoxicated, or just puts you to sleep right away, don't worry, you won't get hooked on that. I have patients who are overly concerned that they may become addicted to opiate pain medications once they start taking them. I try to allay their fears by explaining to them that there is a genetic predisposition as to why someone gets hooked, that most people are not susceptible, and what the signs are that one may be susceptible.

Once they understand what addiction is and why someone becomes addicted, they will often take the pain medication more appropriately and improve their own quality of life. For those who are susceptible to the drugs' allure, they can realize that they may be getting hooked before it's too late. These are the patients who tell me, "I better stop, because I am starting to like it too much!" as their pain starts to subside.

One common trait when it comes to alcohol and opiate addictions is that instead of the sedation most of us feel, those who are susceptible to these drugs initially experience a heightened sense of energy and stimulation when taking the drug at a low dose. For most people, both alcohol and opiates are sedatives; they make us tired and groggy right off the bat. However, for those who are susceptible to these drugs, the drugs have the opposite effect and act as stimulants, at least at a low dose. At high doses, they do cause sedation, but only after the initial high starts to fade. Otherwise, no one would overdose on them. But this difference at a lower dose is the distinguishing feature between those who are susceptible versus those who are not.

On the other hand, cocaine, amphetamine, and crystal meth are uppers or stimulants, and everyone becomes energized by them. Unlike alcohol and opiates, they do not cause opposite reactions in those who are susceptible versus those who are not. These drugs do not sedate those who are susceptible. However, for most, this heightened sense of energy is not accompanied by a feeling of euphoria. For those who are susceptible, not only do they feel energized, they also become extremely euphoric. At higher doses, those who are not susceptible find these drugs make them feel jittery and unpleasant. For those who are susceptible, the higher the dose, the more euphoric they become. However, as the high fades, they too become jittery and wired.

Whereas someone coming down from an alcohol or opiate high may become groggy and intoxicated, someone coming down from a cocaine or crystal meth high becomes jittery and wired rather than intoxicated. That's why they don't look "stoned" coming off their highs, whereas someone coming off an opiate or pot high does. Remember that even for them, being stoned is only the aftermath of their high.

A common thread that predicts or explains why someone gets addicted to a drug is that for those who are susceptible, the drug makes them highly euphoric and happy (at first). However, if they understand that something that artificially makes you happy is the true high, they can stop before they get sucked in. Because many people mistake the high to be that dopey feeling, they do not realize that they are actually getting high when something makes them feel extremely happy. And because they do not realize that they are getting high, they will chase such an experience. When someone understands that such a sensation is the true high, a trap, an early warning sign, he can often make the right choice and stop before it's too late.

A patient once told me that getting high on cocaine was better than sex. It gave her the intense feeling like she was having multiple orgasms that lasted an hour. If you felt such an experience, wouldn't you want to repeat it? This person was a 72-year-old retired schoolteacher. If something makes you feel that good, it is easy to understand why you would want more of it.

I have another patient who told me that when he first started drinking, he felt like Superman. After 17 years of heavy drinking, he was finally able to quit with the help of AA. He also got extremely high on pot, but opiates did nothing for him.

The movie *When a Man Loves a Woman*, starring Meg Ryan and Andy García, depicts alcohol addiction better than most, because it shows the different stages of alcoholism. In it, there is a scene when Meg Ryan's character, an alcoholic at the end of her addiction, stands up in her first AA meeting and describes her initial reaction to alcohol, which tells us a lot about why someone becomes addicted to anything. She stands up and says, "When I was 15, I had my first beer, and I liked it. So, I had another and another." Most of us do not remember our first drink, because it was not a very memorable experience. We may have gotten tipsy, but that experience was not powerful enough to imprint it in our memories.

The character played by Andy García shows how fun and exciting Meg Ryan's character was early on in their courtship. She is portrayed as the life of the party, quite sociable, and fun to be around. Andy García's character falls in love with Meg Ryan's character because of how exciting and fun she was when she was drinking. Later on, when alcoholism takes full hold, her life spins out of control. Early on, alcoholics make even those of us who are not susceptible to alcohol's allure have more fun. We have more fun because of them. We want to be like them. It is only as addiction takes full hold that you see the life of an alcoholic unravel and fall apart.

Most people don't understand why others get addicted because they do not have the same response or experience with that drug. They say, "Gee, all it does for me is make me groggy and nauseous." They think that others must have the same experience as they do. They ask, "Why can't Johnny just quit?" Of course, if Johnny had the same reaction to the drug they had, he wouldn't have gotten hooked. On the other hand, if they felt the way same Johnny did, they may have gotten hooked as well. In order to understand why someone got hooked, you really need to understand how the drug made them feel!

The Genetics Behind Addiction

In 2004, a genetic marker for alcoholism was finally isolated.[1] In 2008, a genetic marker for tobacco addiction was also isolated.[2] These discoveries should put to rest the argument between nature versus nurture as to why someone becomes addicted. Unfortunately, they have not!

Even when faced with such revelations, some people still argue that addiction is not a disease but a personal failing. How can anyone still feel that way even after the genetic links for these additions have been discovered? Faced with facts that may contradict your own belief systems, you have a choice. Either you can accept these facts and reexamine your own belief system, or you can choose not to believe them and question their validity. In the course of human history, it is not uncommon to find that many have chosen the latter approach when it comes to many new discoveries or scientific facts.

Why would anyone choose not to believe these new findings? There are many possible reasons. Some people may not grasp the implications of such findings. Others may choose to ignore them because it's easier to do so. Entrenched belief systems are intrinsically hard to change. One only needs to see the resistance to new discoveries over the course of human history to understand this. Two obvious examples are:
- The earth is not the center of the universe. The earth revolves around the sun.
- The earth is not flat. It's round.

I chose these examples because everyone now accepts them as facts. Although most of us would find resistance to the above facts to be quite ludicrous today, at the time, many people strongly resisted these new scientific facts. They threatened many entrenched core belief systems. Often, when one's own belief systems are challenged, one may find oneself instinctively fighting back rather than trying to examine the new data with an open mind so as to look at its validity. When one is challenged, it is often the first instinct to resist and fight back. Often, it is easier to ignore the facts rather than having to rethink or relearn something we thought we already knew. Indeed, it took a generation or more to accept these new scientific facts.

Unfortunately, science has only recently revealed the genetic links for some addictions. Although with our modern technologies the dissemination of information is almost lightning-fast, if our past history teaches us anything, for some people it may take a generation for these facts to become accepted. Only when we truly examine our entrenched belief systems and discuss them openly can we help more people accept what makes sense in the light of these new discoveries and help facilitate changes in their ingrained beliefs.

Environmental Influences on Addiction

Of course, environmental factors do play a role in addiction. Even if we understand that addiction is based on genetic predisposition, we have to acknowledge that the environment does play a role. We know there are environmental and outside influences that can affect any addiction. For example, stress can often trigger a relapse in an alcoholic who may have been clean and sober for years. However, we have also known that the same stress does not cause addictions for most people.

What most books on addiction do not understand is that without genetic predisposition, the environment plays no role! Many addiction treatment centers seem to insinuate that somehow the environment plays just as important a role in addiction as genetics. Nonsense! The environment only plays a role if there is a genetic predisposition.

Because we have misunderstood why addiction takes place, we have given the environment equal weight with genetics as the cause of addiction. When you truly understand addiction, you begin to understand that the environment only plays a role for those who are genetically susceptible to the drug.

Of course, outside influences such as poverty, depression, and feelings of utter despair and helplessness may subject some to seek solace in the escape drugs may offer them. This would explain the high rate of alcoholism and drug use among the inner-city poor as well as the mentally ill. During economic downturns, alcohol and drug usage goes up.

However, the common misconception that there is a fundamentally increased risk of opiate addiction among the mentally ill or within a certain socioeconomic group needs to be reexamined. The fundamental risk may be the same as the risk within the general public. Only increased exposure skews the increased number.

Studies show that most of the Vietnam vets who were thought to be hooked on heroin while in Vietnam were able to quit on their own when they returned home.[3] Seventeen percent of Vietnam vets admitted using heroin on a regular basis while they were in Vietnam. However, a 1974 study showed that only 2% of Vietnam vets (12% of the 17%) were still using it three years after coming home.[4] This is an amazing statistic, given that most people who are truly hooked on heroin rarely seem to quit on their own. However, some did not or could not stop their habit. It is easy to understand why some people would turn to drugs to numb their senses and escape from their reality when trapped in the harsh environment of war. Of course, they were all abusing the drug, but only a few got truly hooked.

Common Early Signs That You Are at Risk of Addiction (to Opiates or Alcohol)

I look for three basic things. SIG is the mnemonic.
Stimulate
Insomnia
Good

Does a low dose of the drug **stimulate** or energize you rather than sedate you? Do you act like the Energizer bunny when you take them?

Does the drug cause **insomnia**? Are you cleaning the house in the middle of the night after you took a drug you thought would help you sleep? Remember, at a high enough dose of opiate or alcohol, everyone will eventually get sedated. Otherwise, no one would overdose on these drugs.

Pièce de résistance (The Ultimate Reason)
Did the drug make you feel really **good**, euphoric, or high (at first)?
Did it make you feel ten feet tall, invincible, or on top of the world?
Did you think that this was the best thing that God put on this green earth?
Did it seem like an elixir of life?
Did it make you feel like Superman?
Did it make every other problem go away?
Did it make you feel younger?
Was it better than sex?
Did it make sex better (at first)?
Did it promise you the moon?
Did it make you feel better than you would feel otherwise?

Unless something makes you feel that good (*really* good), you will not get hooked. Why would you? Eureka! For those who got hooked on a drug, it produced such a euphoric experience that they wanted to keep repeating it without realizing that doing so would eventually enslave them in its

snares. Once the brain is so stimulated by repeated exposure to such a highly euphoric experience, the brain becomes rewired and becomes dependent on the drug.

When that happens, the addict is no longer in control;
the drug is. Then, the desire for the drug becomes an all-
consuming demand. By then, the craving has taken hold.
The addict no longer feels that he can live without it. The
addict will do anything to get it regardless of the consequences. Only then the behavior that we now call addiction
becomes apparent to outside observers. By then, addiction
has taken full hold, and the grip it has on that person may
seem like a death grip. Unfortunately, many pay for their
mistakes with the ultimate sacrifice: their own lives.

Most Who Got Hooked Did Not Realize That They Were Getting Hooked!

The irony is that because we have done such a poor job describing what a high is, most people who got addicted did
not realize they were getting addicted early on. They did
not realize they were getting hooked because they did not
realize they were getting high. Most who do not suffer from
addiction will find these concepts hard to believe. But if
you think about it, it makes all the sense in the world. Let
me try to explain it this way.

Most people who smoke pot think they are high. Because we have always portrayed the high as a dopey, intoxicated, and altered state of mind, it's natural that most
people will confuse their reaction to pot as the high. Because most people think they got high on pot, when they
experience something that excites and makes them happy,
they do not realize they are getting high. They say to
themselves, "Gee, I feel great!" but do not think they are
high.

If you see a roomful of people smoking pot, most look
stoned and intoxicated by pot. But there are usually one or
two who look excited and happy. They will look at their
friends and think, "These idiots are high, but I am not!"
when in fact they are the only ones getting high. They are

usually the ones who got everyone to smoke in the first place. Eventually, they will get addicted to pot if they don't stop, but their friends will move on, having never gotten hooked on it. It's precisely because of this upside-down view of what the high is that so many fall victim to addiction without realizing it.

By educating the public about what a true high is, we should be able to prevent many people from getting hooked in the first place. When you understand the true reason behind any addiction, not only is treatment a more logical way to approach this problem, but prevention becomes possible. The more people we can prevent from falling into this trap in the first place, the less we will ultimately have to treat!

References

[1] www.medicinenet.com/script/main/art.asp?articlekey

[2] albertalocalnews.com/.../Tobacco_addiction_has_genetic_link_study.html

[3] 'Vietnam veterans' rapid recovery from heroin addiction: a fluke or normal expectation? *Addiction*, Volume 88 Issue 8, pages 1041-1054. Jan. 24, 2006.

[4] www.reason.com/news/show/28809.html

Chapter 4 Alcoholism

THE BEST WAY TO UNDERSTAND any addiction is by looking at alcoholism. It is the most studied and best understood of all addictions. There is a lot we understand about alcoholism, but a lot of misconceptions still persist.

Societal Perception of Alcoholism

So how do we define alcoholism? There is a joke in medical school that an alcoholic is someone who drinks more than you. In all seriousness, at what point do most of us think that someone else's drinking becomes excessive? Whether we realize it or not, most of us do have an opinion about at what point someone else's drinking reaches this point.

When you ask people whether they believe one drink a day is excessive, most people will say, "No." How about two? The answer is again, "No." How about three? The answer, this time, is "Probably not." How about four, six, or eight? You get the picture. Most of us will draw a line in the sand at some point and say that, beyond such a point, someone else's drinking becomes excessive.

Does that mean anyone who drinks more than that arbitrary cutoff point on a daily basis is an alcoholic? Many may say "Yes" with hesitance because, although they may hold such a view, they may not quite know why. What about a person who drinks one less drink a day than your arbitrary cutoff point?

I am not dismissing such behavior. After all, at some point, most people will get drunk. Since we really don't know how many drinks it took for that person to get drunk, most of us assume he must have had at least a certain amount (over a certain span of time). Once again, when push comes to shove, most of us seem to hold an arbitrary number when this will take place for most people; our keen eyes for observation tell us so. We have seen it happen many times. We also hear on the news that a blood alcohol level above the legal limit of 0.08% means that the person has had more than two drinks within the last hour. Does that mean that all of these people were drunk? According to the law, the answer is yes. You may or may not agree with this, but we all seem to have an opinion about when someone else's drinking becomes a problem.

The Truth Isn't Always What It Seems

In school, we are taught the scientific method, which uses observations of repeated experiments to come up with a conclusion. We look at a cause and effect and then draw a conclusion from such an observation if we can consistently reproduce the same result. By no means am I suggesting that such a method does not work. It does work very well, most of the time. The basis for many of our scientific discoveries as well as our own core beliefs are based on such observations of similar events of cause and effect over our lifetimes. That's why they are so hard to reexamine when they are challenged.

Some of our deeply held biases, prejudices, and illogical beliefs are also based on such observations of perceived cause and effect. Sometimes, we observe something over and over, but draw the wrong conclusions based on faulty or incomplete information. There is an old joke that shows the danger of how such a faulty conclusion can come about. Obviously, it's a joke, so it carries this point to an extreme. The joke goes like this:

A not-so-bright scientist was doing an experiment on frogs. He told a frog to jump, and it jumped eight feet. The scientist wrote this down on his clipboard and then cut off one of the frog's limbs. Again, he told the frog to jump. This time, the frog only jumped six feet. After carefully documenting his finding, once again, he cut off another limb.

This time, the frog jumped only four feet. Off with the third limb, and the poor frog was only able to jump two feet sideways. He then chopped off the last limb, and shouted, "Jump!" When the frog didn't jump, the scientist kept shouting "Jump!" over and over.

As any good scientist, he repeated the same experiment on other frogs with the same exact result. When he was convinced that he had enough data, he wrote down his finding: "When you cut off the last limb, frogs go deaf!" Your data may be correct, but your interpretation is absolutely wrong.

Unfortunately, many of us make the same kind of illogical conclusions from the things that we see every day because we don't have all the facts or because we misinterpret them. When such belief systems become ingrained over time because other events that follow seem to reinforce your first faulty conclusion, these beliefs become harder to challenge. However, just because you believe something to be true because you have witnessed it happen many times, it does not mean that you may not have misinterpreted it completely. The bases for many biases and prejudices are based on just such faulty logic. Yet, for those who harbor such views, they make perfect sense. Everything seems to reinforce, not negate, their views.

When you only see a person's behavior but do not understand the true reason behind his actions, you tend to misinterpret his behavior. For many, this is the reason why they equate alcohol abuse with alcoholism. For them, the act becomes the disease itself. Using only the person's behavior to try to understand any addiction is what contributes to many misunderstandings about addiction. Unfortunately, for many this is not an easy thing to unlearn.

The Current Medical Definition of Alcoholism

DSM-IV defines alcohol abuse as "repeated use despite recurrent adverse consequences" and alcohol dependence as "*alcohol abuse* combined with tolerance, withdrawal, and an uncontrollable drive to drink."[1] One often-used screening tool to identify alcoholic patients is the CAGE[2] questionnaire:

- Have you ever felt you needed to **C**ut down on your drinking?
- Have people **A**nnoyed you by criticizing your drinking?
- Have you ever felt **G**uilty about drinking?
- Have you ever felt you needed a drink first thing in the morning (**E**ye-opener) to steady your nerves or to get rid of a hangover?

Two or more "Yes" responses are believed to indicate that the person may be an alcoholic. Once again, such an approach can only identify someone once the disease (in this case alcoholism) has taken full hold. It also confuses those who may abuse alcohol with those who are truly hooked. Because it uses behaviors to diagnose alcoholism, it fails to distinguish a true alcoholic from someone who may be abusing alcohol for other reasons, such as depression or anxiety. Abuse does not necessarily mean addiction. It also fails to explain why anyone gets addicted in the first place.

Early in my career, I came face to face with alcoholism firsthand. One of my first receptionists was an elderly woman. She was sweet and kind-hearted. Patients loved her. She was tardy a few times, but I thought nothing of it. A few months after she started working for me, my patients and co-workers started complaining that they smelled alcohol on her breath. I chose not to bring this up with her because I didn't know how to address it. One day, she came back from lunch highly intoxicated. It was so obvious that I could not avoid addressing it any longer. I had to let her go.

A few months later, she was hospitalized with end-stage liver disease. I visited her at the hospital. She looked up at me from her hospital bed with sadness in her eyes. I could see how ashamed she felt about seeing me in her condition, about having to show her weakness to this vice. I comforted her as best I could. I told her how patients missed her and asked about her. I held no animosity toward her. I knew she was a good person, but somehow this disease had consumed her life.

I spoke with her son, who had been aware of her drinking problem for years but had felt helpless about it. Apparently, she had struggled with it most of her adult life. She passed away soon afterward.

Years later, I had another receptionist who was in her twenties. She was bright and excelled at her work. Once again, I heard complaints from patients and co-workers that they smelled alcohol on her breath. One day, she shredded all the incoming mails before opening it. It was obvious that she was intoxicated.

I told her that I felt she was talented and had a lot going for her, but I had to let her go. I asked her to get help. She told me that she had been attending court-ordered AA meetings after receiving several DUIs. The court also had her install a Breathalyzer in her car that would prevent her from starting her car if her alcohol level was too high. I wished her well and encouraged her to stay with AA.

In each of these instances, I could see that there must be something that made these two succumb to alcoholism. They weren't bad people and didn't have obvious character flaws. Years later, once I began to understand addiction, I was able to understand why they too had become addicted.

The Difference between Alcohol Abuse and Alcohol Addiction

By definition, all who are addicted to alcohol are abusing it. However, not all who abuse alcohol are addicted. Confused? The best way to understand this is to first look at it like that old Venn diagram where circle B is completely inside circle A. Everything inside circle B is a part of circle A, but not everything inside circle A is a part of circle B. For example, all zebras are mammals, but not all mammals are zebras.

People may abuse alcohol for many reasons. Some use it to treat their anxiety or depression. Others may abuse it to deal with psychological pain, such as the loss of a loved one or other psychological trauma. Some of these people will get addicted to alcohol, but not everyone will. The difference is their genetic susceptibility. Those who are genetically predisposed will become addicted. For others who are not, once their stress or depression lifts, often such behavior stops.

Obviously, there are those who got hooked on alcohol not because they started out using it to treat other ills in their lives, but because they tried it and liked it—a lot. Eventually, many of these people may become deeply depressed once alcoholism takes full hold.

Abuse is defined only by behavior. Because most of us only see behavior without understanding the true reason behind the behavior, we tend to equate all abuse with addiction. Because the outcome that we see is the same, we confuse the two as one. However, when you understand that not everyone who abused alcohol got extremely euphoric on the alcohol early on, then you can distinguish those who may be abusing alcohol but are not truly addicted.

It does not mean that even for those who are not truly hooked that their behavior is not a problem. Of course it is. The chronic overconsumption of alcohol will take its toll on the body in either case. However, for those who are not truly hooked, their problem is much easier to deal with. Once their life's ills or depression lifts, such behavior may resolve on its own, or they can be easily taught to change. For those who are truly hooked, their problem is much harder to address. Understanding the fundamental difference between the two groups makes it possible to understand the struggle that true alcoholics face.

Stats and Facts
- Statistically, 64% of adults in the United States drink.[3]
- About 7.4% of adults meet the diagnostic criteria for alcoholism.[4]

- 30% of suicide victims are alcoholics, indicating at least a four-fold increase in the risk of suicide among alcoholics.[5]
- Alcohol is the most commonly abused substance in the world.[6]
- Alcohol is the most commonly abused drug among young people.[7]
- Alcohol kills 6.5 times more youth than all other illicit drugs combined.
- 50% of high school seniors reported drinking in the last 30 days, and 32% reported being drunk at least once.
- The World Health Organization (WHO) estimates that around 140 million people around the world suffer from alcoholism.[8]
- In the US, 500 million workdays are lost each year to alcoholism.
- More than 100,000 deaths are caused by excessive alcohol intake in the U.S. each year.[9]
- 95% of alcoholics die from their disease and die approximately 26 years sooner than their normal life expectancy.
- Alcoholism is the third leading cause of preventable deaths in the US.
- Alcoholics Anonymous (AA) was founded in 1935.[10]

The Tax Windfall is a Myth

Many believe that legalizing illicit drugs and taxing them would generate a tax windfall for the government and the states. However, the money we collect in taxes from the sale of alcohol and tobacco has never matched the societal cost we incur from their use. For example, in 1992, alcohol dependence and abuse cost the United States an estimated $246 billion.[11] In 1992, the federal government collected a little over $3.5 billion in taxes from the sale of alcohol.[12] Even if you add all the state and local taxes on alcohol, the taxes we collect from the sale of alcohol only pay for a fraction of the societal cost we incur from its use.

So Why Does Anyone Get Hooked on Alcohol?

Do you remember your drinking buddy in high school or college, the party animal, the one who always seemed to have much more fun than anyone else when he drank? That's the person who will turn out to be an alcoholic down the line if he does not stop. There is a reason why they were having such a great time when they drank; their experience with alcohol was totally different than that of most people.

If a roomful of people who are not susceptible to alcohol addiction start drinking, the volume in the room goes down. Everyone becomes mellower. However, if a person who is susceptible to alcohol addiction walks into the room and starts drinking, the volume goes up, and everyone starts having more fun. If you ask the person with the alcohol gene, "Is everyone having just as good a time as you are?" he will say yes. However, if you ask the rest of the people, "Are you having as good a time as that person?" they will say no. They will say, "Gee, I wish I could have as much fun as he is having!"

It is much more fun to party with such people, because their energy and euphoria lifts everyone else's spirits. They would do things that you would never do even when you were loaded. They were everyone's friend. They were more popular in school. They had more fun. And others had more fun because of them. However, if you run into them 10–20 years later, you can often see the changes in their lives. They are more reclusive. Their lives are often a mess.

Because alcoholism takes years to take hold, with better public education and discourse, we should be able to help prevent many young people from going down the same path as their parents. Often, children of alcoholic parents resent their parents for their addiction, but they view it as a personal failing on their parents' part. They do not realize that their parents started out the same way as they are early on. Their parents who were the life of the party in their 20s become angry drunks by the time they were 40 or 50 years old.

By the time a child becomes a young adult, his parent's

addiction has taken full hold, and the relationship between them begins to sour. The child can't see how his parent's addiction has anything to do with how the alcohol affects him. The child only sees his parent's life spiraling out of control and how miserable he is, and thus how miserable he is to everyone else. Often, the child of an alcoholic resents his parent, but does not think that the relationship will be the same with his own children. Often, it is too late by the time he realizes that he is his parent and the cycle continues.

Alcoholism was once thought to be a recessive trait. Now, we know it to be a dominant trait. The perception that alcoholism must be a recessive trait probably arose out of the fact that some children of alcoholic parents do not fall victim to alcohol's snare, but it often resurfaces in the grandchildren of the alcoholics. Some children of alcoholics do see the damage that alcohol has done to their parents and avoid it themselves. But when they don't understand the true nature of this disease, they often fail to prevent their children from falling into the same trap.

However, when it comes to alcohol addiction, because it takes a long time for addiction to take hold, many seem unaware of what is happening early on. They are having too much fun to realize what is happening to them until it's too late.

Co-morbidities

There are co-morbidities associated with alcoholism. In fact, this is true with all addictions. There are many studies that show that the occurrence of psychiatric illness such as depression and other behavioral disorders is much higher in the alcoholic population than the general public. There are other studies that show that among the mentally ill, the rate of alcohol and drug usage is higher than in the general public as well. Some use this data to show that mental illness causes alcoholism and other addictions.

However, a Duke University study in 1990 showed that when approximately 2000 college students were followed for 20 years using the Minnesota Multiphasic Personality Inventory (MMPI) that the incidence of mental illness did not change over time.[13] Any parent can tell you that a child is born with his or her own personality. A happy child grows up to be a happy adult, and vice versa. An exception to this was when someone became addicted to alcohol or suffered a traumatic event, such as PTSD. Then, the incidence of mental illness went up.

Which came first, the chicken or the egg? Addiction or mental illness? The answer is addiction. Once addiction is treated, the incidence of mental illness falls back to a normal level. One caveat to remember is that those suffering from depression and anxiety and other ills are more likely to try alcohol or other drugs to deal with their problems. The higher the percentage of people who try these drugs, the higher the number of people who are likely to get hooked. There is no cause and effect when it comes to depression and alcoholism.

Delirium Tremens (DTs)

The physical withdrawal from alcohol is called delirium tremens (DTs). Unlike physical withdrawal from opiates, DTs can be fatal. This is because DTs can result in seizures. DTs have a lot of similarity with symptoms of opiate withdrawal, such as agitation, sweating, tachycardia, and hypertension. However, there are major differences between the two as well. These include visual, auditory, and tactile hallucinations. DTs can happen to people coming off benzodiazepines and barbiturates as well.

Even a person going through DTs may not be truly addicted to alcohol. Most medical textbooks will disagree with me on this point. According to most medical textbooks, the fact that someone went through DTs is proof beyond doubt that such a person is an alcoholic. It is viewed in the same light as if someone tried to commit suicide; it would clearly indicate that such a person must be depressed. In most cases, they are right. However, once again, if we truly define addiction as what is going on inside the brain and not just as a set of behaviors, then we cannot look at any behavior alone, no matter how detrimental or hideous it may be, as proof of the disease.

Just as going through physical withdrawal from prolonged opiate use does not necessarily mean that the person is addicted to opiates, we cannot say that just because someone is going through DTs that this must mean that he/she became addicted to alcohol. If the reason behind that person's prolonged alcohol abuse was depression or anxiety or mental illness, but the person never experienced the truly euphoric feeling from the alcohol, he is not addicted even if he is going through DTs.

Vivitrol

In 2006, the FDA approved Vivitrol, a once-a-month injectable naltrexone, for the treatment of alcoholism.[14] Naltrexone is an opiate blocker. Because alcohol releases dopamine in much higher quantities for those who are susceptible to its allure, naltrexone helps block its euphoric effect. Alcohol releases dopamine and by blocking this, naltrexone blocks the euphoria derived from alcohol in alcoholics and thus gets rid of their desire to chase that high. Unlike Antabuse, which makes an alcoholic violently sick when he drinks, Vivitrol just blocks the extreme euphoria from the alcohol. It basically makes the alcoholic experience alcohol like the rest of us.

For those who still enjoy their alcohol too much, they wouldn't want to give up their fun without a good reason. By educating them about what addiction is and what the true high is and pointing out that their fun will eventually snare them in its trap, we can help prevent them from falling victim to this disease.

When someone is undergoing Vivitrol treatment, he must be told to stop drinking altogether. Although he may think that he can become a social drinker like everyone else, as long as he is drinking, he is likely to relapse once the Vivitrol treatment ends. Once an alcoholic feels normal when he drinks, he soon forgets why he wanted to quit in the first place and often relapses. In my experience, unless the Vivitrol treatment is combined with an outpatient treatment such as AA, it rarely works. It's strange that something that makes things easier doesn't always mean that it's better.

The struggle that someone goes through to stay clean and sober often helps that person remain sober. Easy fixes may seem to work better early on, but they make the person more likely to relapse. Without a strong education and reinforcement of why they wanted to quit in the first place, no drug will cure these patients. The only real cure we have is through education and counseling.

In 2010, the FDA approved Vivitrol for the treatment of opiate addiction as well.[15] I have even used it for cocaine addiction, and it seems to work.

References

[1] *APA Dictionary of Psychology*, 1st ed., Gary R. VandenBos, ed., Washington: American Psychological Association, 2007.

[2] Ewing, John A. "Detecting Alcoholism: The CAGE Questionnaire." *JAMA* 252: 1905-1907. 1984.

[3] http://www.cdc.gov/nchs/fastats/alcohol.htm

[4] /ncadistore.samhsa.gov/catalog/facts.aspx?topic=3

[5] http://www.afsp.org/index.cfm?fuseaction=home.viewpage&page_id=050fea9f-b064-4092-b1135c3a70de1fda

[6] Gabbard. "Treatments of Psychiatric Disorders." Published by the American Psychiatric Association: 3rd edition, 2001. ISBN 0-88048-910-3

[7] http://www.marininstitute.org/Youth/alcohol_youth.htm

[8] WHO European Ministerial Conference on Young People and Alcohol.

[9] http://www.about-alcohol-abuse.com/Alcohol_Abuse_Statistics.html

[10] http://alcoholism.about.com/od/history/a/The-Founders-Of-Alcoholics-Anonymous.htm

[11] http://www.nih.gov/news/pr/may98/nida-13.htm

[12] http://www.ttb.gov/statistics/1stqtr92.pdf

[13] I.C. Siegler, A.B. Zonderman, J.C. Barefoot, R.B. Williams Jr., P.T. Costa Jr., and R.R. McCrae. Behavioral Medicine Research Center, Duke University Medical Center, Durham, North Carolina 22710. *Psychosomatic Medicine*, Vol 52, Issue 6 644-652, Copyright © 1990 American Psychosomatic Society.

[14] http://alcoholism.about.com/od/meds/a/Vivitrol-Treatment-For-Alcoholism-And-Addiction.htm

[15] http://abcnews.go.com/Health/MindMoodNews/month-vivitrol-shot-opioid-addicts/story?id=118651

Chapter 5 Alcoholism and Genetics

FOR CENTURIES, MANKIND HAS ARGUED whether it is the environment or genetics that lead one to become addicted to alcohol. Many Americans with their Puritanical values of self-determination and individualism have long viewed alcoholism as a failing, a sin, an overindulgence, secondary to a lack of self-control, moral compass, and value. Unfortunately, such a value system tends to make people hide their family's dirty secret and prevents many from getting the help they need.

Even today, many Americans hold such views. Such views are so ingrained in our society that many people who became alcoholics feel deep guilt and shame because they share these views. Even after I explain to many of my patients that we have found a genetic marker for alcohol addiction, many patients cannot let go of their own guilt and shame at having fallen victim to this trap. This is true even though we as a society have "accepted" alcoholism as a disease. This is even more true when it comes to other addictions that we have yet to publicly accept as a disease.

Many who do not suffer this affliction often view those who get addicted with disdain and consider them weak-willed or suffering from some character flaw. This is especially true when it comes to many people's views on alcoholism among the Native Americans.[1] When we truly accept alcoholism as a disease, how it affects one ethnic group should not make any difference. Only because deep underlying prejudices and biases about alcoholism still persist is it possible to view alcohol affliction in one ethnic group with disdain and contempt and attribute such a group's problem to their own laziness or inherent badness.

To this day, I vividly remember my shock when I was confronted with such blatant prejudice many years ago.

During my second year of medical school at Rush Medical School in Chicago, a few of my friends and I decided to celebrate the end of our grueling finals week by renting a cabin up in northern Minnesota to go fishing. Although I used to go fishing with my dad in Wisconsin, Minnesota held an allure for me as the ultimate fishing destination in the Midwest. We stayed at a place called Bender's Camp on one of the thousand lakes in Minnesota. It was close to the Canadian border. It was also right next to an Indian reservation. One night I was making small talk with the camp owner's daughter. She couldn't have been more than 18 or 19. She was sweet, in an innocent sort of way. I remember her telling me that she was attending a local community college nearby and was helping her father run the camp during the summer.

Somehow, the subject turned to the local Indian population, and I still remember how astounded I was when she told me that old racial slur, "The only good Indian is a dead Indian." I was shocked. Being Korean American, over the years I have experienced my share of racial prejudice and slurs, but I had not come face to face with such a blatant racial statement in some time. I asked her why she felt that way, and she told me it was because every Indian she knew was either lazy or drunk, or worse, both.

Although many people may not share such a hateful sentiment today, the undercurrent of bias and prejudices when it comes to alcoholism is still very strong. Otherwise, I would not be seeing so much guilt and shame among the people who got sucked into this disease. It is because they share these common misconceptions about their own illness that they feel ashamed; they believe they got to where they are because of their own failings.

Alcoholism and the Role of Family and Society

It has been understood, even early on, that alcoholism runs in the family. Many people viewed this as a sign that alcoholism was a learned behavior, a byproduct of the environment; loose morals that condoned heavy alcohol consumption and other vices were passed down from one generation to another. So goes the logic. Some who do not succumb to the allure of alcohol may believe that it was their higher moral scruples and upbringing that made them immune to such folly. Without realizing why, the fact that alcoholism does run in the family made some believe that it must be their upbringing that protected them, whereas those who fell victim to it did so because it was a learned behavior. Once again, the data is correct. The conclusion drawn from it is wrong. It's based on the faulty premise that everyone is susceptible to alcohol's allure. Therefore, the only reason why some succumb to it is because of their weak will, character flaws, or upbringing.

Of course, there are cultural disparities that encourage or discourage the consumption of alcohol as well, and many factors play a role in the number of people becoming addicted to alcohol. Yes, societies that consider it the norm to drink on a regular basis do contribute to more people becoming addicted to it. There are higher incidences of alcoholism in France and Russia, where alcohol consumption is high. In Japan, where alcohol consumption is considered a must while engaging in a business deal, the incidence of alcoholism among Japanese businessmen is much higher than it is among the general public.

On the other hand, a culture that discourages any form of self-indulgence or mind-altering drugs decreases the incidence of alcoholism. Contrary to popular belief, Buddhism and Hinduism do not prohibit alcohol. They discourage it as they do tobacco use. They view such pleasures as self-indulgence. Since enlightenment comes from self-sacrifice and abstinence, such experiences are discouraged.

The Science Behind Alcoholism as a Disease

By the early 1970s, the argument for the genetic basis behind alcoholism was winning. A study showed that adopted children of biological parents with alcoholism had a much higher incidence of alcoholism as adults than the general population.[2] The opposite was also true. If the biological parents did not have a history of alcoholism, then the adopted children had a much lower rate of alcoholism even when they were raised by adoptive parents with alcoholism. It finally proved that alcoholism was not a learned behavior. For those who are susceptible, whether their adoptive parents drank or not, did not matter. Adopted children had rates of alcohol addiction that closely resembled those of their biological parents and not their adoptive parents.

There was another study that proved this point even more clearly. Adopted identical twins had much higher concordance of becoming (or not becoming) alcoholics than fraternal twins even when they were separated at birth.[3] Previous studies showed that adopted children mimicked their biological parents when it came to their rate of alcoholism. This study showed that identical twins had a near-identical incidence or concordance of alcoholism later in life, even when they were separated at birth. Such was not the case with fraternal twins. Yet, naysayers still persisted (and persist today). Many said they still needed that proof, the smoking gun, the genetic marker. However, even when the smoking gun was finally found, some people would not be swayed.

The Genetic Marker

In 2004, the genetic marker for alcoholism was finally found in a village in Russia, where there was a preponderance of alcoholism.[4] It turns about to be a G-variant of the A118 polymorphism of the OPRM1 gene, one of the genes responsible for a mu-receptor (one of the dopamine receptors) expression.

Children with the G-variant of the A118 polymorphism of the OPRM1 gene have much lower levels of beta-endorphins in their blood. Beta-endorphins are responsible for feelings of well-being, contentment, and euphoria. Does this mean that these children were less happy or well-adjusted? The answer is no. It turns out that their G-variant receptors bind three times more tightly to the beta-endorphins than the A-variant type. Thus, fewer beta-endorphins are needed to achieve the same level of euphoria and the feeling of well-being.

However, when children with the G-variant of the A118 gene were exposed to alcohol, they released three times the level of the beta-endorphins than their A-variant counterparts, and thus experienced a much higher feeling of euphoria, stimulation, and ultimately intoxication, explaining their profoundly different experience when they drank.

Finally, science has confirmed what we have suspected for ages, that those who are likely to get addicted to alcohol seem to enjoy it much more than the rest of us (at least early on). Those who became addicted to alcohol have described this in numerous books and articles and it has been repeatedly discussed by members of AA. Now, we understand why.

Science has finally shown us why they have much more fun when they drink. The alcohol stimulates their pleasure center much more powerfully than it does the rest of us. The alcohol takes them places the rest of us can only imagine. Sure, alcohol takes away many people's inhibitions, but for the rest of us, it does not make us feel invincible or like being on top of the world. They were more fun because alcohol made them feel that way. They were more amorous and funny because of alcohol.

Yes, with enough alcohol in their system, they too became drunk. Usually, their final intoxicated state was much worse than for the rest of us because they had the extreme high that made them want to chase the high. Remember, the higher the high, the lower the low.

Unfortunately, like all addictions, such intense euphoria can't be sustained. Over time, such overstimulation of the pleasure center leads to a need rather than a want. Eventually, they can't live without it. With alcohol, this takes years to take hold. However, over time, what made them extremely happy takes away the happiness in the end.

There may be more than one genetic marker for alcoholism. However, the argument whether it is nature versus nurture as to why someone becomes addicted to alcohol should finally be put to rest.

False Perceptions about Alcoholism

Even now, there are books published and heavily promoted about how alcoholism (as well as other addictions) is "not a disease" but just a maladjusted coping mechanism. They say that they can cure alcoholism and other addictions. They say that anyone can get addicted to anything and that you got addicted because you were using the drug to deal with depression and anxiety and other ills in your life, and by showing you the errors of your ways you can get yourself out of it, and that addiction can be cured. Such foolish beliefs exist because they confuse abuse with addiction, and because they use only behavior to diagnose addiction.

Most people who are truly addicted to anything will tell you that there is no cure for what ails them. Yes, they can learn to control it, but there is no cure. They must stay vigilant if they are to prevent themselves from slipping back into their addiction.

Contrary to popular belief, Prohibition did decrease alcoholism and alcohol-related illnesses.[5] I am not proposing that we revert back to Prohibition, but I point this out as an argument against legalizing illicit drugs. Although most people will not get hooked on most illicit drugs, the possible increase in the sheer number of people exposed to them will increase the number of those who will become addicted to them. While alcoholism can take years to take hold, addiction to some drugs can happen rather quickly.

References

[1] http://alcoholism.about.com/cs/genetics/a/blacer031116.htm

[2] D.W. Goodwin, F. Schulsinger; N. Moller; L. Hermansen; G. Winokur; & S.B. Guze. "Drinking problems in adopted and nonadopted sons of alcoholics." *Archives of General Psychiatry* 31:164-169, 1974.

[3] Z. Hrubec & G.S> Omenn. "Evidence of genetic predisposition to alcoholic cirrhosis and psychosis: Twin concordances for alcoholism and its biological endpoints by zygosity among male veterans." *Alcoholism: Clinical and Experimental Research* 5:207-212, 1981.

[4] Alcoholism: Clinical & Experimental Research (2004, December 30). A Genetic Difference At The Opiate Receptor Gene Affects A Person's Response To Alcohol. *ScienceDaily*.

[5] http://www.druglibrary.org/Prohibitionresults.htm

Chapter 6 Opiates

IN ORDER TO UNDERSTAND OPIATE addiction, one must understand what opiates are. Opiates were originally derived from compounds found in the opium plant. Now, we also have manmade opiates, both semi-synthetic and fully synthetic. All opiates exhibit characteristics similar to those of morphine. Although most opiates have a similar molecular structure to that of morphine, not all do. Some manmade opiates were first classified as non-opiate pain medications because their molecular structures were so different from that of morphine. Others that look very similar to morphine are not considered opiates, because although they may look like morphine, they don't behave like it.

The most commonly found opiates in the opium plant are morphine, codeine, and thebaine.[1] Morphine is the most abundant. From morphine, heroin is synthesized by adding two acetyl groups.[2] In the body, heroin is converted back into morphine. Morphine breaks down into hydromorphone (Dilaudid). Codeine is a weak opiate.

Thebaine in its natural state is highly toxic to humans, but from it, we get hydrocodone (Vicodin, Norco), oxycodone (Percocet, OxyContin), and oxymorphone (Opana). Oxycodone breaks down into oxymorphone. From thebaine, we also get buprenorphine (Suboxone/Subutex). However, buprenorphine is not considered a true opiate because it lacks the similar effects of morphine. It is a partial opiate agonist.

Another useful alkaloid found in opium is paparverine. It is not classified as an opiate because it lacks the morphine-like effects. It is a gastrointestinal anti-spasmodic drug. Diphenoxylate HCl, an active ingredient found in Lomotil, a popular anti-diarrheal medication, is an isomer of meperidine (Demerol). It's not classified as an opiate. However, Demerol is. Just because its chemical structure looks like an opiate does not mean that it acts like one. Another example of this is dextromethorphan, an active ingredient in many cough medications. It's a stereoisomer of levomethorphan, which is an opiate, but dextromethorphan is not.

Although the term opioids and opiates are often used interchangeably, strictly speaking, opiates refer to only those that are derived from the opium plant. Opioids encompass opiates as well as semi-synthetic and fully synthetic substances that exhibit the characteristics of morphine.[3] Opioids also include the endogenous ones in the brain.[4]

Opioids are classified into four categories:
- **Natural** opiates found in the opium plant, including morphine, codeine, and thebaine
- **Semi-synthetic** opioids are derived from natural opiates and include hydromorphone (Dilaudid), hydrocodone (Vicodin), oxycodone (Percocet, OxyContin), oxymorphone (Opana), and heroin
- **Fully synthetic** opioids are those that are manmade and may bear no resemblance to naturally occurring opiates except that they produce similar effects as morphine. They include fentanyl (Duragesic), meperidine (Demerol), methadone, tramadol (Ultram), Nucynta, and propoxyphene (Darvon, Darvocet)
- **Endogenous** opioids are produced naturally in the body, such as endorphin, enkephalin, dynorpin, and endomorphin

All naturally occurring opiates as well as the semi-synthetic opiates are in the same class as heroin. If one can get addicted to heroin, one can get addicted to all naturally occurring and most semi-synthetic opiates. If one is immune to them, one is immune to heroin.

When discussing opiate addiction, we are referring to all opioids except for the endogenous ones. We have not been able to reproduce endogenous opioids in a large enough quantity to see if one can become addicted to them. The effects that opiates have on us depend on how they interact with the opioid receptors in our brain. As stated before, their effects can be profoundly different from one person to another. Even the amount of analgesic (pain-relieving) effect one opiate can have can vary greatly from one person to another.

Physicians have known that most patients do not seem to derive any euphoric feeling from opiates. Most patients will tell you that all opiate pain medications do for them, other than helping alleviate their pain, is to make them groggy and sedated.

However, for those who are likely to get hooked on opiates, it has profoundly different effects early on. At a low dose, it stimulates them and makes them highly euphoric. At a high dose, it eventually sedates them. We have not isolated the genetic marker for opiate addiction as of yet. However, given the profound differences in the way people react to opiates, genetic differences must exist.

Opioid Receptors[5],[6]

There are five known opioid receptors: Mu, Kappa, Sigma, Delta, and Epsilon.

Mu Receptors
- mediate euphoria, analgesia, respiratory and physical depression, meiosis
- reduce GI motility
- μ1 mediate euphoria and analgesia
- μ2 mediate respiratory depression
- The μ1 receptor is morphine selective and is responsible for euphoria

Delta Receptors
- mediate   spinal   and   supraspinal   analgesia,

dysphoria (feeling of doom), psychomimetic effects (e.g., hallucinations), and respiratory and vasomotor stimulation
- These receptors have been sub-typed as $\delta 1$ and $\delta 2$ and are thought to be relatively unimportant in terms of euphoria

Kappa Receptors
- mediate spinal analgesia, sedation, miosis, respiratory depression, and dysphoria
- K1 mediates spinal analgesia
- K3 mediates supraspinal analgesia
- K2 function is unknown

Sigma Receptors
- implicated in psychotomimetic (hallucinations)
- causes dysphoria
- possible dilation of pupils

Epsilon Receptors
- least understood of all opiate receptors

Opioid Receptors and their Roles[7,8]

Receptor Types	Mu/Delta	Kappa	Sigma
Supraspinal	++	+	
Spinal	+	+	
Analgesia	++	+	-
Respiratory suppression	++	+	
Pupil constriction	-		
Pupil dilation	++	+	
Reduced GI motility	++		
Smooth muscle spasm	++		
Behavior effect	Euphoria++/+	Dysphoria++	
Physical dependence	Sedation++	Sedation+	

Psychomimetic	++	+	

The above chart makes it obvious that opiates probably trigger different opioid receptors in different people in varying degrees. Otherwise, we would not see such profound differences in people's reactions to opiates.

Classes of Opioid Pain Medications

There are three major classes of opiate pain medications based on their molecular structures: morphine (phenanthrenes), phenylpiperidines, and diphenylheptanes groups.[9]

1. Morphine (phenanthrenes) group are the most prevalent and the most commonly used opiates. They include codeine, hydrocodone, oxycodone, oxymorphone, morphine, hydromorphone, nalbuphine, butorphanol, levorphanol, pentazocine, heroin, etc.
2. Phenylpiperidines group contains meperidine (Demerol), fentanyl (Duragesic patches), sufentanil, remifentanil, etc.
3. Dipenylheptanes group includes methadone, propoxyphene (Darvocet), etc.

If you are truly allergic to one of the drugs in the morphine group, then you are allergic to all of the drugs in that class. It is rare to have a true allergy to morphine or its derivatives. As a pain specialist, I see patients who tell me that they are allergic to codeine, but OxyContin works wonders. Such a patient may not know what a true allergy is. They often confuse side effects such as nausea and itching (without hives) as a true allergy. Sometimes, when a patient names a specific drug like OxyContin as the only opiate that he is not allergic to, there may be an ulterior motive.

Because morphine-based medications are often used in an emergency setting, for those who are truly allergic to the morphine group, it could be lethal if the emergency staff is not aware of this fact. For them, I recommend that they wear a medical alert bracelet indicating their allergy.

Once again, let me point out that if you can get high on any of the opiates in the morphine group, then you can get high on heroin. The opposite is also true. If you don't get high on any of these opiates, then you can't get high on heroin.

Mice Study

When Dr. George Uhl at the National Institute of Drug Abuse bred mice without a gene for mu opioid receptors, the mice "showed a profound indifference to morphine and a striking reduction in their response to alcohol and other stimulants."[10] They also failed to thrive, most of them dying prematurely unless they were force-fed.

Endogenous opioids and their interactions with opioid receptors are necessary for survival. They are the natural painkillers and provide us with the tools to give us a sense of contentment, well-being, and happiness, and they foster those behaviors that are good for us such as eating, socializing, and sex by rewarding such behaviors through the release of dopamine in the mesolimbic pathway. However, when it comes to addiction, this reward system is hijacked to such an extreme level that it creates a demand for that drug that is not healthy.

There is work underway to find a vaccine for opiate and other addictions. It may be the panacea we are looking for. However, if Dr. Uhl's mice study teaches us anything, such a vaccine must not affect our own mu receptor sites. Otherwise, the cure will be worse than the disease.

The Difference between Normal and Abnormal Reactions

The difference between normal interactions and what happens in addiction is the degree to which these opioid receptors are stimulated. With addiction, there is such a powerful stimulation of euphoric feelings that, with repeated exposure, the brain becomes enslaved by the need to chase that feeling. Without such a highly euphoric experience early on, addiction will not take place. This, then, is the basis for any addiction.

The craving that follows such overstimulation of this pleasure center over time, which is the hallmark of any addiction, happens in part because the number of dopamine receptors increases over time.[11],[12] While the number of dopamine receptors increases, the brain's ability to produce its own endogenous dopamines (endorphins) decreases as addiction takes full hold.[13] There are more receptors looking for it, but there is less natural dopamine available to meet the demand. We think of tolerance to a drug as the liver's ability to metabolize the same drug faster with repeated exposures. However, with addiction, the increased number of dopamine receptors explains why it becomes harder and harder to satisfy all the dopamine receptors clamoring for them and why the craving ultimately sets in. This is also why everyday activities no longer bring any joy.

References

[1] http://www.britannica.com/EBchecked/topic/430129/opium
[2] http://en.wikipedia.org/wiki/Heroin
[3] http://en.wikipedia.org/wiki/Opiate
[4] http://medical-dictionary.thefreedictionary.com/opioid
[5] http://en.wikipedia.org/wiki/Opioid_receptor
[6] http://www.opioids.com/receptors/index.html
[7] http://en.wikipedia.org/wiki/Opioid_receptor
[8] http://archives.drugabuse.gov/pdf/monographs/71.pdf
[9] http://ocw.tufts.edu/data/41/530115.pdf
[10] http://whyfiles.org/225drug_receptors/index.php?g=4.txt
[11] http://www.ncbi.nlm.nih.gov/pmc/articles/PMC281732/pdf/pnas00293-0337.pdf
[12] http://bjp.rcpsych.org/cgi/content/full/182/2/97
[13] http://www.hhs.gov/asl/testify/t980728a.html

Chapter 7 Pain Medication and Addiction

CAN SOMEONE GET ADDICTED TO opiate pain medications, even if they are taking them for pain? In my experience, the answer is an emphatic yes. I know at least a few physicians who will emphatically say no. Who is right and who is wrong? More importantly, how could such opposing views exist when it comes to this topic?

The Urgency to Better Understand This Beast

According to the Center for Disease Control, in 1999, over 16,000 people died from an opiate overdose in the US.[1] By 2005, the last year for which we have the complete available data, that number had increased to more than 22,000, and this trend has been rapidly growing over the last two decades.[2] By the way, the majority of these deaths were from prescription opiate pain medications and not from heroin.[3] An unofficial number of overdose deaths for 2006 in America is estimated at over 31,000.[4] For the first time, in 2009, 15 states reported having more people die from an opiate overdose than from motor vehicle accidents.[5] This is an ominous trend. We are not dealing with an innocuous problem. It is a growing epidemic. As awful as these numbers are, deaths from opiate overdoses represent only the tip of the iceberg.

Increase in the Prescribing Habits of Physicians

The trend in the exponential growth of overdose deaths related to opiates is mirrored by the trend in the increased prescribing habits of physicians over the last two decades, particularly regarding prescriptions of opiate pain medications.[6] One of the reasons behind such a change in the prescribing habits of physicians is thought to be a push by both the pharmaceutical industry as well as many pain specialists in the early 1990s who claimed that chronic pain was being undertreated. To a large extent, they were probably right.

Even now, many physicians are leery of prescribing any opiate pain medications because they are afraid that anyone who takes them for too long will become addicted. However, a growing number of physicians were brought up to believe that no one gets addicted to opiate pain medications when they are used for pain. Unfortunately, I have to say that both groups are wrong. Although most patients being treated for pain do not get addicted to opiate pain medications, some do.

Without understanding why some patients become addicted while most do not, it is as if physicians have to either believe everything their patients tell them or be suspicious of every pain patient who walks in through their door. This leads to either overprescribing of opiate pain medications or under-treatment of legitimate pain. Neither scenario is healthy.

Unfortunately, with little training, some physicians found it easy to become a pain specialist. How hard is it to give your patients what they want? They are happy, and your life is easier. Unfortunately, there are also great financial incentives to overprescribe.

Not only did overprescribing make such physicians' lives easier, but it also grew their practices. Many of these self-defined pain specialists started to do cash-only practices and saw their income blossom. Some even started to charge for every prescription they wrote. Although some highly publicized (and often corrupt) physicians got in trouble, many of these practices still exist. Unfortunately, most physicians are not trained to understand addiction or how to treat pain. Looking back, God knows I wasn't, even though a part of my training was in pain management and addiction. Some feel the need to fill the void left by other physicians' refusal to help treat those pain patients who truly deserve help. Some physicians, however, have taken advantage of such a void.

Contrary to popular belief, the majority of those who overdose are not teenagers or drug addicts living on the street, but working-age adults with jobs.[7] Most addicts lead normal lives, at least superficially. Most addicts have jobs, maybe in part because they need to work in order to sustain their habit. And most people, including family members, are not aware of their problem until it's too late.

For every fatal opiate overdose, there are countless more non-fatal ones. Only when a loved one becomes a victim to this tragedy or when we hear about a celebrity who overdosed recently do we focus on this epidemic. However, the public's attention span is short and the focus on this epidemic fades quickly with each change in the news cycle. We quickly forget how big this problem really is. There were over 245,000 visits to emergency rooms across the United States in 2009 because of opiate overdoses.[8] Most patients survived, but some paid the ultimate price for their mistakes. Only when we realize the scale and the magnitude of this problem will we as a society finally sit up and pay attention to this crisis. Only when we finally understand addiction can we get this epidemic under control.

In 2012, Americans consumed 80% of all opiate pain medications produced in the world![9] The pendulum has swung the other way. Yes, the medical community is largely at fault for this. Because we have handed out pain medications too carelessly, we have fostered an expectation by patients that it's OK to pop a pill for every ache and pain. This expectation by patients then leads to more and more pain pills being prescribed.

Opposing Views on the Addictive Nature of Opiate Pain Medications

There are doctors as well as a great number of the general public who think that anyone using opiate pain medication long enough will eventually get hooked on it. They often equate tolerance and physical dependence with addiction.

The literature is full of such misconceptions. For them, using any narcotic pain medication poses danger. Such doctors tend to under-treat their patients' pain. Such patients tend to under-treat themselves. But if they understood why some may get hooked and the signs that one may be susceptible or not, they could approach this more rationally and with less fear.

Others think that no one gets addicted, and that it is not a disease, but rather a vice, a behavior that can be controlled, modified, and managed. Many believe that as long as they are using opiates to control their pain, they will not get addicted. Unfortunately, this is also not true. Doctors who believe this about opiate pain medications have often contributed to their patients' addiction.

Unfortunately, these opposing views are both wrong. The truth, as it often does, lies somewhere in the middle. Most patients who take pain medications do not get hooked. That's true no matter how strong the drug is or how long the patient has been taking it. However, some will become addicted even when their drug is considered a weak opiate like Vicodin. If anyone could get hooked on opiate pain medications, we wouldn't be using them to treat pain; it would be too dangerous!

One study that is often cited to show that patients do not get addicted to opiate pain medications when they are used for pain was done on post-op patients. They were followed only while they were in the hospital. No follow-up studies were done after they were discharged. Patients were asked whether they thought they got hooked while they were in the hospital, and the study also asked the medical staff whether they saw any telltale signs of drug-seeking behaviors. This was an extremely fraudulent study, especially because it followed patients for such a short period of time.

I agree that if treated appropriately, patients are less likely to get addicted. If pain medications help decrease the pain to a tolerable level but do not get rid of the pain completely, the chance that someone will get addicted is much lower. However, when pain medications are given above the dose necessary to bring the pain to a reasonable level, one of two things will happen.

For those who are not genetically susceptible to becoming addicted, all they will experience is grogginess and sedation. However, for those who are susceptible, they will become stimulated and euphoric at first. Even for those who are susceptible to becoming addicted, sedation may eventually follow the initial high at a higher dose. Otherwise, no one would overdose on opiates when they are getting high. However, this only happens as the high fades.

Most addicts overdose at night. They get extremely high, but the sedation that follows may be so powerful that it shuts down their brain and their breathing stops and they don't wake up the next day. However, for those patients who are just trying to survive day to day without getting extremely high, insomnia is often the hallmark of their addiction. The fact that Michael Jackson suffered from chronic insomnia on a $30,000-per-month drug habit is not unusual.

A person who tells me that he can't sleep after taking a pain pill that he thought would help him fall asleep is the one who I warn about getting addicted. A patient who I was treating for OxyContin addiction once told me that his parents knew he had gotten high because he would be up all night cleaning the house afterward.

For those who are susceptible to opiate addiction, treating pain with opiate pain medications has an added plus (at least superficially). Not only do the pills get rid of the pain, it makes them feel better (much better). By this, I am not talking about feeling better or normal because there is no pain. For them, they feel much better than just having no pain. They feel great! They feel like "Hey, this is the best I have ever felt!"

Most of us couldn't take enough pain medication to make the pain go away completely. If we did, we would be so groggy we couldn't function. Those who can take enough pain pills to make the pain go away completely and still function are the ones who can get hooked on the pain pills.

Most patients who get hooked on opiate pain medications know it. Some may not want to admit it. For some there is a lot of guilt and shame admitting they got hooked.

Unfortunately, this is not an uncommon reaction. They believe how the mass media portrays addicts and can't see themselves in the same light. The mass media portrays addicts as homeless, destitute, and depraved. Why would anyone want to be likened to such people? But addiction comes in many shades and disguises. In fact, most addicts lead a seemingly normal life. Most go to work. Many fool lots of people, including themselves, about their own addiction.

I treated a 72-year-old gentleman named Clay for chronic low back pain for about a year. He had severe spinal stenosis. After months of spinal injections and therapy, he underwent a low back surgery. His pain improved but never went away. I first saw him after the surgery. His surgeon, who wanted me to manage his pain, referred him to me. The patient was on a high-dose opiate pain medication.

Clay had been on the same dosage of pain medications for about a year when he revealed to me that he was hooked. He sat down in front of me, with his wife next to him, and started to cry. He told me that he read my article on addiction and understood it. He was hooked.

I was flabbergasted. I wanted to make sure he understood the difference between addiction and physical dependence. If someone has been on opiates for a while, he will go through physical withdrawal if he stops or decreases the medication too quickly. Some patients think that this means they got hooked. Clay understood the difference.

Clay told me that, about six months earlier, his pain finally went away, but he didn't stop his pain pills. Not because of the withdrawal symptoms, but because the pills made him feel good. He felt 20 years younger. He felt that his golf game was better. His sex was better. But after a while, he began to notice that things changed. He had to constantly fight the urge to take more pain pills because he wanted to feel the burst of energy and euphoria he once felt. For the last six months, he had struggled with the fact that he was getting hooked. He thought that someone his age shouldn't get hooked. He had never been hooked on anything in his life. Why would he get hooked now? He thought he was stronger than that. His wife noticed the change in him as well. He was not the same happy person; he was more irritable and depressed.

I apologized to my patient for not picking up on this sooner. I have discussions with all my chronic pain patients about addiction and why some people can get addicted during almost every visit. Unfortunately, as I learned earlier, the only person who truly knows what is happening early on is the patient (and sometimes the patient's immediate family). I was glad to help Clay get off opiate pain medications and put him on Suboxone (which we will discuss later). Clay and his wife send me Christmas cards every year telling me how well he is doing.

The Proper Use of Opiate Pain Medication

When a patient takes opiate pain pills to bring their pain down to a tolerable level but not mask it completely, it shouldn't do anything other than help decrease the pain. The pain medication is to be used to make the pain tolerable, not eliminate it completely. You may ask why not completely eliminate the pain? There are three reasons for this.

First, if you mask the pain completely, you may do things that you shouldn't be doing and make the condition worse. Remember, the pain is there for a reason. It's there to stop you from doing things that may make the injury worse. I tell patients that they should take pain pills like the NyQuil commercial. Take it so you can rest at night. Sometimes, the reason why someone is not getting better is because he is taking pain medications and doing things he shouldn't be doing and further injuring himself.

The second reason for not trying to completely eliminate the pain is because what first gave you that complete pain relief will soon no longer work. The pain has a way of resurfacing after a while. The patient, then, will have to increase the pain medication again, and the cycle continues. Even if these patients do not get addicted, they will develop a huge tolerance to the pain medication.

The third reason is that when you completely mask the pain, the pain medication will either make you groggy or stimulated and euphoric. Neither scenario is good. For those who get groggy right away, they are not susceptible to getting addicted. However, for those who get stimulated and euphoric, they are.

For those who got sleepy right away, I tell them that they don't have to worry about getting hooked. For those who are not at risk, but refuse to take any opiate pain medications because they are worried about getting hooked, this should allay their fears. For those who got stimulated and euphoric on opiate pain medications, I tell them they must be careful. If they keep chasing that high/euphoric feeling, they will get hooked. Knowing this, they can prevent themselves from getting hooked in the first place. All they have to do is decrease their opiate pain medications to a level where their pain is tolerable without overtaking it. And when the pain subsides, they should stop the pain pills.

Over the years, I have had many patients who have told me that they should stop their pain pills as their pain started to subside because they are starting to like it too much. Once they understand that this is an early warning sign that they can get hooked unless they stop, they can make the right choice and stop. Knowledge is power.

I have a colleague who once told me that while he was in a hospital recovering from a surgery, he felt a great urge to keep pushing the button on his pain pump that delivered the pain medication because he liked the way it made him feel. Instinctively, he knew it probably wasn't the right thing to do and talked himself out of it. Looking back on that experience, he realized why some would get hooked. Not everyone realizes this, and by the time some realize what's going on, it may be too late.

Ethical Issues about Treating Pain

We have a moral and ethical obligation to treat pain adequately. This is true even when treating patients with past or current opiate addiction. There are many patients who believe that because of their past opiate addiction, they can never take opiate pain medications again. This cannot be the standard by which physicians operate.

If a heroin addict comes to an emergency room with a broken leg or a third-degree burn, should we not treat the pain? Of course we should. What if he comes in complaining of back pain? This time, the answer will depend on many factors, such as the cause of the injury, the severity of the injury, and signs of physical trauma. What if the same patient shows up at your office months after the initial injury, but with no discernible pathology to explain the ongoing pain? Such dilemmas confront those of us who treat pain on a daily basis.

If the pain is great enough, we must provide adequate pain relief, even if there is a likelihood of addiction. As I mentioned before, if the pain is not completely eliminated by the pain pills, the chance that a patient will get hooked is much lower. However, we must be vigilant about how opiate pain medications are prescribed to help prevent addiction. The only way this can be done successfully is by educating our patients. I often find that patients will make the right choice and stop the pain pills when their pain starts to subside if they understand what addiction is and recognize the signs that they may be getting hooked. Before addiction takes full hold, the patient still has a choice.

Unfortunately, because there is no true measure of pain, we must rely on our not-so-foolproof method of observation to see if the patient's usage of opiate pain medication matches what we see clinically. There are those who believe that it is probably better to err on the side of trying to provide adequate pain relief rather than trying to prevent every addiction from taking place. I believe that this is probably the right course. But this, too, is not without its perils. When you show your patients that you trust them to help guide you and explain to them the goal of proper pain management, as well as the above concepts, more often than not they will make the right call.

This does not mean that, as physicians, we should give a person as much pain medication as he wants because he says he is in pain. We have to use our judgment, as flawed as it may be. As long as the physician acts in the best interest of the patient with the best understanding and training required of him, few will fault him for his actions. As physicians, we are bound by our Hippocratic Oath to "provide aid and comfort" to our patients, but we are also bound by the same oath to "but *first* do no harm."

This is a fine line we have to walk when it comes to treating pain, one that most physicians probably have faltered with from time to time. Yes, I have contributed to some patients getting hooked and have turned away others whom I believed were hooked. I admit that I probably have wronged some patients. Some of my angriest patients are those whom I have discharged because I honestly felt that I could no longer help them, and did not want to continue enabling their addiction. Ultimately, each physician has his own comfort level and is answerable to his own conscience. Treating pain is a delicate balance between providing adequate pain relief without getting patients hooked.

Some believe that under-treatment of pain because of the fear of getting some hooked is a bigger problem than getting some patients addicted. There is some truth to this. Many physicians are too afraid to prescribe any opiates for fear of the ethical and legal ramifications.

Some, on the other hand, believe that no one gets addicted when they use opiates to treat pain. Some of these physicians have lost their medical licenses because of their generous prescribing habits, and some have even been prosecuted and jailed. On the other hand, there are well-publicized accounts of physicians being sued for inadequate treatment of their patients' pain. Such an atmosphere makes many physicians afraid to treat any chronic pain patients.

Physical Withdrawal from Opiates and Pain

Most patients who are not addicted to opiates will go through physical withdrawal with very little pain. They may complain of mild muscle aches and flu-like symptoms, but not severe pain. However, those who are truly hooked on opiates often experience severe pain. This is true whether they were using opiates for pain or for recreational use. The rest of the physical withdrawal symptoms, between the two groups, are comparable. However, for those who are hooked, the pain is tenfold worse. Does it mean that anyone who experiences severe pain is addicted? In my opinion, the answer is yes.

Pseudoaddiction versus True Addiction

Pseudoaddiction is a term used to describe a condition when a patient may exhibit all of the signs of addiction, such as frequent early refills, shopping around for doctors, hoarding his pills, etc., when he is not truly addicted. How do you know? It's because when the pain is adequately treated, these behaviors go away, indicating that the patient was probably not addicted in the first place, according to this theory.

When you look at addiction only as a set of behaviors, it's impossible to distinguish addiction from pseudoaddiction. Pseudoaddiction happens when a physician under-treats a patient's pain. It is due to a lack of trust between the patient and the doctor, which, unfortunately, is not uncommon and happens for a myriad of reasons.

On one hand, many patients think that their doctors will not believe how bad their pain is. In their eagerness to show their doctors how much pain they are in, they overplay their symptoms. When asked to rate their pain from a scale of one to ten, these are the patients who say "20." They may even walk with an exaggerated limp or jump even at the lightest touch.

In medicine, we call this pain magnification. There is also a sign that we use called the Waddell signs,[10] which indicate whether the patient's pain is truly organic or not. Unknowingly, many patients, in their eagerness to make their physicians understand how much pain they are in, fall victim to this trap. It is truly ironic that in response to their behavior, many physicians will tend to discount their pain. What they try to accomplish in earnest backfires on them.

On the other hand, when it comes to treating pain, there are a lot of barriers to a healthy doctor-patient relationship right off the bat. Many physicians are too scared that the next pain patient who walks through their door is already addicted, is diverting his/her drugs, or will become addicted to the pain medication.

If you were to play the devil's advocate, couldn't you just say that if you gave an addict as much opiates as he wanted, his behavior of addiction would go away as well? Maybe—or at least at first! How, then, can you tell the difference?

The current logic goes like this. For those who are truly addicted, any benefit from an increased dose is only short-lived. Soon, the same dosage will no longer work, and aberrant behaviors will return. For them, there isn't a high enough dose to quench their cravings. Or is that really the case? Maybe you just haven't reached the right dose yet! Unfortunately, these are questions that many physicians struggle with because they were taught to diagnose addiction only using the patient's behavior.

If the only tool a physician has to evaluate whether his patient is addicted or not is the patient's behavior, then there is no absolute way to tell the difference between addiction and pseudoaddiction. Only when we define addiction as what is going on inside the patient's brain can we tell the difference. That's why the traditional way medical professionals have been taught to recognize addiction does not work. It pits doctors against patients.

Either you believe that your patient is in pain when he tells you so, or you don't. Sometimes even an addict is in real pain. Sometimes addiction may be the cause of the pain. Sometimes the patient is just plain lying to get his drugs or is trying to divert them. Most physicians understand that most of the time, patients are telling the truth.

However, as physicians, we can be sanctioned or have our licenses revoked if we indiscriminately hand out opiate pain medications to anyone who wants them, while at the same time being liable for malpractice if we under-treat patients who truly need pain medications. This either leads to overprescribing of opiate pain medications, which may lead to getting some patients hooked, or pain medications being diverted, or to denying some patients the legitimate care they need. As physicians, this is the dilemma we face.

Only when we start asking, "How did the drug make you feel?" can we distinguish those who became addicted to the pain pills versus those who are exhibiting pseudoaddiction behaviors.

For most physicians, there is no way to tell who is getting hooked early on. Because we have been trained to diagnose addiction only as a set of behaviors, it's impossible to diagnose addiction until it has taken full hold. However, if we truly understand addiction, we will ask that all-important question, "How did it make you feel?" The better the medical community understands addiction, the better we will be able to help our patients not get hooked in the first place. Instead of relying only on our observations of the patient's behavior, which often only allows us to diagnose addiction when it's too late, we can learn to spot those who are susceptible and help them avoid getting hooked in the first place.

We need to stop looking at our patients as potential adversaries from whom we are trying to weed out the addicts. Instead, by educating our patients about what addiction is and why some people get hooked, we can become partners with our patients in trying to help some avoid getting hooked and offer those who are already hooked a way out. Once the patient understands addiction, he will know whether he is susceptible to getting hooked or not. Unfortunately, this does not apply to everyone, and it obviously does not apply to those who are diverting their drugs.

High-profile celebrity drug overdose deaths bring our national focus on this epidemic for a while, but soon the discussion fades into the background. These celebrity deaths, as unfortunate as they are, are only the tip of the iceberg, and should point out the enormity of this communal problem and should prompt more discussions about how to tackle this growing epidemic.

It is easy to understand why some doctors would be enamored by celebrity patients and bend over backward to comply with their every whim and desire. The huge financial incentives cannot be overlooked either. They may argue, "Hey, if I don't give him what he wants, there are a dozen others who will." However, such justification cannot defend that doctor from the argument that he provided his client substandard care rather than providing his client the best medical care he deserves, even if that is not what his client asked for. Sometimes, saying no is the right thing to do.

A physician cannot be a patient's buddy, pal, or an employee beholden to his every wish. We are supposed to be mentors and healers who have the patient's best interest in mind, even if that's not what the patient wants at the time. When we see that the patient is involved in a self-destructive behavior such as addiction, our job is not to further enable that person, but to try to counsel and offer constructive help out of his addiction. If the help is not wanted, unfortunately, whether your patient is a celebrity or not, you must stop enabling that patient and stop further giving credence to his belief that the medical community condones what he is doing.

Barriers to Sorting out Addiction When It Comes to Treating Pain

There are many barriers to educating patients about addiction. There are many ingrained beliefs and prejudices patients bring with them that often make discussing addiction difficult.

Often, trying to make patients understand that their own experience with a drug may be quite different than that of others is not easy. Only when they start asking other people about their own experiences and hear how others had profoundly different experiences from their own do they finally begin to understand this.

Another obstacle when dealing with patients who got hooked on prescription pain medications is overcoming the media stereotypes of addicts. Because the media often portrays addicts as depraved and truly down and out, it is often difficult to make patients understand that most addicts have jobs and carry on seemingly normal lives and can fool a lot of people, sometimes even themselves.

Sometimes, patients can't seem to overcome the stigma they associate with being addicted. Some build an insurmountable barrier that prevents them from even considering the possibility that they may have gotten hooked. They believe that as long as they are taking their pain pills to treat their pain that they can't be hooked.

Can Addiction Perpetuate or Increase Pain? (The Theory Behind Hyperalgesia)

This is an interesting concept that surfaced in the pain management field a few years ago. Of all the things I will cover in this book, this will be the most controversial and generate the most heated debates and disagreement. I offer no definitive scientific proof on this subject, but offer my own insights and observations, as flawed as they may be, along with some incomplete scientific data.

The theory behind hyperalgesia states that, for some patients, prolonged exposure to opiate pain medications actually increases their perception of pain. This is different than tolerance, where opiates are not as effective as they used to be. For patients with hyperalgesia, the perception of pain actually increases with prolonged exposure to opiate pain medications. This theory states that for those who become addicted to opiate pain medications, there is no amount of pain medications that actually makes the pain go away or even manages it adequately (except for a very brief period when you increase the dose again). We as pain specialists have known that, for most patients, we can achieve adequate pain control without constantly having to increase the dose, but for some, this elusive pain control is never achieved.

Once someone is put on opiate pain medications, sometimes the pain never goes away, and over time it becomes worse, even when there is no discernible pathology to explain the escalating pain. Once the patient is started on opiate pain medications, often the physician may feel compelled to continue prescribing the pain medication as long as the patient states that he is in pain and as long as the patient does not exhibit aberrant behaviors indicating that he may be getting hooked. Of course, most physicians will try to keep the pain medication at a reasonable level.

What may have started out as an attempt to improve the quality of the patient's life by providing adequate pain relief may ultimately lead some patients to become dependent on pain medications for the rest of their lives. Such dependency is not just metaphorical, but one of enslavement. Although opiate pain medications may help the pain and improve the quality of life for many, for some the pain may never become manageable. Although for many people, these medications improve quality of life, for others they do not. For some people, it becomes a love-hate relationship.

Many of these chronic pain patients are unhappy in spite of how much pain medication they are on. I am not saying that all chronic pain patients are unhappy or that most cannot find adequate pain relief—most do. However, for some, pain pills do not improve their quality of life but enslave them. Even when they exhibit no outward appearances of having gotten addicted, some of these chronic pain patients are deeply unhappy. Since most chronic pain patients can find adequate pain relief and are happy with their pain pills, what needs to be asked is what's different about these patients. Yes, I understand that chronic pain can bring on depression. But this is a different subset of patients.

Let me clarify. Many patients can adequately control their pain, and their quality of life improves. However, for some, no matter how much pain medication they are on, there seems to be no improvement in their quality of life. These are the patients who tell me, "Get me off this stuff, but give me more." Let's assume for a moment that they are not trying to get high on the pain medication but are trying to use it to treat pain.

For these patients, the question that needs to be asked is, "Why is the pain not subsiding and why can't the pain be adequately controlled?" Most injuries heal on their own, and the pain often subsides. Most people learn to adapt and live with some pain. Why, then, doesn't some people's pain improve or why can't it be adequately managed? The answer is complex and multifaceted. However, one possibility that should be raised is that addiction to the opiate pain medication itself may be perpetuating the pain.

This is the basis for this fairly new concept in pain medicine called hyperalgesia to pain medications. As I stated earlier, it is a controversial concept with many lining up for or against it. It states that a *prolonged exposure to opiate pain medications may subject some patients to become hypersensitive to the pain.* What a normal brain will perceive as discomfort can become unbearable pain when exposed to prolonged opiate use. Because there is no scientific proof to back it up, this is just a theory.

Whether you believe in hyperalgesia or not, the question that I want to ask is why some patients' pain can never be adequately managed, even with high doses of opiate pain medications, especially when there are no strong physical explanations for their ongoing pain? What started out as a minor injury can often become a chronic and disabling pain in some patients, even when adequate pain relief was achieved early on (usually for a very brief period).

When severe pain is not adequately alleviated early on, sometimes chronic pain can set in. There is scientific evidence that points to a lack of adequate pain relief early on as a cause of the chronic pain. However, even when adequate pain relief was achieved early on, why does some people's pain become chronic, and why does these patients' pain never become fully manageable?

As I have stated earlier, in those patients who got hooked on opiates (because they were chasing their highly euphoric feelings), the number of dopamine receptors in their brains increases over time. For patients who got addicted, this may explain, in part, why they may experience severe pain with physical withdrawal. However, this concept does not explain it all. Since the number of dopamine receptors decreases much more slowly over time than the seven to ten days that physical withdrawal usually lasts, this does not explain this phenomenon fully. If the increased number of dopamine receptors was the only reason for the heightened pain, then the pain should theoretically last much longer.

However, let's assume for a moment that the increased number of dopamine receptors does somehow play a role in the pain associated with the physical withdrawal. Then it wouldn't be hard to postulate that, for those patients who did become addicted to opiates, there may be an increased perception of pain to any painful stimulus. In other words, these patients may be hypersensitive to normal pain that you and I perceive as annoying discomfort rather than a disabling pain. I understand that this is just a theory, but one with some scientific basis.

However, there is another problem with this theory. I will be the first to admit that most people who get addicted to opiates for recreational uses do not report a heightened sense of pain unless they are in physical withdrawal. They do have increased dopamine receptors in their brains. Therefore, there must be more than just the increased number of dopamine receptors to explain the hyperalgesia. It's as if the brain is fooling the patient into believing that he needs the drug that it craves. Yes, I know. It's just a theory, and one that I can't possibly substantiate at this point.

Since the premise of any addiction is that it only happens to those who experienced a highly euphoric response to the substance early on, we must examine the above theory in that context. What I have been asking my chronic pain patients who have no discernible reason for their on-going pain, especially when their pain seems to be disproportionate to the dose of their opiate pain medications, is, "How did the pain medication make you feel early on?" If the answer to this question is that the patient did experience highly euphoric feelings early on, then I raise the possibility that hyperalgesia may exist.

Suboxone Challenge

I tell these patients that I believe that their pain is as real as any physical pain and should not be minimized. However, the answer to their problem may not lie in further increasing their pain medication, but in treating the underlying addiction (and thus the hyperalgesia to the opiate pain medications). For these patients, I have been offering them what I call the Suboxone Challenge. I will discuss Suboxone in more detail in a later chapter. For now, let me just say that Suboxone is a drug that we have been using to treat opiate addiction.

The Suboxone Challenge goes like this. If the patient is willing to get off the pain medication and go on Suboxone, one of two scenarios will happen. One possibility is that the patient's pain will become much more manageable or will even be eliminated with Suboxone. In that case, it means that the patient did develop hyperalgesia to the pain medication and was addicted to the pain pills. Or, the pain will become much worse, and there is no hyperalgesia. If the pain worsens, I promise to put the patient back on their pain pills.

It is surprising how many of my chronic pain patients have taken me up on my challenge, and even more surprising how many have actually gotten off their pain medications with their pain becoming much more controllable or being completely eliminated once they have gotten off their pain pills.

Let me state that I only bring this up as a possible option when there is a strong possibility that the patient may have gotten hooked on their pain pills (based on their initial reaction to opiates), and I never force anyone to take the challenge. Most of these patients took the challenge eagerly, probably because they realized that the pain medication was not the answer for them long before I raised the possibility of them being hooked. I also let them know that I believed their pain was real.

Before I have a patient take the Suboxone challenge, I promise him that, if the pain becomes worse, I will put him back on the pain pills. Although Suboxone can be used as a pain medication, it is a relatively mild pain medication. Its true use is in the treatment of opiate addiction. If the patient's pain becomes much better on Suboxone than it ever was on a high dose of opiate pain medications, this suggests that the patient did get hooked and developed hyperalgesia. For these patients, once they are weaned off Suboxone after a prescribed period of time, their pain does not return or worsen.

I had to put some of these patients back on opiate pain medications, but the majority of the patients who took the Suboxone Challenge actually did get off their pain pills, with their pain being much better or completely eliminated.

However, for those patients whose pain became much worse on Suboxone and had to be put back on the opiate pain pills, does it mean that none of them were hooked to begin with? Maybe. Maybe not. It may mean that their pain was a bigger problem than their addiction at the time. Once the physical reason for the pain subsides, they too may be candidates for the Suboxone Challenge at a later time. Remember that even a heroin addict can have real pain.

Even for those patients whose pain went away once they were started on Suboxone, they may develop pain while they are on Suboxone. If the pain is bad enough, the patient may need to be taken off Suboxone and put back on the pain medication. I have done this on many occasions. As I explained earlier, when patients understand that as long as they take their pain medication below the level of their pain and do not try to completely eliminate their pain, often there is no euphoria and they should not get sucked back into their addiction. Once their pain starts to subside, often these patients can be easily taken off their pain pills and put back on Suboxone to finish their prescribed treatment.

Some of my patients who got better after coming off their pain pills and going on Suboxone have told me that they did exaggerate their pain to justify getting their pain medications. However, some have told me that their pain was as real as any pain they had ever felt before and are amazed that their pain actually went away once their addiction was treated. Yes, I do believe addiction to opiate pain medication can magnify and perpetuate pain. This is the basis of the hyperalgesia theory.

As I mentioned before, it is my belief that the only person who is truly aware of whether he is getting addicted to opiate pain medication early on is the patient, once he understands what addiction is. That is why it is so important to educate everyone about addiction and why it happens.

There are tools that have been developed to help physicians detect which patients may be at risk of becoming addicted to opiate pain medications. Unfortunately, in my opinion, they do not work. I used to use them regularly early in my career. When I finally started understanding addiction, I saw why they did not work.

Two of the more popular ones are the Screener and Opioid Assessment for Patients with Pain – Revised edition (SOAPP-R) and the Current Opioid Misuse Measure (COMM). In my opinion, such tools fall short of their intended goal because they mistake commonality as a shared causality. They tend to lump all risk factors or risky behaviors together without understanding what may have contributed to such risky behaviors. Once again, these tools use the patient's behavior (past and present) to diagnose addiction rather than trying to understand what is going on inside the patient's brain. None of these tools ask the right question, "How did it make you feel?" Because both of these are commonly used by many pain specialists (as well as some primary care physicians), I have listed them in their entirety so I can go over what I believe are the problems with these two particular screening tools.

SOAPP-R[11]

SOAPP-R is a set of 24 questions, each given a score from 0 to 4, with the higher the score indicating the more you agree with such a statement.

Never	Seldom	Sometimes	Often	Very Often
0	1	2	3	4

Here are the 24 questions:
1. How often do you have mood swings?
2. How often have you felt a need for higher doses of medication to treat your pain?
3. How often have you felt impatient with your doctors?
4. How often have you felt that things are just so overwhelming that you can't handle them?
5. How often is there tension in the home?
6. How often have you counted pain pills to see how many are remaining?
7. How often have you been concerned that people will judge you for taking pain medication?
8. How often do you feel bored?
9. How often have you taken more pain medication than you were supposed to?
10. How often have you worried about being left alone?
11. How often have you felt a craving for medication?
12. How often have others expressed concern over your use of medication?
13. How often have any of your close friends had a problem with alcohol or drugs?
14. How often have others told you that you had a bad temper?
15. How often have you felt consumed by the need to get pain medication?
16. How often have you run out of pain medication early?

106

17. How often have others kept you from getting what you deserve?
18. How often, in your lifetime, have you had legal problems or been arrested?
19. How often have you attended an AA or NA meeting?
20. How often have you been in an argument that was so out of control that someone got hurt?
21. How often have you been sexually abused?
22. How often have others suggested that you have a drug or alcohol problem?
23. How often have you had to borrow pain medications from your family or friends?
24. How often have you been treated for an alcohol or drug problem?

Scores from the above 24 questions are added. A score of 18 or higher is supposed to indicate that the patient is at a high risk of becoming addicted (or is addicted) to the opiate pain medication.

The problem I have with this approach is that it uses a broad stroke to capture those traits that people believe contribute to addiction. Such traits include depression, feelings of loneliness, boredom, anger/irritability, stress, being ill-tempered, history of sexual abuse, etc. Because we generalize what we see without understanding why addiction takes hold, we misunderstand such traits as hallmarks of addiction. This is the basis of the addictive personality theory.

Question 13, "How often have any of your close friends had a problem with alcohol or drugs?" takes this to an even higher level of absurdity. It's guilt by association. Is this question implying that addiction is a learned behavior?

The only questions that have anything to do with pain medications themselves are:

2. How often have you felt a need for higher doses of medication to treat your pain?
6. How often have you counted pain pills to see how many are remaining?

7. How often have you been concerned that people will judge you for taking pain medication?
9. How often have you taken more pain medication than you were supposed to?
11. How often have you felt a craving for medication?
12. How often have others expressed concern over your use of medication?
15. How often have you felt consumed by the need to get pain medication?
16. How often have you run out of pain medication early?
19. How often have you attended an AA or NA meeting?
22. How often have others suggested that you have a drug or alcohol problem?
23. How often have you had to borrow pain medications from your family or friends?
24. How often have you been treated for an alcohol or drug problem?

Of these, the only questions that have anything to do with addiction are:

11. How often have you felt a craving for medication?
15. How often have you felt consumed by the need to get pain medication?
19. How often have you attended an AA or NA meeting?
22. How often have others suggested that you have a drug or alcohol problem?
24. How often have you been treated for an alcohol or drug problem?

I would reword the above questions with "Have you ever had" rather than "How often have you" and make them yes or no questions. I would reword question number 11 with "craving for pain medication" rather than "craving for medication," question number 19 to say just "NA" meeting and not "AA or NA" meetings, and change question number 24 to just say "drug problem" and not "alcohol or drug problem." A "Yes" answer to any of the above questions would indicate to me that the patient has a high likelihood of becoming addicted to opiate pain medications if they are not taught how to take them properly. Question number 22, "How often have others suggested that you have a drug or alcohol problem?" deserves special attention. It should be reworded to say, "Have you ever thought that you have a drug problem?" Combining drug and alcohol problems suggests that there is a link between the two. Although in my later chapter, I will show you that there is a link between alcohol and opiate addiction, that link is not one-to-one. One can become addicted to one and not the other. Yes, some may be susceptible to both, but there is no direct link. A "Yes" to the above question as it stands should alert the physician to delve further as to whom and in what context this was said. If a person who said this is a close family member or a loved one, I would take such a statement seriously and try to determine the validity of such a statement. I would recommend bringing that person in to talk to them personally to determine the true nature of their concerns.

COMM[12]

COMM is a set of 17 questions, each given a score from 0 to 4, with the higher the score indicating the more you agree with such a statement.

Never	Seldom	Sometimes	Often	Very Often
0	1	2	3	4

1. In the past 30 days, how often have you had trouble with thinking clearly or had memory problems?
2. In the past 30 days, how often do people complain that you are not completing necessary tasks? (i.e., doing things that need to be done, such as going to class, work or appointments)
3. In the past 30 days, how often have you had to go to someone other than your prescribing physician to get sufficient pain relief from medications? (i.e., another doctor, the emergency room, friends, street sources)
4. In the past 30 days, how often have you taken your medications differently from how they are prescribed?
5. In the past 30 days, how often have you seriously

thought about hurting yourself?

6. In the past 30 days, how much of your time was spent thinking about opioid medications (having enough, taking them, dosing schedule, etc.)?

7. In the past 30 days, how often have you been in an argument?

8. In the past 30 days, how often have you had trouble controlling your anger (e.g., road rage, screaming, etc.)?

9. In the past 30 days, how often have you needed to take pain medications belonging to someone else?

10. In the past 30 days, how often have you been worried about how you're handling your medications?

11. In the past 30 days, how often have others been worried about how you're handling your medications?

12. In the past 30 days, how often have you had to make an emergency phone call or show up at the clinic without an appointment?

13. In the past 30 days, how often have you gotten angry with people?

14. In the past 30 days, how often have you had to take more of your medication than prescribed?

15. In the past 30 days, how often have you borrowed pain medication from someone else?

16. In the past 30 days, how often have you used your pain medicine for symptoms other than for pain (e.g., to help you sleep, improve your mood, or relieve stress)?

17. In the past 30 days, how often have you had to visit the emergency room?

A score of 9 or higher is supposed to indicate that you may be abusing or misusing your opiate pain medications. Some of the above questions make sense. However, others miss the mark because they confuse the patient's behavior as the disease itself. According to the above tool, a dementia patient (question number 1), who is often argumentative (question number 7), and who may be often angry (question number 13) must be abusing or misusing his pain medications! Obviously, that doesn't make any sense.

When one looks at addiction only as a set of behaviors,

such misunderstandings can exist. When one truly under-stands what addiction is and why it takes place, one need not resort to such methods to diagnose or detect it.

Unfortunately, the above tools have high sensitivities but low specificities, meaning that anyone who is addicted to opiate pain medications will score high on these screen-ing tools. However, many people who score high on such screening tests are not necessarily addicted. These screen-ing tools cast a wide net to ensure that those who are ad-dicted do not fall through the cracks, but at the same time they ensnare too many people who may not be truly ad-dicted to opiate pain medications. In practical terms, such screening tools offer no real advantage in a clinical setting. Unless you want to deny all of your clinically depressed patients opiate pain medications, even when they are war-ranted, these cannot be the sole tools you rely on to deter-mine who is truly at a high risk of developing an opiate addiction and who is not.

We also cannot assume that everyone will answer the-se questions truthfully. Those physicians who think that such screening tools protect themselves from legal and eth-ical liabilities when it comes to prescribing opiate pain medications may not be correct.

My advice is to try to truly understand what addiction is and why it takes place. Don't be afraid to educate your patients about what addiction is and why it happens, and many will be glad to tell you whether they got hooked or may be getting hooked. When you make treating pain as well as addiction a partnership between you and your pa-tients rather than an adversarial role between the two of you, you are more likely to find your patients cooperating with you in your effort to help them. Learn to ask the right question: "How did pain pills make you feel early on?"

References

[1] http://www.sciencedaily.com/releases/2006/07/060721180821.htm
[2] http://www.cdc.gov/nchs/fastats/acc-inj.htm

[3] http://www.cdc.gov/washington/testimony/2008/t20080312a.htm

[4] http://ezinearticles.com/?Frightening-Drug-Overdose-Statistics---No-One-Thought-it-Would-Happen-to-Them&id=3280971

[5] http://lansing.injuryboard.com/fda-and-prescription-drugs/drug-overdoses-overshadow-number-of-deaths-caused-by-auto-accidents-in-15-states.aspx?googleid=271956

[6] http://www.findingdulcinea.com/news/science/July-August/Prescription-Drug-Related-Deaths-on-the-Rise---.html

[7] http://www.hhs.gov/asl/testify/2008/03/t20080312b.html

[8] http://cleveland.injuryboard.com/medical-malpractice/adverse-drug-reactions-result-in-over-700000-er-visits-per-year.aspx?googleid=207616

[9] http://www.narconon-news.org/blog/2012/09/americans-consume-eighty-percent-of-the-worlds-pain-pills/

[10] http://en.wikipedia.org/wiki/Waddell's_signs

[11] http://www.painedu.org/soapp.asp

[12] http://www.painedu.org/soapp.asp

Chapter 8 Opiate Epidemic

"They call it an epidemic because white folks are doing it!"
- Richard Pryor

WHEN IT COMES TO OPIATE ADDICTION, national expenditure is measured in billions of dollars. This is not including the socioeconomic impact on lives that are ruined by it, the loss in productivity, or the cost of health-related expenditures for treating drug-related illnesses and emergency room visits.

As of 2000, the illicit drug trade was thought to be a $300–400 billion global industry annually.[1] In the US, over 50% of all opiate addiction is to prescription drugs.[2] In 2001, a national survey showed that more than three million adolescents have reported having tried heroin to get high.[3] More than three million adolescents have tried over-the-counter (OTC) cold medications to get high. More than three million people have used LSD. More than 2.4 million have used crystal meth. Remember, most probably did not get high!

More than 50% of those who are incarcerated in our federal prison systems are there for nonviolent drug-related offenses. We spent more than $40 billion incarcerating these prisoners in 2000, which was more than what we spent on all of our primary education that year. The same year, we also spent in excess of $40 billion on our war on drugs.

Even with this enormous expenditure, we are losing the war. In 2009, it's estimated that more than 40,000 people died from opiate overdoses in the US, most involving prescription opiate pain medications. In 1990, that number was 17,000. The first time the number of people who died from opiate overdoses shot past the number of people killed from motor vehicle accidents in some states was 2009. Some of the more famous people who paid the ultimate price for their addiction in the past few years include Michael Jackson, Anna Nicole Smith, Danny Gans, and Philip Seymour Hoffman.

One of the reasons behind this doubling of opiate overdose deaths over the last two decades is thought to be the increased prescribing habits of opiate pain medications by physicians over this time. In the early 1990s, there was thought to be an under-treatment of chronic pain. The CDC classified chronic pain as a disease itself. There was a big push to educate physicians about the need to treat pain more aggressively. The pendulum has swung to the opposite extreme over the last two decades.

Stats and Facts

According to the Substance Abuse and Mental Health Services Administration (SAMHSA), a branch of federal government, we have the following stats:

- 149,000 new addictions to heroin (1999)
- 980,000 persons using heroin at least weekly (1998)
- 810,000–1,000,000 chronic users of heroin (1999)
- Only 170,000–200,000 heroin addicts receiving treatment (< 20%) (1999)
- In 2000, there were approximately 17,000 deaths, secondary to accidental overdose of illicit drugs[4]
- More than 2 million chronic users of heroin in the US (2005)

The dramatic increase in heroin addiction from 1999 to 2005 is thought to be secondary to the influx of cheap heroin, known as black tar heroin, from Mexico.[5] This proves that the greater the availability and the cheaper the drug, the higher the incidence of addiction. This should point to an argument against legalizing drugs.

Contrary to popular belief, I want to point out that not everyone who has tried heroin becomes addicted to it. In 1971, 17% of Vietnam veterans admitted using heroin on a regular basis while in Vietnam,[6] but only 2% of the Vietnam vets were still using heroin three years after they came home. In 2007, 1.7% of high school graduates admitted to having tried it within the past year, but the incidence of heroin addiction in the US is not 1.7%. Given the US population of 300 million and the fact that there are two million chronic users of heroin in the US, the incidence of heroin addiction is about 0.6% or six per thousand.

Is There a Racial Bias in How People are Punished for Drug Violations?

Unfortunately, the answer is yes. Even though racial relations have come a long way, racial disparities still exist. One only needs to look at the racial disparity within our prison population to understand this. According to the Human Rights Watch, in 2003, we have the following statistics from the US Department of Justice:[7,8,9,10]

- More than two million men and women are in our prisons.
- The United States has the highest percentage of its population behind bars in the world.
- The ratio of prisoners per general population has quadrupled from 1970 to 2000.
- The biggest reasons behind the growth of the prison population have been the "war on drugs" and the "three strikes and you are out" laws.
- More than half (51%) of those incarcerated are there for nonviolent, drug-related offenses.
- Although blacks account for 12% of the US population, they account for 44% of all prisoners.
- Hispanics account for 13% of the US population, but they account for 18% of the prison population.
- 38% of blacks are incarcerated for nonviolent drug-related offenses vs. 27% of blacks are incarcerated for violent offenses.
- 24% of whites are incarcerated for nonviolent drug-related offenses vs. 27% of whites are incarcerated for violent offenses.

- Although only 13–15% of all nonviolent drug-related offenders were black, they account for 63% of all nonviolent drug-related offenders who are imprisoned for their crimes.

We are squandering our national resources on incarcerating these nonviolent drug offenders. The racial bias evident in how we dole out punishments speaks volumes on the ills of our socioeconomic problems. However, there are many complex issues underlying such lopsided, irreconcilable, and blatantly racial inequalities. The war on drugs may have had less to do with our prejudices against blacks and Hispanics, but rather our inability to deal with the inner-city poor, who just happen to be of color.

Unfortunately, among the inner-city poor, where there have always been high unemployment, rampant poverty, deep despair, and feelings of helplessness, rates of drug (and alcohol) use and subsequent addictions have always been high. The failure to address the problems of our urban, inner-city poor and disenfranchised is a major contributing factor to both the high incidence of abuse/addiction and the disparity in their incarceration rates. The disparity in how crack cocaine use (mostly by the inner-city poor) is punished much more harshly than regular cocaine use (by rich suburbanites) has contributed to this as well.

Instead of dealing with issues of poverty, race, and the underprivileged who live in our inner cities, we have chosen to lock them away. The war on drugs has been largely launched on the urban poor, who are disproportionately of color, whether they are black or brown. The "three strikes and you are out" laws enacted in many parts of the country made the rest of us feel safer by locking the "undesirables" away. But it was a false sense of security and came at a great price to our society.

From an economic standpoint, it is a hell of a lot cheaper to treat an addict than to incarcerate him. The cost to society is not just in the cost of incarceration, but also in lost productivity and the breakdown of the social fabric of the family, and cannot be measured in dollars and cents alone. Not only is treatment more humane, it is also more commonsensical and cost-effective. We spend over $40 billion a year incarcerating nonviolent opiate drug offenders. Offering treatment, on the other hand, would cost pennies to the dollar. For our own self-interest, if not for the broader good of society, treatment should be an obvious choice. It's time to abandon the "lock them up and throw away the key" mentality. If not for altruistic reasons, but for our own self-interest, we must reverse this insane direction we have set ourselves on.

Hopefully, a better understanding of addiction will bring about more intelligent discourse about how to approach those who are addicted. Instead of incarcerating them out of desperation and fear, hopefully we can offer them hope and help them climb out of the hole that they have dug for themselves. It will be far better for all of us.

Prison: A Growth Industry

Unfortunately, during the last four decades, there has been a boom in the prison industrial complex, brought on by seemingly diverse special interest groups such as politicians, prison guards, and bail bondsmen each pursuing their own self-interest. As mentioned before, the ratio of prisoners to the general population has quadrupled since the 1970s. The prison industrial complex is expected to grow by 5–10% annually for the foreseeable future.[11]

Politicians have used fearmongering, accusing their opponents of being soft on crime, in order to get votes. Others fail to support reasonable changes to the three strikes law out of fear of appearing to be soft on crime.

In California, prison guards and their union helped bring down Proposition 5 in 2008 to preserve their own jobs.[12] Prop. 5, called the Nonviolent Offender Rehabilitation Act (NORA), was a ballot measure that was trying to bring down the state's bloated prison system by bringing a sensible reform to the three strikes law and letting thousands of nonviolent offenders out. It would have saved the state billions of dollars. However, it would have meant a job loss for many prison guards.

For just as bizarre and perverse a reason, the relationship between the bail bond industry and our prison systems keeps many poor, nonviolent offenders in prison.[13] The bail bond industry has lobbied against letting many poor nonviolent offenders out on their own recognizance.

Why Is Narcotic Addiction Punished When Alcoholism Is Not?

One obvious answer is because alcohol is legal but narcotics for recreational use are not. Another reason is that we have accepted alcoholism as a disease but we have not accepted narcotic addiction as a disease. We also fail to distinguish abuse from addiction.

The Harrison Narcotics Tax Act of 1914 regulated the use of narcotics for the first time.[14] It allowed physicians to prescribe narcotics for the treatment of pain, but forbade its use in the treatment of addiction as well as recreational use. A careful look at its passage reveals its racial undertones and fearmongering. Cocaine was added to this list because it was felt to "drive black men to become sexcraved and rape white women."[15] In 1913, marijuana was added to the list of banned substances. Its addition was largely used to expel migrant Mexican workers in the south for economic reasons.[16] In 1970, the Controlled Substances Act replaced the Harrison Act and allowed the inclusion of other illicit substances including LSD, methamphetamine, Ecstasy, etc.

The Controlled Substances Act of 1970

The Controlled Substances Act gave the federal government the power to regulate the manufacturing, sale, and distribution of all narcotic substances as well as any such substances that were deemed likely to be misused or abused. It gave two federal agencies, the Drug Enforcement Agency (DEA) and the Food and Drug Administration (FDA), the sole power to enforce the law as well as the power to determine which substances should be included in or excluded from this list.

It basically created five categories, called Schedule I, II, III, IV, and V classes, to which drugs with potential for abuse were classified. Drugs in Schedule I are deemed to have the most potential for abuse and misuse and are deemed not to have any appropriate medical use. Schedule V, on the other hand, is for those drugs that, although they can be abused, have the least possible abuse potential.[17],[18]

Schedule I
Includes heroin, MDMA, LSD, Quaalude, as well as marijuana.

Schedule II
Includes morphine, hydromorphone, oxycodone, oxymorphone, fentanyl, methadone, amphetamine, Nucynta, pure codeine, pure hydrocodone, as well as cocaine and PCP.

Schedule III
Includes Tylenol with codeine, Vicodin, Vicoprofen, Marinol (synthetic THC), as well as buprenorphine. In 2013, the FDA reclassified hydrocodone (Vicodin and Vicoprofen) as a Schedule II drug.

Schedule IV
Includes drugs such as Xanax, Klonopin, Valium, and Ambien.

Schedule V
Here, we have promethazine with codeine, Lyrica, and even Lomotil (an anti-diarrheal medication).

Why Not Legalize Drugs?

For those who argue that we should legalize all drugs, I share this caveat. As flawed as our drug policy is, legalizing them will only make matters worse. A lot more people who otherwise would have never tried them will try them, and although most will not get addicted, more people will be exposed to them and ultimately more will become addicted to them.

Instead of legalizing drugs, we need to stop criminalizing them, educate people about why people get addicted to help minimize the number of people getting hooked, and treat those who do get addicted. Dry up the demand, and the supply will not matter. Trying to stop the supply when the demand is high never works. Get rid of the guilt and the blame game, and offer addicts treatment.

Can you decriminalize the recreational use of illicit drugs without making their use legal? Can you criminalize distribution and sale of these drugs, but not their use? How can you distinguish a user from a dealer? How much does one have to possess to make it a crime of intent to distribute and sell? These questions have no easy answers. However, we can approach these problems from a more logical vantage point.

Instead of incarcerating those who are addicted, we can offer them treatment and counseling: offer them a more humane and fiscally sound way out. Small steps in this direction have already begun. More and more judges are directing addicted felons into drug rehab programs rather than jail. However, in order to make this work nationally, we must overturn the three strikes law in many of our states and redefine it to apply only to those criminals who have committed serious, violent crimes. We must give judges the freedom to overlook the minimum sentencing guidelines when it comes to nonviolent, drug-related crimes. And, yes, we must educate our judges as well as the public about what addiction is and why people do what they do when they are enslaved by their addiction, and let them know that there are treatments available to free them from the grip of their addiction.

Yes, we do need to abandon the "War on Drugs." It hasn't worked since its enactment by Richard Nixon in the '70s. The "Just Say No" campaign has also been a dismal failure. Instead, our effort should be focused on educating the public about what addiction is, why some get hooked while most don't, what are the signs that one may be susceptible, and what can be done about it once it happens. If we educate the public, we can finally start to make a fundamental difference in this war that we have been losing for generations. We can make everyone understand what an addict is going through. With education, we can offer an addict a lifeline out of the sinkhole he has gotten himself into. With education, we can finally bring down the human and financial costs addiction has on our society. We can teach people the signs that they may be susceptible to a given drug's allure and help many avoid getting hooked in the first place. We can dry up the demand and finally win the war on drugs! Yes, knowledge is power, and an idea can change the world!

References

[1] http://www.pbs.org/wgbh/pages/frontline/shows/drugs

[2] US Department of Health and Human Service's National Household Survey on Drug Abuse, 2001.

[3] SAMHSA report on prevalence of opiate addiction, 2004.

[4] http://drugwarfacts.org/cms/?q=node/30

[5] www.botulismblog.com › Botulism Watch

[6] www.bookrags.com/research/vietnam-drug-use-in-edaa-03

[7] http://www.hrw.org/reports/2000/usa/

[8] http://www.ojp.usdoj.gov/bjs/abstract/pjim02.htm

[9] http://www.hrw.org/reports/2000/usa

[10] http://www.ojp.usdoj.gov/bjs/abstract/p01.htm

[11] Schlosser, Eric. 1998. "The Prison Industrial Complex." *Atlantic Monthly*, December, pp. 51-77.

[12] http://www.huffingtonpost.com/daniel-abrahamson/jerrys-brown-nosin-with-c_b_139293.html

[13] http://www.npr.org/templates/story/story.php?storyId=122725771

[14] http://en.wikipedia.org/wiki/Harrison_Narcotics_Tax_Act

[15] http://en.wikipedia.org/wiki/Cocaine#CITEREFMadge2001

[16] http://www.pbs.org/wgbh/pages/frontline/shows/drugs

[17] http://www.adph.org/publications/assets/ControlledSubstancesList.pdf

[18] http://en.wikipedia.org/wiki/Controlled_Substances_Act

Chapter 9 OxyContin

I HAVE CHOSEN TO ADDRESS concerns about OxyContin because there is enough public interest in this subject. OxyContin has been in the news a lot lately. Some call it the "hillbilly heroin" because of its easy accessibility and because when crushed and snorted or smoked, it gives the same intense high as that of heroin (for those who are susceptible). Some people get extremely euphoric even when they take the pill whole. In fact, many of my patients who got hooked on OxyContin started out by getting high even when they took it the way they were supposed to. For them, they only started to crush and snort it after their addiction started to set in. There is a misconception out there that only those who intentionally try to abuse the drug by crushing, snorting, or smoking it get hooked. That's not true.

OxyContin was first introduced in 1996 by Purdue Pharma.[1] Since then the illicit use of OxyContin for non-medical use has grown exponentially. Some have said that OxyContin has become the single most important source of new opiate addiction in America. From only 20,000 cases in 1997, by 2004, the non-medical use of OxyContin has exploded to over 600,000.[2] It has mirrored the prescribing habits of physicians during the same period. From 1996 to mid-2001 alone, OxyContin brought in more than $2.8 billion in revenue for Purdue Pharma.[3]

The question that needs to be asked is why has OxyContin been such a phenomenal success over the last 15 years? Why are physicians prescribing more and more OxyContin each year? My theory is that there are two basic reasons.

The first reason was the brilliant campaign strategy by Purdue Pharma to convince physicians that because OxyContin was a long-acting opiate pain medication, it was safer than a short-acting opiate pain medication.[4] Physicians were also led to believe that treating patients with a long-acting medication controlled the pain better. Both arguments made sense.

It was also easy to convert someone from Percocet (oxycodone with Tylenol) to OxyContin. All you had to do was count how many Percocet someone was taking and convert it milligram for milligram to OxyContin. For example, if someone was taking eight Percocet 5/325 (5 represents the 5 mg of oxycodone and 325 represents the 325 mg of acetaminophen) a day, that meant they were taking 40 mg of oxycodone a day. All you have to do is switch the patient to OxyContin 20 mg twice a day for (supposedly) safer and better pain relief.

The second reason for OxyContin's success was that as more and more people were getting hooked on it, it created its own demand. Later on, as more people got hooked, instead of this making physicians less likely to prescribe OxyContin, the number of OxyContin prescriptions actually increased. This follows the simple law of supply and demand. Many patients who were hooked kept demanding OxyContin from their physicians, saying that nothing else worked. When physicians do not understand why OxyContin is more likely to be abused than other opiates (and many still don't), it is easier to just give into patients' demands rather than suggest that they try something else. Often, these patients' responses would be that they have already tried the other drugs, and they didn't work, or they had serious side effects or were allergic to all other opiate pain medications. Instead of fighting with their patients, most physicians just gave in and kept writing prescriptions for more and more OxyContin over the years.

With an increase in the demand for OxyContin, we also started seeing a lot more patients doctor-shopping to get OxyContin for diversion. With a street value of OxyContin at a dollar for each milligram, these pills had serious monetary value. Forty-milligram OxyContin goes for $40 a pill.

Eighty-milligram OxyContin goes for $80. If someone is getting 60 tablets of OxyContin 80 mg per month, that translates into $4800, minus the cost of the prescription and the office visit, as profit for someone who is diverting his drugs. That's over $57,000 a year in extra income. Some doctors prescribe four or six OxyContin 80 mg a day. Why, you ask? If OxyContin were truly a 12-hour drug, why would anyone need to take so many? It's because most physicians found out (later) that OxyContin really does not work for 12 hours. Patients had found this out much earlier.

Although Purdue Pharma marketed OxyContin as a 12-hour medication and extolled this as the reason why someone would be less likely to get hooked on it compared to other short-acting opiate pain medications, this turned out to be false. In fact, the reason why OxyContin became such an abused drug is because of its delivery system. Most medications that are designed to last 12 hours release their medication gradually over the course of 12 hours fairly evenly. However, OxyContin releases the majority of its medication rather quickly, especially at a high dose, and tapers off rather quickly.[5] Most patients have been complaining to their physicians for years that OxyContin does not last more than six to eight hours. This is even when patients are taking OxyContin the way they are supposed to and not chewing them, crushing them, snorting them, or smoking them.

Because the majority of the medication is released fairly quickly, even when taken orally, these pills either make the patient really groggy early on and then wear off too quickly, or make the patient extremely euphoric early on and then wear off too quickly. Neither scenario is good, but for those who are susceptible to opiate addiction, many got hooked.

Theft versus Diversion

According to the SAMHSA, in 2004, there were 615,000 new OxyContin users taking the drug for non-medical uses.[6] During 2000–2003, 4,434,731 doses of OxyContin were stolen on the East Coast, mostly from pharmacies and pharmaceutical distribution centers.

The population of the East Coast accounts for 53% of the US population. If so, you can postulate that there were probably approximately 8,367,416 doses of OxyContin stolen from the entire US during the same period. Accounting for just the new users, if 615,000 new users of OxyContin for non-medical purpose used only one dose of OxyContin a day (a pretty low estimate), it would take 18,450,000 doses of OxyContin to account for just one month of use. If you take the 8,367,416 doses of OxyContin that were stolen and divide that number over three years, and divide by 12 months, it accounts for only 232,428 doses of OxyContin a month. This means that all the thefts account for only 1.25% of OxyContin that they was being used for non-medical use.

If you postulate that the theft of OxyContin probably grew exponentially, like the sales of OxyContin, as well as its use for non-medical purpose, and multiply the 232,428 by a factor of ten, it would still only account for 12.5% of all the OxyContin that is being misused. So, where am I going with this? The question that needs to be asked is where is all this OxyContin coming from?

Remember your Economics 101 about the law of supply and demand. We know the demand is out there for OxyContin. The average street price for OxyContin is $1 per milligram. The most common dosages that are being abused are the 40 mg and 80 mg tablets. Meaning, they carry a street value of $40 and $80 each.

I had a married couple who were both being prescribed four OxyContin 80 mg tablets a day for pain who were selling half of their OxyContin. I also have a patient who was buying OxyContin from other patients and selling it for them. They were all able to enjoy a higher level of living by doing so. Some senior citizens have been quoted as saying that they are supplementing their meager social security income by selling their prescription drugs.[7]

I run into some of these patients. Their physicians refer them to me. They have been getting high doses of Oxy-

Contin for a long time. After a while, their treating physicians feel uncomfortable treating them and refer them to a pain specialist like me. Most of them seem to have a legitimate story behind their chronic pain medication usage. I do a urine drug screen on all my new chronic pain patients, and sometimes it shows that they are not taking the drugs. I will contact them to go over the test results or ask them to come back in for a follow-up without telling them about the test results. Invariably, most of them just move on.

By law, I have no obligation to report them to the police. But the real reason why I don't is because I can't prove that they are diverting. They may think that there is no harm done by what they do. They may think they are just supplying the demand that is out there and making a buck. However, I wish I could convey to them that what they are doing is not without harm. Someone is getting hooked on these drugs. Someone is dying from the use of these drugs.

Unfortunately, we as medical professionals are contributing to this problem. We need to do a better job of monitoring our own patients. Some will get hooked, and some will divert their medications. This does not mean that we should stop treating patients with legitimate pain, but we must understand these problems exist and try to educate our patients about these potential pitfalls.

The reason why I bring up diversion in this chapter is because diversion has become a bigger and bigger problem over the years as OxyContin addiction has become an epidemic. The greater the demand, the greater the monetary reward. Over the years, my encounters with those who are diverting their drugs have grown in large part because of the OxyContin epidemic. The majority of those I have encountered over the years who were diverting their drugs were diverting OxyContin.

Preventing Drug Diversions

The only way to stop the diversion of opiate pain medications is by being aware that it happens. It happens a lot more often than most physicians seem to believe. We, as medical providers, are the gatekeepers who can help prevent this from happening. When someone walks into your office and asks for a pain medication by name and states that nothing else works, this should set off an alarm bell. This doesn't mean that all such patients are out to scam their doctors. It just means that one needs to ask, "Why is this the case?" Is this really true? Is there a possible ulterior motive behind such a statement?

Most patients who are diverting their drugs are very savvy. They come prepared with their story down pat. They have already been to many doctors before they got to you and know all the tricks in the book. Since none of us are mind readers, we can only rely on our sense of due diligence to prevent such scams from happening. We must be vigilant that such scams go on every day.

One tool I have at my disposal is a drug screen. Most patients who are diverting their drugs are not actually taking their drugs. For one, if they were hooked themselves, they would find it hard to part with their drugs. So when we do a urine drug screen on such a person, the urine drug screen comes back negative for the drug. However, many patients will have a ready-made answer when this happens. Oh, they ran out a few days before they saw you. I learned this the hard way. Now, I ask and document when the patient told me he last took the drug before I ask for the urine drug screen. That way, they can't go back and change their story, although some will try.

Even when the urine drug screen comes back positive for the drug, it doesn't always mean that the patient is actually taking the drug. Many have learned to trick their doctors by dissolving a small amount of the medication in their urine so it will test positive for the drug. However, what they fail to understand is that the liver converts the drugs to metabolites before the kidney excretes the drugs. Because most medications break down into metabolites when they are taken orally, medications we are testing for should have their metabolites present when we do a urine drug screen.

When the urine drug screen shows the medication but

none of its metabolites, there are only two possible explanations. One, the patient is taking something he does not want the doctor to know about and brought in someone else's urine and dissolved the medication in it. Or, the patient is not taking the medication, but dissolved it in his own urine sample. In either case, you need to discontinue prescribing opiates.

Sometimes, I wish I could scream at the top of my lungs, "Why are you doing this? Don't you know the harm you are doing?" I know that, for most of these people, nothing I say will matter. When I refuse to fill their prescriptions because obviously they are not taking it, they don't make a fuss. They are not angry like most of my addicted patients when I refuse to fill their prescription. I even had one person tell me, "What's the fuss? It's just pain pills." I was too shocked to show my disgust at such a naive, careless attitude. They just walk away and look for their next unwitting accomplice.

Drug Diverters (Who and Why)

Yes, when it comes to drug diverters, it's a cat and mouse game we play. Most don't see themselves as the drug dealers that they are. Just like addicts, the drug diverters come from all races, sexes, ages, and socioeconomic statuses (maybe with the exception of the very rich). Some are middle-aged housewives or businessmen. Some are elderly on a fixed income. The only commonality I see is that most of them are not themselves hooked on the drugs they are diverting, and because of this they do not see (or choose not to see) the harm in what they do. There are exceptions to this rule. Obviously, there is an ulterior motive behind why they do it. Usually, it's greed. But it can be for an even more sinister reason, such as love (or sex). Some have been known to trade drugs for sexual favors. One person once told me that she needed the drug for her loved one, because he was hooked. I can only imagine the co-dependency issues at play.

For many who are diverting their drugs, they truly

seem to believe what they are doing is not that big of a deal because they are selling a legal product and not an illegal one. Some may even see themselves like the bootleggers during the Prohibition era. They should have to endure the suffering of one of their victim's families when their client dies from an overdose. They must think that since they didn't make the person addicted to the drug in the first place, that they are not personally responsible.

It's ironic that such a cavalier attitude exists, precisely because of our misconceptions about what addiction is. Because those who are diverting the drugs are usually not hooked on the drug themselves, they can't see the true harm done by the drugs. They have probably experimented with the drug themselves, but found themselves not attracted to the drug. It didn't make them highly euphoric because they are not genetically susceptible. When they don't understand that others may find the drug highly euphoric and fall victim to it, they are more likely to think the drug is not the problem, but that the problem lies with the person himself, and that it is a character flaw or failing. When the person is to blame for his own weakness or stupidity, there is no need to feel guilty about what role you may have had in that person's addiction.

This is one group of patients for whom I feel no empathy. I can understand the plight and suffering of those who get hooked, and this motivates me to go out of my way to help them. The same is true of chronic pain patients. However, I have no good will toward those who are diverting drugs to make a buck.

Sometimes, even after they themselves get addicted and they finally seek help, some may continue to divert. This may seem like a bizarre contradiction. If you know firsthand how devastating addiction can be, why would you do this to others? Obviously, it's a purely monetary reason. How can they do such a despicable thing when they know the price someone else may pay just to make a buck? How do I know that this happens? I have had patients over the years whom I was treating for opiate addiction with Suboxone, who were also getting OxyContin from other physicians so that they could sell it to others. They themselves did great while they were on the Suboxone program with me. However, I found out they were still getting OxyContin from other physicians while they were seeing me for their addiction. I found out what they were doing only because they got sloppy and started using the same pharmacies for both their Suboxone and OxyContin prescriptions. Until 2012, Washington State did not have a statewide database where all pharmacies could report controlled substances being filled. Such a system would have made these behaviors much easier to detect earlier. Such a system would also have alerted physicians about patients who were doctor shopping.

At first, it didn't dawn on me what was going on. These patients never tested positive for opiates including oxycodone (the active ingredient of OxyContin). One such patient was selling part of his OxyContin before he got hooked on it himself. Once addicted, he was using it all himself. He told me so on our first visit. However, even after he sought help for his own addiction, he did not stop getting OxyContin from other doctors. I had no reason to suspect that he was doing this. His urine drug screens showed no traces of opiates. They tested positive for Suboxone (and its metabolite) only.

However, when I found out that he was getting OxyContin from other physicians, it became clear what was going on. It was obvious that he was not using OxyContin himself. Then, why would he still be getting OxyContin from other physicians? The answer was simple. He was selling it. I discharged such patients from my Suboxone program.

I am not saying that I view myself as the arbiter of justice, but I just could not, in good conscience, continue treating them. If I did, it would be the same as tacitly condoning their behavior. I did not turn them in. I conveyed to them my disappointment in their actions. I told them that they should stop such behavior and continue to seek help for themselves.

I later treated a patient who was buying OxyContin from one of these diverters. He told me the name of his supplier, who turned out to be a former patient whom I had previously discharged for the above reason. If you know how devastating this disease is, how could you knowingly get others hooked for money? Obviously, for some the allure of easy money is too hard to resist even when you, yourself were a victim of the same disease.

Over the years, I have learned there is no profile that can predict who may be diverting their medication or not. I have had professional people such as nurses, accountants, and lawyers who were diverting their drugs. Some are elderly patients who are trying to supplement their meager social security benefits. Some are people who got hooked themselves.

Whenever I get a chance to ask them (most don't return for their follow-up visit once they are found out) why they divert their drugs, the answer is usually the same. There is a need, a demand for the drug, and they are just making a few bucks meeting the demand. Often, they say this with no guilt or remorse. They seem to think, "Hey, if I don't provide this to them, they will just get it from someone else." I try to convey to them the harm they are doing to others, and that others are getting hooked on these drugs, and that some are dying from their addictions. Most of the time, my plea for them to stop falls on deaf ears. They just move on.

There are brazen criminal elements as well. For them, it is a career, much like a drug dealer getting his stash of drugs so he can sell it to his clients. Sometimes, they operate in small groups, moving from one town to another until they have exhausted their welcome and the local medical community becomes suspicious. They often switch aliases and use stolen identities to carry out their crimes.

Most of my patients whom I have treated for opiate addictions were addicted to OxyContin. Many have died from their disease. It is false for any one of these drug diverters to think what they are doing is harmless. They are deluding themselves. They are drug dealers. Their guilt as well as their punishment should be no less.

In the spring of 2011, Purdue Pharma came out with a reformulated version of OxyContin that made it harder for someone to tamper with the drug, making it harder to chew, snort, or smoke it.[8] The unintended consequence was that most addicts who were abusing OxyContin switched to heroin.[9]

Although the reformulated OxyContin is more difficult to abuse, patients can still get addicted to it even when they are taking it the way they are supposed to. Unfortunately, Purdue Pharma did not change the way the drug is released; it still has a higher plasma concentration early on and tapers off too quickly. For those who are susceptible to opiate addiction, it still produces extreme euphoria. However, the reformulated OxyContin has driven down the demand for the drug. I am seeing a lot less patients demanding OxyContin by name, and I am seeing a lot less diversion of the drug.

References

[1] http://www.ehow.com/facts_5340353_history-oxycotin.html

[2] http://www.asipp.org/documents/PrescriptiondrugabuseWhatisbeing.pdf

[3] http://www.nytimes.com/2007/05/11/business/11drug.html?_r=1&ex=1180065600&en=f388818f2c0f0db5&ei=5070

[4] http://www.pbs.org/newshour/bb/health/jan-june07/oxycontin_05-11.html

[5] http://industry.bnet.com/pharma/10005955/who-signed-off-on-purdues-misleading-oxycontin-chart-judge-could-ask-for-an-answer/

[6] http://www.oas.samhsa.gov/2k6/pain/pain.cfm

[7] http://seniors-site.com/index/Articles/News/News+for+Seniors/Seniors+Selling+Prescription+Drugs

[8] http://www.nytimes.com/2011/06/16/health/16oxy.html?_r=0

[9] http://articles.latimes.com/2012/jul/11/news/la-heb-oxycontin-heroin-drug-abuse-20120711

Chapter 10 The Downfall of Any Addiction

The drug that made you happy at first will eventually take away the happiness.

SO WHAT'S WRONG WITH GETTING high on a drug, especially when something is legal, readily available, and relatively inexpensive, like alcohol? What's wrong with having a good time? There is nothing wrong with feeling good when it is done naturally. However, when drugs make you feel good, they can stimulate the pleasure spot in your brain much more powerfully than normal stimulations. When you scratch that pleasure spot too strongly too often, eventually you rewire the brain.

We now understand that with repeated overstimulation of these pleasure spots, there is a structural change that occurs in the brain of an addict. For those who become addicted, the number of dopamine receptors in the brain actually increases over time.[1] This has been proven with both heroin and cocaine addictions. It is probably true for other addictions as well. At the same time, the person's ability to produce his own endorphins (the natural feel-good neurotransmitters) diminishes.[2] These two opposing structural changes are ultimately the basis for the craving as well as the reason for addiction's downfall. This double-whammy effect is why normal activities such as eating and sex do not provide any joy over time for these patients, and why depression and a deep sense of unhappiness set in as addiction takes full hold.

With all addictions, the euphoria can't be sustained. It takes more and more to achieve the same high. Not only that, but after a while, you don't feel normal without it. There is a scene in a movie *Things We Lost in the Fire* when Benicio del Toro, an actor playing a heroin addict, says that the first time you get high is like "being kissed by God," but you can never get that feeling back. You chase that elusive "perfect high" but can never come close to it again. Unfortunately, the inability to attain that perfect high is not the only downfall of addiction. It gets much worse!

Once addiction takes full hold, you are no longer in charge—the drug is. As I pointed out earlier, depression and other mental illnesses often set in. A person who is addicted is not the same person that he was before the addiction took hold. The drug consumes him. You no longer get to decide when you get high. You need the drug to just survive. An alcoholic will tell you that he is not having a drink in the morning to get drunk. He has to have a drink in the morning so he can wake up and go to work. Once addiction takes full hold, opiate addicts will tell you the same thing. Most of us do not like being out of control. The loss of control often leads to a sense of failure and anxiety.

When I ask my patients to write down the reasons they want to quit and become clean and sober, most will write that they are tired of the all-consuming aspect of being addicted, always having to worry about their next fix, worrying about getting it and not running out, the physical withdrawal, the financial cost, the sense of their own failure to control themselves, and the lack of self-control or willpower to help themselves get out of the grip of addiction. Most will list their desires to make their loved ones proud of them again, to win back their trust and love, and to get back their lives, as well as to have money in their pocket and a sense of control. Although all of these are good reasons for wanting to quit, in my opinion they are not the true reason why someone finally wants out.

In my opinion, the common thread among all the patients who come looking for a way to end their enslavement to their addiction is their deep sense of unhappiness, and not just because of the deep despair they feel at the direction their lives have taken. Fundamentally, they are unhappy. What gave them happiness earlier seems to have taken the happiness away in all aspects of their lives. Let me repeat! What made them extremely euphoric at first eventually robs them of their ability to feel joy from anything else. They are unable to feel happiness from normal day-to-day activities. This is the cause of their depression and anxiety and unhappiness. Eventually, the bad outweighs the good. This, in the end, is the true reason why addicts finally want out. And this is the lesson they cannot forget, or else they are likely to relapse.

The most important reason why I believe people eventually want to quit is because of their sense of great unhappiness, because normal things that used to give them pleasure no longer can. They lose interest in others, sex, and other normal things in life that make us happy. Often, family members and those closest to the patient notice the change first. Spouses will often remark that this is not the same person they married years ago. They are easily irritated, not as happy, and deeply depressed. Addiction changes the personality.

When a family member thinks that someone I am treating for chronic pain became addicted to opiate pain medications, I take it seriously. They are often right. Since I don't see the patient outside of my office, I rely on family members to let me know how opiate pain medications are affecting their loved ones. Sometimes the patient may be the last to admit that there is a problem.

With the increased number of opiate prescriptions being prescribed by physicians over the last few decades, we have seen an increased number of patients becoming addicted to them. More people are overdosing and dying from them as well. The only sensible way we can turn this trend around is not by punishing physicians for overprescribing, but by educating both the medical community as well as the general public about what addiction is and why it happens.

Once you educate physicians, their habits will change. Once you educate the public, less people will get hooked!

The DEA and state licensing boards must believe that the only way they can curtail the prescribing habits of physicians is by punishing the extreme overprescribers. This has happened over the last few years. In my years of practice, I had never seen so many physicians being sanctioned or losing their licenses to practice medicine because of their excessive prescribing habits of opiate pain medication as I have in the last few years. In the western Washington area alone, there have been more than a dozen physicians who have lost their medical or DEA licenses because of this. However, these physicians represent extreme cases. Most of us were shocked at how freely they were handing out opiate pain medications. There have also been some highly publicized cases across the country over the last few years of physicians not only losing their licenses, but also going to jail for their overprescribing habits. Most of these cases involved some form of fraud or criminal activities.

One such case was a California physician who was basically selling each prescription for money. He charged according to the strength of the prescription. For example, for a prescription of OxyContin 40 mg twice a day (for a week's supply), he would charge $40, and for 80 mg OxyContin, he would charge $80. Another physician in Florida was convicted of selling his prescriptions to drug dealers. Obviously, such physicians deserve to be thrown in jail. They are a disgrace to the profession. More chilling are the cases when physicians are indicted for murder when their patients overdose and die from the pain medications.

However, some of these physicians were not guilty of criminal acts or malpractice. Their sin was that they did not understand what addiction is. They lacked common sense. They believed that no one gets addicted to opiate pain medications when they are taking them for pain. Their prescribing habits were extreme, even by a generous standard. As with all things, there are extreme cases in everything. Yes, there probably are some overzealous prosecutions of physicians for what may be merely poor judgment rather than any true criminal intent. Luckily, such cases are usually rare.

However, some in the medical community as well as some in big Pharma have used such cases in spreading fear among the medical community as well as the general public to suggest that the government is trying to take away physicians' rights to prescribe opiate pain medications, thus taking away the legitimate use of opiate pain medications by patients with legitimate pain. One only needs to see the steady increase in the number of opiate pain medications being prescribed annually as well as the steady increase in the number of people overdosing on opiate pain medications each year to know that such fearmongering is unfounded. Only when we truly understand what addiction is and why it happens can we get this problem under control.

When one truly understands addiction, one can begin to understand why all addictions eventually lead to their own downfall. In a way, an addiction's success leads to its own subsequent failure. Because it made that person feel so good, that person kept chasing such an extreme high. Unfortunately, over time, like many other forms of sensory overload, it becomes harder and harder to experience the same thing. However, with addiction, something even worse happens. It's not just the tolerance. One loses the ability to feel joy from normal day-to-day activities. What made the person extremely happy at first eventually takes away that happiness and makes the person unable to feel happy with normal day-to-day activities, and eventually makes that person miserable. This is the ultimate reason for addiction's downfall.

This is the reason why eventually most want to get off the roller coaster ride. By the time I see them, they are unhappy. Not only are they unhappy about the downward spiral that their lives have taken, but most are depressed and miserable as well. However, when their addiction is brought under control, their depression and anxiety lift and they return to their old selves. No, depression and anxiety do not cause addiction; they are just the byproducts. However, in order not to relapse, addicts must not forget their misery.

References

[1] http://bjp.rcpsych.org/cgi/content/full/182/2/97
[2] http://www.ncbi.nlm.nih.gov/pmc/articles/PMC3104618/

Chapter 11 Suboxone/Subutex

BEFORE I GET STARTED ON buprenorphine, in the interest of full disclosure, I want to point out that I have no financial ties to the manufacturer of buprenorphine (that I am aware of). I own mutual funds that may have pharmaceutical companies invested in them. However, I do not know which ones they are. I have been trained to prescribe buprenorphine and have treated over 800 patients with buprenorphine. Yes, I have given talks to other physicians about addiction and buprenorphine and have been paid an honorarium for these talks, but I have no financial ties to the company.

My interest in promoting this drug is because of how well it has worked for my patients and how it has changed their lives for the better, as well as how it has helped me by providing me with another tool to treat chronic pain and addiction.

If you treat pain, you are dealing with addiction, whether you want to admit it or not. Some of your patients are already hooked, and others will inevitably become addicted to these drugs even with your due diligence to prevent this from happening. Most patients are immune to the drug's allure, but some will find it quite irresistible. You have to be honest with yourself that this is a possibility for some, and try to educate your patients about what addiction is in order to help prevent them from getting hooked in the first place and to help others to get off their drugs once they are hooked.

For those patients who are hooked on opiates (whether to prescription medications or street drugs), now we have a more effective treatment option. Before Suboxone and

Subutex came on the market, the only medication available to treat opiate addiction was methadone.

Treatment of Opiate Addiction with Methadone

Methadone is a synthetic opiate first introduced in Nazi Germany in 1937 to meet the shortage of other opiate pain medications.[1] It was introduced in the United States in 1947 for use as a pain medication.[2] It is a full opiate agonist, whereas Suboxone is a partial agonist. By the 1960s, methadone was found to be an effective treatment for heroin addiction. In 1973, with the passage of the Controlled Substances Act, Congress authorized the formation of methadone clinics to treat heroin addiction. Physicians are allowed to use methadone to treat pain, but are forbidden to use it to treat opiate addiction outside the confines of methadone clinics. Since its inception, methadone has come to treat all opiate addiction and not just that of heroin.

Most people associate methadone with the treatment of heroin addiction, and because of this, there are a lot of negative connotations associated with it. However, methadone did not turn out to be the panacea for opiate addiction. The reasons why methadone did not bear out its promise are multifold. One of the reasons is that some patients who get high on other opiates can get high on methadone as well. As my data will later show, of the patients who can get high on regular opiates, about a third can get high on methadone—not an insignificant number. For these patients, it can be a deadly drug because of its overdose potential.

However, an even bigger problem with methadone is that, for many, it is a lifelong treatment. Many patients are enrolled in a methadone maintenance program for life. For many patients, when they stop methadone, the craving is still there. Many patients still experience cravings after coming off methadone, even if they had been on methadone for years.

Another problem that has emerged with methadone is

that addicts have figured out they can use methadone to help them get through their withdrawal symptoms. They can get high on their opiate of choice, and then use methadone to help with the withdrawal until their next fix. When buprenorphine was first introduced, there was a fear that buprenorphine would be abused the same way. Naloxone was added to help prevent this as well as to prevent IV injection of buprenorphine.

Advantages of Buprenorphine over Methadone

With Suboxone and Subutex, we can finally successfully treat cravings. The therapeutic ingredient in both Suboxone and Subutex is buprenorphine. Buprenorphine is a partial opiate agonist, which means that it mimics opiates but is not a true opiate. Unlike methadone, it binds to the opiate receptors but does not trigger them. Think of it as a key that fits in the lock, but can't turn. It binds to opiate receptors but does not release the dopamine. Thus, it satisfies the craving the brain has without triggering the release of chemicals that gives rise to the feeling of euphoria and high.

Another advantage buprenorphine has over methadone is that it can be prescribed in the privacy of a physician's office. Those who are on methadone for addiction must receive their daily dose of methadone at a government-sponsored methadone clinic. However, the most important difference between methadone and buprenorphine is that, with prolonged use of buprenorphine, the craving finally goes away.

Buprenorphine is approved for the treatment of both the physical dependence as well as the opiate addiction. Remember that physical dependence happens to anyone who is on opiates long-term. When treating physical dependence, patients can be weaned off Suboxone/Subutex in a matter of weeks. When treating addiction, patients need to be on it for a longer time, usually six months to a year. This is because it takes that long for the craving to finally go away. After six months, you can taper off Suboxone.

However, if the craving comes back as soon as you come off Suboxone, you should plan on being on it for a full year. Buprenorphine can also be used for pain. However, it is a relatively mild pain reliever.

A note of warning: If you have been off opiates for more than a month, and you decide to go back to using them for whatever the reason, I tell my patients that they should not go back to the same dose they were using when they stopped. IT CAN KILL YOU! The tolerance they developed over time is now gone. That 80 mg of OxyContin that you used to smoke on a regular basis will now kill you. Unfortunately, some of my patients learned this lesson the hard way.

So How Does Buprenorphine Work?

For those who are susceptible, when opiates attach to the mu opiate receptors, they release dopamine, causing euphoric feelings. As the opiates leave the mu receptors, the euphoric feelings fade and the craving begins. The craving comes on before true withdrawal. For those who are not susceptible, opiates do attach to the mu receptors as well, but they do not trigger the release of dopamine.

Buprenorphine attaches to the mu receptor sites and suppresses the withdrawal symptoms as well as the craving. Because it is a partial opiate agonist, buprenorphine does not trigger the release of dopamine. Thus, there is no feeling of euphoria associated with it. Some people do find it mildly stimulating, but not euphoric. It is as if it tricks the brain into thinking that it got what it wanted without further stimulating it. Because buprenorphine binds stronger to the mu receptor sites than it does to opiates, it blocks other opiates from binding to these sites.

While the brain was being overstimulated, the number of dopamine receptors increased.[3] With prolonged use of buprenorphine, the number of dopamine receptors eventually declines. For most patients, this takes 6–12 months, and at that point, the patient can be weaned off buprenorphine without the craving still being there.

Buprenorphine comes in three formulations:
- Suboxone
  - buprenorphine + naloxone (4 to 1 ratio)
  - naloxone is an opiate blocker
  - naloxone was added to prevent abuse
- Subutex
  - buprenorphine (without naloxone)
  - is used in those with known naloxone allergy or side effects
  - is used for pregnant females rather than Suboxone because naloxone has been shown to cause birth defects in mice
- Buprenex (IV buprenorphine)

Suboxone is a combination of buprenorphine and naloxone (an opiate antagonist). Subutex, on the other hand, is just a plain buprenorphine. Unless the patient is pregnant or has a known allergy or sensitivity to naloxone, Suboxone is prescribed. Naloxone was put in to prevent abuse and deter the IV injection of buprenorphine. It was also put in to discourage patients from switching back and forth from their opiate of choice to Suboxone. The biggest fear with buprenorphine was that it might be abused like methadone.

Unlike methadone, buprenorphine binds stronger to the mu-receptor sites and prevents other opiates from binding to them. Thus, as long as buprenorphine is in your system, you can't get high with other opiates. It also helps prevent overdoses from opiates for the same reason. This is not true of methadone. An addict can get high with other opiates even if he has methadone in his system. He can also overdose and die on opiates while on methadone.

Because naloxone is an opiate antagonist, if someone uses Suboxone too close to the last dose of the opiate, it will actually dislodge the opiates from the mu-receptors and cause full physical withdrawal. Thus, unlike methadone, it is not easy to use Suboxone as a stopgap measure to help with the withdrawal symptoms between the highs. However, this does not mean that it cannot be successfully used in such a manner. Unfortunately, many have figured out that if they wait long enough to be in mild to moderate withdrawal before they take the Suboxone, it is quite effective in eliminating the severe withdrawal symptoms.

Buprenex was an IV form of buprenorphine that was first introduced in the 1970s as an opiate analgesic. Buprenex was a dismal failure as a pain medication. However, for those patients who were hooked on pain pills, it got rid of their cravings. Thus began the path for buprenorphine to be later used to treat opiate addiction.

The Drug & Alcohol Treatment Act (DATA) of 2000[4]

The DATA is an amendment to the Controlled Substances Act. Prior to the passage of the DATA in 2000, physicians were not allowed to treat opiate addiction outside the confines of the methadone clinic. Prior to its passage, all those receiving treatments for opiate addiction had to get their daily dose of methadone through government-sponsored methadone clinics.

With the passage of the DATA, physicians, after undergoing a proper certification process, are allowed to use buprenorphine to treat opiate addiction in an office setting. We are still prohibited from using methadone to treat opiate addiction outside the realm of methadone clinics. However, the DATA has revolutionized the treatment of opiate addiction.

Does Buprenorphine Really Work?

On August 15, 1989, the *Science Journal* published a Harvard study done on rhesus monkeys that showed that monkeys that were hooked on cocaine were able to kick their habit by using buprenorphine.[5] Cocaine is not an opiate. It actually acts on the opposite side of the dopamine chain. Whereas opiates release dopamine, cocaine prevents the reuptake of the dopamine. The result is the same—an increased of dopamine in the brain. I have treated patients who got hooked on cocaine with Suboxone, and it works. Why it works still needs further research. Unfortunately, it doesn't seem to work for methamphetamine or pot addiction.

On September 3, 2003, the *New England Journal of Medicine* (NEJM) published another Harvard study, this time using human subjects.[6] Three hundred and twenty-six heroin addicts were enrolled in a multi-center, double-blind, randomized study between a Suboxone and a placebo group. Outcome measures used cravings and the urine drug screen. The study was terminated early because the Suboxone group was found to be far superior to the placebo group. All of the patients were then enrolled in an open label study. Between 35–67% of the patients remained clean while on Suboxone. Although these numbers may not seem like a miracle cure, they represented a much higher success rate than had been found with any other previously studied drugs.

Reckitt Benckiser, the maker of Suboxone/Subutex, published their own study in 2002.[7] They enrolled 326 heroin-addicted adults and divided them into Suboxone 16 mg a day, Subutex 16 mg a day, and a placebo in a double-blind, randomized trial. Outcome measures were cravings and the urine drug screen. Once again, they found far superior outcomes in both the Suboxone and the Subutex groups versus the placebo group.

The FDA approved the use of Suboxone and Subutex for the treatment of opiate addiction in 2002.[8] Since then, there have been other studies comparing Suboxone and Subutex to methadone.[9] In most studies, Suboxone/Subutex fared far better than methadone. The advantages of using Suboxone or Subutex over methadone are many, not the least of which is that patients can be treated in the privacy of a doctor's office, rather than having to get their daily dose of methadone at a methadone clinic. And with buprenorphine, the craving finally goes away.

French Data

In France, Suboxone has been in use since 1996.[10] There,

any doctor can prescribe Suboxone. With a population of 60 million people in France, it is estimated that there are about 150,000 to 300,000 heroin addicts.[11] Of these, about 50,000–60,000 are enrolled in treatment programs. Patients have a choice of either Suboxone or methadone. By 2003, most of the patients had chosen to enroll in the Suboxone program rather than the methadone program by a margin of 93% to 7%. During the same period, accidental overdose deaths dropped by half (>500/yr prior to 1993 compared to <250/yr by 2003).[12]

Does Suboxone Work Too Well?

Yes, the biggest problem with Suboxone is that it works too well. Let me clarify. Its strength is also its weakness. Because Suboxone makes it easy for those who are addicted to opiates to quit, it also makes some forget how difficult it was for them to quit on their own before. It makes some complacent. Some patients have told me that they don't remember what the big deal was about getting hooked. It makes some forget why they wanted to quit in the first place. When they forget, they often tend to relapse.

Without some way to keep them from forgetting what it was like when they were truly down and out, addicts often relapse. The average number of times that a person at an inpatient drug rehab unit has already gone through this process before is 3.5 times. All it takes is one dose to send them spiraling back down the path of addiction. There are many studies that show that the relapse rate for heroin addiction over a lifetime is nearly 100%. Suboxone gives patients a second chance, a new lease on life. It gets rid of the craving, but often patients forget their past struggles. There has to be a happy medium between struggling with the monkey on your back every day and the false sense of complacency that Suboxone can give you. Therefore, I insist that all my new Suboxone patients attend AA or NA meetings on a weekly basis.

One day, we may have vaccines that will turn off addiction genes. Until that day, we must remind these patients of the reality that their disease has no cure and that they will always be susceptible to being sucked right back into the depths of despair. The only thing that will prevent them from falling victim to their drug again is their memory of what it was like for them when their addiction truly took full hold and the reasons why they wanted to get off their drug in the first place.

Can You Get Addicted to Buprenorphine?

When coming off buprenorphine, you can have physical withdrawal similar to opiate withdrawal. Does this mean that you have just switched one addiction with another? The answer is no. Remember that physical dependence and physical withdrawal do not mean addiction. Because buprenorphine binds to opiate sites without triggering the release of dopamine, there is no euphoria, and thus no cravings. Most people will say that it just makes them feel normal. As long as you are gradually weaned off buprenorphine, the withdrawal symptoms are mild.

However, a small number of patients can get highly euphoric on buprenorphine as well. I have had a few patients who did get extremely euphoric on buprenorphine. Two of them tried crushing it up and injecting it into their veins. They both got extremely sick from it. The only reason why someone would do something like that is because it made them extremely high, even when they took it orally. But, in my opinion, this number is pretty low. Suboxone and Subutex now come in generic forms. Vivitrol, a once-a-month injectable naltrexone, is now also FDA-approved for the treatment of opiate addiction.

References

[1] http://science.blurtit.com/49690/when-was-methadone-invented-

[2] http://en.wikipedia.org/wiki/Methadone

[3] E.J. Nestler & R.C. Melenka. "The Addicted Brain." *Scientific American*. March 2004: 78-85.

[4] linkinghub.elsevier.com/retrieve/pii/S0376871605000165
[5] *Science* 25, August 1989.
[6] NEJM 9/3/2003.
[7] www.centerwatch.com/patient/drugs/dru804.html
[8] http://www.fda.gov/Drugs/DrugSafety/PostmarketDrugSafetyInformationforPatientsandProviders/ucm191521.htm
[9] opioids.com/buprenorphine/index.html
[10] http://www.sciencedirect.com/science/article/pii/S0376871601001612
[11] http://www.seedwiki.com/accounts/Ekgren_Joe_Siri_13424/Auriacombe,%20et%20al,%202004.pdf
[12] www.medicineau.net.au/clinical/womenshealth/womenshealt84.html

Chapter 12 Why Do People Relapse?

If we had memory like an elephant's, no woman would have more than one child.

RECENTLY, JIM, A CURRENT SUBOXONE patient, told me about Paul, whom I had treated years ago. Jim told me that Paul had recently overdosed and died. He attended Paul's funeral. Paul had referred Jim to me to go on the Suboxone program. You see, Paul had done well on the Suboxone program. He was attending NA meetings. He had sponsored others. When he saw that Jim was struggling to stay clean, he told him about Suboxone, and how I had helped him get his addiction under control. Jim was shocked that Paul had relapsed; he had no idea. Such is the tragedy that I hear too often.

Every year, I hear about a former patient or two who have recently overdosed and died. Over the years, I have learned that relapse is too common, but I can't help but grieve for each one of these patients.

There are a lot of theories as to why some (if not most) patients relapse. You may even say that it is a part of one's recovery and that most will relapse many times before (if ever) staying clean and sober. Usually, there are triggers that precipitate the relapse. Something stressful happens or one runs into a situation that reminds one of how good it felt to get high. But in my opinion, the true reason why addicts relapse is because they forgot how bad things were for them and the reasons why they wanted to quit in the first place.

The difference between a trigger and a craving is that a craving is constant, whereas a trigger is fleeting. The craving is the monkey on your back that makes you feel like you have to have the drug. A trigger is a reminder of how good the drug made you feel. Fighting cravings may take superhuman strength, but all it takes to fight triggers is to remember how bad things were to outweigh the good memories of getting high. With sobriety, the craving eventually goes away, but triggers persist.

When I ask my patients why they think they relapsed, I hear a myriad of reasons. Many have told me that something stressful happened to them. However, I have also had patients tell me they were bored and wanted some excitement in their lives. Some patients have told me they were happy and celebrating because they had gotten a raise. I had one patient tell me she was celebrating her engagement, and this made her relapse. She was happy and wanted to celebrate!

If you look at these so-called reasons, they can't all be true. If stress and depression lead to relapse, then happiness and excitement can't cause it as well. In my opinion, none of these is the real reason why these patients relapse. The true reason for their relapses is that they allowed themselves to forget the bad memories and the reasons why they wanted out of their addiction in the first place. You see, when you forget the bad memories, the good memories will make you fall victim to addiction again.

Memories are often faulty, especially the bad ones. If bad or painful memories did not fade over time, no woman would have more than one child. Our daughter recently gave birth to our first grandchild, a beautiful baby girl. For the last few months of her pregnancy, my daughter complained about her back pain and a myriad of ills. She swore that she would never go through it again. Her labor was just as bad. Her last ultrasound, done just days before her due date, showed a baby weighing about eight pounds. My daughter wanted to experience a natural childbirth. After 20 hours of agonizing labor, she begged for an epidural. The baby was nine pounds and ten ounces and 24 inches long. It's a good thing that we soon forget the painful memories. If women never forgot their first birthing experience, why would any woman want to go through that again? But luckily, they do, and we as a species carry on.

If you don't get over the pain from your last breakup, would you ever start a new relationship? The reason why a relationship ends is because the bad outweighed the good. However, we often remember our old relationships fondly.

Bad memories are meant to fade over time, whereas the good ones linger. This has an evolutionary advantage. There was a woman who once appeared on *Oprah* who explained how miserable her life was because she had a perfect memory. If we never got over the loss of a parent or a child, we couldn't survive. Luckily, *time heals all wounds*.

My wife recently lost her mother to breast cancer. She cried every day for weeks. But with time, the wound healed, and the sorrow faded. Now, she remembers her mother with joyful memories more often than with tears. However, some lessons carry too high of a price if one forgets.

One of my patients told me that she was clean and sober for years before she relapsed. The reason she got clean in the first place was because of a tragic event that happened one fateful day years earlier. She was getting high with her best friend, when her friend overdosed and died in front of her. That finally got her to quit. She went through an inpatient drug rehab and attended NA meetings for years. Eventually, she stopped attending meetings, and eventually her memory of her friend and her struggle with this demon faded.

After years of sobriety, she found herself back on drugs. She told me that she had a miscarriage and was prescribed opiate pain medications. She liked it. She had forgotten the lessons she had learned previously. She kept taking the drugs more and more, and when her doctor cut her off, she found herself getting opiates off the street. She was hooked back on heroin for a year before she sought treatment.

At our first meeting, I asked her why she wanted to quit now. Why not six months ago? She told me that she wasn't ready six months ago, but she was ready now. Now she remembered all the bad things about being truly hooked. Now, she remembered her old friend. Such is the power of this disease. If you forget how truly bad it was when you were down and out in the depth of your addiction, you are likely to repeat your mistake.

"Those who cannot remember the past are condemned to repeat it." - George Santayana

I have patients who have been clean and sober for years after going through the Suboxone program who call me because they have relapsed and want to go back on Suboxone. Interestingly, I never get a call immediately after they first relapse. Usually, it's months after they have relapsed before they call. I always ask them why they didn't call me sooner. The answer is always the same: it felt too good to stop at first. They thought they could control it, that it would be different this time.

Studies show that people who attend AA or NA meetings are more likely to stay clean and sober.[1] Because of the high dropout rates in both AA and NA, these claims have been challenged. However, I do believe that attending meetings on a regular basis does help people from relapsing, but not for the reasons that the AA or the NA associations may believe. Both AA and NA follow the twelve-step program and believe in a higher power to help you stay clean and sober.

I believe it is the meetings themselves that remind addicts of how bad it was for them and why they want to stay clean. When you see someone just getting off drugs, you see their misery. Seeing someone else's misery can remind you of your own past misery. Bad memories are supposed to fade. The only way you can keep the bad memories alive is by revisiting them on a regular basis. The meetings help you not to forget. You can find local meetings by going to www.AA.org or www.NA.org.

I had a 72-year-old patient whom I treated for opiate addiction. He told me he had been clean for 40 years. He said he attended meetings on a weekly basis for 40 years. When he turned 70, he told himself he was done with the meetings. He told himself, "Why would I relapse after 40 years?" He told himself, "I wouldn't know where to get the drug even if I wanted to." After a year, he relapsed. The patient was back on heroin when I first met him. I put him on Suboxone and had him go back to the meetings.

For those patients for whom these meetings are not the answer, I ask that they do something else to remind themselves of how bad it was. This may take the form of a diary or a list of all the bad things that happened to them because of their addiction. I ask them to read this on a regular basis. Having a spouse or a family member who understands addiction and the triggers that may cause one to relapse can also help greatly. I have patients who, when they feel sad or stressed out, turn to their loved ones to help them through with words of encouragement and gentle reminders as to why they do not want to use their drug as a quick fix.

One of the great pitfalls of a drug like Suboxone is that some patients can become too complacent. Suboxone works so well that patients can sometimes forget what it was like when they were truly down and out. Unfortunately, this is more common with younger patients. They are more likely to relapse.

Suboxone, by taking the struggle away, makes it easier to quit, but at the same time, it makes some patients forget what it was like to struggle with their demons. Therefore, the Suboxone program has to be tied to some type of counseling to make the patient not forget. This could take the form of attending AA or NA meetings on a regular basis or individual drug counseling, or some form of a regular self-reminder.

I am not stating that we need to treat addiction as some form of a mental illness that needs never-ending talk therapy. I believe that we need to treat addiction as a medical illness and not a mental illness. We also need to take the guilt out of the conversation, and help everyone understand that those who get hooked are not somehow weak-willed or lack a moral compass. Unfortunately, in the past the focus has been too much on the failure of the patients themselves. This is even true in the underlying principle behind AA and NA.

Forgiveness

Self-forgiveness is necessary for addicts not to relapse. Addiction will make even the saints among us do things that they would not be proud of. Mothers will give up their children because of their addiction. Addicts will lie, steal, and debase themselves to unimaginable levels to get their drugs. While they are in the throes of their addiction, no logic or reason will prevail. The need for the drug is greater than the need for life itself.

Addicts must be made to understand that their past behaviors were byproducts of their disease and do not define who they are. Unless addicts forgive themselves, they cannot recover from their illness. Their own guilt and shame often make them think that they must be what their past behaviors defined them to be—bad people. When they believe that they are inherently bad, they will allow themselves to fall back into their old habits. Their low self-image makes some use any excuse to relapse.

When addicts understand that they did what they did because the grip the addiction had on their souls was more powerful than any mortal power to withstand it, then they can be taught to forgive themselves for their past misdeeds and finally become who they were before they became addicted. Unfortunately, this journey of self-healing and forgiveness takes time.

I recently had a patient who relapsed. He had been clean for about six months on the Suboxone program. I got a call from his father saying that he believed his son relapsed. I had the patient come in so I could talk to him about this. When I raised his father's concern, the patient admitted he relapsed. When I asked him what made him relapse, he told me he relapsed because he is an addict!

This is a patient who had been telling me how well he was doing on Suboxone. He told me that he felt like his old self. He told me that he would never relapse again. Although he promised to attend AA or NA meetings, he never did. Although he promised to read my book, he never got around to it.

I learned a long time ago that unless an addict learns to forgive himself for all the bad things he did while he was addicted, he will have a hard time dealing with his addiction. Such a person can't face his past because it brings up too much guilt and shame. He would rather pretend it never happened, but this will set him up for failure. Unless an addict can put a distance between his misdeeds and himself, he can't revisit those memories that will help prevent him from relapsing. He must forgive himself for all the bad things he did while he was addicted, but must not forget the bad things that happened to him because of his addiction. This may seem like a contradiction, but it's not. He must learn to understand that he is as much a victim of addiction as the loved ones he may have harmed.

Even when the craving is finally brought under control and addicts learn to forgive themselves, there has to be a way to keep the memory of what it was like to be truly addicted alive. Most of the time, it's healthy to forget the bad things that happen to you. Those who can't do that usually can't get on with their lives. In medicine, we call this neurosis. However, some lessons, if you forget, will lead you to repeat that mistake. There is a fine line between obsessing about something bad that happened to you and remembering the lessons you need to take away from that experience. It can be done and must be done in order to help prevent a relapse.

Unfortunately, when patients relapse, the price can be too high. Those who are trying to quit are much more likely to overdose and die when they do relapse. Their tolerance to the drug goes away fairly quickly. When patients don't remember this and go back to taking the drug at the same dose that they used to take, it can KILL them.

Once again, let me emphasize. If you have cravings, the decision to use is not just a mere choice, it's a battle. When the craving is finally gone, the decision to get high is a choice, a bad one, but still a choice. Only by remembering the bad things about being truly addicted can you prevent yourself from falling victim to the allure of the drug again. Most patients who begin their journey to recovery will tell me they will never relapse again. Unfortunately, many will soon forget how desperately they wanted out of their despair and do relapse.

I had a patient who had the words "never forget" tattooed on his hands to remind himself not to relapse. Unfortunately, even that was not enough to prevent him from relapsing. Even the knowledge that if he kept relapsing he may end up in jail did not stop him from relapsing.

It's not the physical scar that's going to remind you of how bad things got for you. It is the psychological ones—the feelings of desperation, loneliness, and hopelessness that come with the onset of full addiction—which you must not forget. It is only when the bad memories outweigh the good ones that you can prevent yourself from relapsing, to falling victim and becoming prey to addiction once again.

There is a saying in AA that recovery is accomplished one day at a time, and that every day you must remind yourself why you do not want to end up where you were. I truly believe that this is the only way one can stay clean and sober. Yes, to stay clean, you must force yourself to remember the depth of despair that you climbed out of every day. They emphasize that sobriety is a journey taken one day at a time. That's why the members of AA and NA celebrate every milestone (30 days, 60 days, etc.) of sobriety.

Not too long ago, I got a call from a patient whom I was treating for opiate addiction. He had relapsed many times over the previous few months. He left a message that one of his friends had recently died from an overdose and that he was going out of his mind. He was stressed out and thought that he might relapse. I called him back, but ended up leaving a message on his voicemail. We played phone tag for three days before we finally connected. He was extremely stressed out, but he had not relapsed. What I told him next surprised him! I told him that, as sad as the passing of his friend was, I was less worried about him relapsing in the last few days than any other time I had known him. I told him that the tragedy of his friend's death would make him less likely to relapse, not more. He just needed to remember this lesson for the rest of his life!

References

[1] www.dickb.com/index.shtml

Chapter 13 Prevention

How to Talk to Your Kids About Addiction

IF WE UNDERSTAND ADDICTION, WE can help others from getting addicted in the first place. That's the reason why I wrote this book.

I have often asked my addiction patients, "Do you think there was anything anyone could have told you about addiction that could have prevented you from getting hooked?" Most say no. However, when I ask them, "Do you think there is anything you could tell your kids about addiction so they don't get addicted?" they say, "God, I hope so." These are contradictory statements. If they believe there wasn't anything anyone could have told them that could have helped them not get hooked, how could they possibly expect to help prevent their kids from falling victim to addiction as well? Luckily, I believe they are wrong about the first question, and, therefore, there is hope for their children.

The reason why I believe this is because when I explain to my new pain patients why some people get addicted to opiate pain medications while most do not, and teach them the early warning signs, they often will come out and tell me (as their pain starts to subside) that they better stop their pain pills because they are starting to like them too much. I discuss addiction with every patient before I give out pain medication. I have been amazed over the years how many patients have prevented themselves from getting pulled into addiction just by knowing these simple concepts. Yes, knowledge is power.

When I ask my addiction patients what they would tell their children about addiction that may prevent them from going down the same path, most have a hard time coming up with an answer. Some will say they will tell their children about how horrible drugs are, what devastation drugs have brought on them, and warn them never to do drugs. When I ask them what their parents told them about drugs, they ponder and tell me the same things they plan to tell their kids. When I ask them, if this didn't work for them, why do they think it will work for their kids, they get the point. Fear only works for a while. True knowledge lasts forever. Let me give you a few examples.

Last year, I saw a young man who sprained his ankle playing basketball. He saw his family physician, who prescribed some Vicodin, a fairly mild opiate pain medication. After a few days, the patient called back and told his doctor that he was out of his pain medication. His doctor refilled the prescription, but told him to decrease his pain medication. A few days later, the patient called back to ask for more pain medication. His doctor then referred him to me.

When I first saw him, I could see that he was in pain. He walked in with a limp. His ankle was swollen. The x-ray showed no fracture. So, I asked him, "How does Vicodin make you feel?" He told me it made him feel great—an honest answer! I told him that most people do not feel that way when they take the pain pill. He asked me, "What do you mean?" So, I explained to him that if you take pain pills to bring down the pain to a reasonable level, but not to mask the pain, all that pain pills will do is help dull the pain. However, if you take enough pain medication to block the pain, it will either make you groggy and tired, or it will start to energize you and make you feel good.

He told me that Vicodin definitely energized him and made him feel good. Then I explained to him this meant that he was genetically susceptible to getting hooked on pain pills. I told him that he was not addicted yet, but if he kept triggering the pleasure spot too long, he would eventually get sucked in.

I went over the following concepts that I go over with all my patients. This is what parents should be telling their children.

- Most people can't get hooked on most drugs, but some people can get hooked on some drugs. Whether you can get hooked on a drug is based on your genetics.
- People can have night-and-day different reactions to the same drug.
- High is not what the media has been telling you. High is not an altered state of mind, or a dopey, drunk, or out-of-control feeling. High is anything that artificially makes you happy, sometimes extremely happy.
- (For older children) The high produces the same chemical reaction in your brain as sex. It releases dopamine, the feel-good neurotransmitter. Just like sex, a high is always exciting and pleasurable.
- If you chase that happy feeling, eventually you will start having cravings for the drug, and will become enslaved by the drug.

The young man then told me that his father had overdosed on heroin and died years ago. He told me that his parents had divorced when he was a child and that he didn't know his father very well, but no one told him that addiction is passed down genetically. No one told him there are early warning signs that can tell you whether you are susceptible to getting hooked or not. No one told him that different people could have profoundly different reactions to the same drug. He thought what he was experiencing was universal.

Once I explained to him the above concepts, he told me that he would never take these pills again. His exact words were, "I will never be like my dad!" I explained to him that when it comes to pain medications, as long as he did not try to mask or overpower the pain, he could take the pills to treat the pain. It's only when you overpower the pain that these pills can make you euphoric. You just need to stop when the pain pills start to make you feel too good. I gave him an ankle brace. He walked out of my office without asking for any more pain pills.

Let me give you another example. I recently saw a 16-year-old who injured his back playing football. I examined him. The injury was minor. I put him on some anti-inflammatory medication and taught him some exercises to do. However, when I looked at his intake form, he had marked there was a family history of addiction. So, I asked him who in his family was hooked on drugs or alcohol. He told me that his father was an alcoholic.

I asked him whether he ever had a drink. He said, "Sure!" So, I asked him how it made him feel. He said, "Great!" He told me that he only drank on weekends, but when he did, he had a great time. He said, "Most of my friends can't keep up with me." So I asked him, "How does your dad act when he drinks?" He told me that his father was a mean drunk.

I asked him, "Do you see a connection between how the alcohol affects you and how it affects your dad?" He said, "No." He didn't know what I was getting at. I am sure in his mind, he thought, *I am having a great time when I drink, and my dad is miserable from it; how can they have anything to do with each other?*

I asked him to ask his grandparents, "What was my dad like when he was younger when he drank?" I told him the answer he would get would surprise him. I told him they would tell him that his father was the fun drunk, the life of the party. I told him that although he was having a great time now when he drank, that it would eventually change. As addiction to alcohol took hold, he would no longer drink to have a great time, but he would need it just to survive. Then, he would become like his father, the mean drunk. I went over the above concepts. After just a few minutes going over these concepts, he told me that he would never drink again. He also said, "I will never be like my dad!"

I asked this young man whether he had ever smoked pot. He said "Yeah!" When I asked him how it made him feel, he told me that it made him high. When I asked him to describe the high, he described feeling buzzed, light-headed, and silly. When I asked him whether pot made him relaxed or energized, he told me that it had a calming effect. I told him that was how most of us feel when we drink, and what he felt with pot was intoxication, not high. I told him what he felt with the alcohol was the true high.

The Paradox of Addiction

I learned a long time ago that most people who got addicted did not realize they were getting addicted until it was too late. This may seem too far-fetched for some to believe. How can people who abuse drugs not know that they are getting addicted? It's because they mistake the high for an altered state of mind, that dopey or loopy feeling. So when they encountered a drug that made them feel extremely happy, they did not realize they were high. And because they did not realize they were getting high, they did not see the danger of getting addicted. Only when the craving started to set in did they realize they were in trouble. By then, addiction had taken hold.

The War on Drugs

So far, the war on drugs has been fought on two fronts. One was a futile attempt at trying to cut off the supply. The other one was an attempt at prevention using scare tactics. Neither of these worked. Anyone who has taken Economics 101 knows that trying to cut off the supply when the demand is high never works. And anyone who has taken Psychology 101 knows that scare tactics only work for a short while.

The reason why we have done such a poor job preventing people from getting hooked in the first place is because the message we have been sending out has been the wrong one. We have been telling people to "Just Say No" to drugs.

This campaign did not work because, at its core, it was a scare tactic. Not only that, it isn't true! When an ad shows a frying egg in a skillet and an actor says, "This is your brain on drugs!" we are saying that anyone dumb enough to try them will get hooked and that everyone's reaction to the drug is the same, both of which are false.

We have also failed to inform people that every drug has a different genetic basis for addiction. Most people are immune to most drugs, and there is a night-and-day difference between how a drug can make one group of people feel versus another. One group can feel extreme joy from the drug whereas the other group will never experience any joy from the same drug, but just intoxication (from downers) or stimulation (from uppers).

We made it even worse by confusing people about what the high is. The high is always portrayed as an altered state of mind, dopey, or loopy on screen. By the time kids are in their teens, they have seen countless depictions of heroin addicts passed out, alcoholics stumbling around intoxicated and slurring their speech, or pot heads with a glazed look in their eyes and a silly grin on their faces. Nothing could be further from the truth. All of these scenes depict the aftermath of the high, but not the true high itself.

I recently saw a movie, *Layer Cake*, in which a character who is supposedly high on Ecstasy has a silly grin from ear to ear, but is passed out and is being held up by two people. Because the media doesn't understand addiction any better than most, it throws everything but the kitchen sink into what it thinks the high looks like. These two emotions of ecstasy and sedation are mutually exclusive. When a person is high, he is awake and alert. Sedation can be the aftermath of the high, but it is not the high.

One may be extremely happy one moment and then later be overcome with sedation as the high fades, but these feelings cannot co-exist simultaneously. Because we never ask the person who got high what he was experiencing, but we can see the sedation that follows, we confuse the aftermath of the high with the high.

It amazes me how many times I have asked my patients, "How did pot make you feel?" and the answer I usually get is "High, of course!" However, more often than not, when I ask them to describe what they felt rather than what they thought they felt, they often describe intoxication, sedation, and just an altered state of mind without the extreme joy. When I ask the same people, "Is pot addictive to you?" most will say, "Of course not!" How can something that makes you high not be addictive? It's because their definition of the high is wrong that such sentiments exist.

This perception exists even among my addiction patients. Most of them also think they got high on pot even when they describe their experience with pot as that dopey feeling. Only when I explain to them the high is never sedating at first, but extremely stimulating and euphoric, do they finally understand the difference.

Because most people think the high is a dopey feeling, when they experience a true high they don't recognize it. When something feels extremely pleasurable to them, they say, "Gee, this feels great!" and think nothing of pursuing such an experience, and have no fear of getting hooked. Only when the craving starts to set in, do they realize something is terribly wrong. Had they been told the high is something that artificially makes you happy, sometimes extremely happy, and not that dopey feeling, they would have been able to understand what was going on.

It is my belief that once we truly understand addiction, we can prevent others from going through the same heartbreaks and tribulations in the first place. With proper education, most people can learn to understand the warning signs and know whether they are vulnerable to a drug's allure or not. Knowing that only those who are genetically susceptible to a drug become highly euphoric on that drug, and that it is the euphoria that lures them in, they can stop before it's too late.

When you think that everyone experiences what you feel, there is no reason to pause and ask whether you should pursue such an enjoyable feeling. It becomes an ego thing to think that if Johnny can handle it, so can I. However, when you know that most people will not get any euphoria from these drugs and that such euphoria is the warning sign you are susceptible to becoming addicted, you can make the right choice and stop. Contrary to popular belief, no one is hooked the first time they try a drug, no matter how strong the drug is, even if that drug makes you feel like "being kissed by God."

Because most people view the world through the prism of their own experience, they think that everyone's reaction to the drug must be the same as theirs. When they experience extreme euphoria, they think that this must be a normal reaction, that everyone must feel that way. If so, they are not likely to think there is anything wrong with repeating such an experience. After all, we are hardwired to seek out those things that make us feel good. Our whole survival instinct is based on this reward system.

Early on, an addict often thinks that the euphoria is a normal reaction and can't understand why anyone would not want to keep chasing such a pleasurable feeling. However, as addiction takes hold and the addict starts to lose control, he begins to realize that something is terribly wrong. Because he does not realize that others do not feel the extreme euphoria that he felt, he believes the problem is with him.

Such people often think that there must be something wrong with them since others do not seem to be suffering from the downward spiral of their addiction. Often, they feel guilty and shameful and blame themselves for letting things get so out of control. Addicts often blame themselves, even when they got addicted to prescription pain medications that their doctors gave them. Such views are widespread in part because of how the society views addiction as a personal failing rather than a disease.

Our war on drugs has been a dismal failure because the focus has been on punishing those who become addicted as well as trying to cut off the supply, while at the same time trying to scare kids away from drugs.

Most parents know from experience that telling a child something is bad does not prevent the child from trying it. Unfortunately, children being what they are, if you tell them not to do something because it is bad, some are more apt to try it. Like a forbidden fruit, it's more tempting when it's bad. Instead, our focus should be on educating our children as well as the general public about the above concepts.

If one understands that there is a genetic basis for any addiction, one can use this information to discern whether one may be at risk. Most people know their own family history. The family may not readily talk about Grandma Mary, who is an alcoholic, or Uncle Joe, who got hooked on pills, but everyone knows about their troubles. Knowing that susceptibility to a given drug is genetic should forewarn those with a family history of addiction to a drug to be more vigilant about their own risks.

There is a time lag from the first exposure to the drug to the point of no return. I truly believe that if one understands why some people get addicted as well as the signs that one is susceptible, most can stop before it's too late. Knowledge is our greatest weapon in fighting this disease. It is imperative that we teach our children (as well as the rest of the public) to understand this. It is the only way we will ever win the war on drugs. Yes, "an ounce of prevention is worth a pound of cure."

Punishing those who get hooked or fighting to cut off the supply when the demand is high never works. Our history with Prohibition should have taught us this lesson. We are repeating the same mistake with the war on drugs. By this, I am not suggesting that we should legalize illicit drugs. When it comes to hardcore drugs, the onset of addiction is too quick and the subsequent cost in harm done to many more people is too great to let this happen. Instead, we must educate the public about what addiction is to help prevent many from getting hooked in the first place. Dry up the demand, and the supply will not matter.

Once you make this connection between how you react to a drug and your own vulnerability, you can be forewarned. Once you realize that you are at risk, you can stop the behavior that will eventually become harder and harder to control. Once you realize that you are genetically susceptible to a drug, you can change your behavior to alter the outcome. We have free will. We also have the power of reason. Once you understand that the glorious banquet laid out in front of you is a trap, you can avoid plunging in headfirst even when you find the drug highly desirable from the first try.

It is one thing to fall into a trap because you didn't know the warning signs; it is another to allow yourself to fall prey to it when you know what is happening before it's too late. It is my belief that most people won't make this mistake when they truly understand what's going on before addiction takes full hold.

Sure, we have been telling everyone about the dangers of drugs, but because the message has been that anyone foolish enough to try these drugs will get hooked, we have missed the mark. Worst of all, because we have done such a poor job explaining or depicting what the high is, those who get dopey on drugs think they are getting high (when they are not) and those who are getting high do not realize they are getting high. Such is the irony of the current message. We must re-educate everyone that the high is anything that artificially makes you feel happy, sometimes extremely happy.

With education, we can prevent many people from getting hooked in the first place. Prevention is the only way we can win the war on drugs! Yes, knowledge is power, and it can change the world.

Dopey Is Not High—Happy Is!

Chapter 14 Alcoholics Anonymous

ALCOHOLICS ANONYMOUS (AA) WAS FOUNDED by a businessman, Bill Wilson, and Dr. Bob Smith in 1935.[1] On a business trip to Akron, Ohio, Bill Wilson met up with Dr. Bob Smith, who was himself struggling with his addiction to alcohol. Each helped the other stay sober, and by word of mouth they founded AA. Wilson later wrote a book called *Alcoholics Anonymous* (often referred as the Big Book), which later became the organization's name. The book describes a twelve-step program to help its members achieve and maintain sobriety.

It is now a worldwide organization with over two million members.[2] It is an informal meeting society composed of recovering and recovered alcoholics whose stated mission is to help its members "stay sober and help other alcoholics achieve sobriety."[3] AA is funded by its members. The society has no membership fees and does not charge to attend meetings, but instead relies on donations from its members to cover basic costs such as room rental and refreshments. A contribution from a member is limited to a maximum annual amount of $2,000, although most contribute only a few dollars per meeting.

The main tenet of AA is that its members follow its twelve-step program for recovery and abstain from drinking by sharing their experiences and camaraderie to help solve their common problem.[4] It teaches that members can help make their own sobriety grow stronger when they share their own experiences with other members. It emphasizes abstaining from alcohol one day at a time.

The Twelve-Step Program[5]

1. We admitted we were powerless over alcohol–that our lives had become unmanageable.
2. Came to believe that a power greater than ourselves could restore us to sanity.
3. Made a decision to turn our will and our lives over to the care of God *as we understood Him.*
4. Made a searching and fearless moral inventory of ourselves.
5. Admitted to God, to ourselves and to another human being the exact nature of our wrongs.
6. Were entirely ready to have God remove all these defects of character.
7. Humbly asked Him to remove our shortcomings.
8. Made a list of all persons we had harmed, and became willing to make amends to them all.
9. Made direct amends to such people wherever possible, except when to do so would injure them or others.
10. Continued to take personal inventory and when we were wrong promptly admitted it.
11. Sought through prayer and meditation to improve our conscious contact with God *as we understood Him,* praying only for knowledge of His will for us and the power to carry that out.
12. Having had a spiritual awakening as the result of these steps, we tried to carry this message to alcoholics, and to practice these principles in all our affairs.

New members are encouraged to get a sponsor to help them go through the twelve-step program. Working the program might include the following:

- Avoiding that first drink. "One is too many and a thousand never enough."
- Regularly attend meetings, and participate by talking or listening.
- Maintain regular contact with a sponsor for support to stay sober.

- Carrying the message to other alcoholics (Step Twelve).
- Meetings usually end with the Lord's Prayer or Serenity Prayer.

There are many people who are turned off by the religious overtone of the AA and NA meetings. I think they are missing the point. Even if you don't believe in God or do not go through the twelve-step program, you can still get something out of these meetings.

Although there is a high dropout rate, there are many studies that show that attending AA and NA meetings does work.[6] [7] Those who attend meetings on a regular basis are more likely to stay clean and sober. One question that has not been answered from these studies is why they are more likely to stay sober. Is it because these people are more committed to their recovery, or is there something intrinsically beneficial about the meetings themselves? I believe the answer is both.

Of course, a person who bothers to show up to meetings must be serious about his sobriety, but I believe that meetings themselves help, but maybe not for the reasons why the AA and NA organizations believe. I see people who come to these meetings who never say a word. They seem to get as much out of the meetings as others. I believe what seems to help is the fact that by merely showing up to these meetings, they remind themselves of the reasons why they are there and why they wanted to quit in the first place. That alone is powerful enough to keep them from relapsing.

If you ever attend these meetings and run across someone who says he has been clean for a long time, you should pull him aside after the meeting and ask, "If you have been clean for so long, why do you still come to meetings?" I have. The answer I get is always the same: because it keeps them clean. They have learned the hard way that, when they stop coming to meetings, they relapse.

I want to point out that I do not agree with every tenet of AA or NA. I believe that there is too much emphasis on the spiritual aspect and that the twelve-step program is usually too cumbersome for many to follow. However, for now, I believe that these meetings are the only cost-effective and readily available means to remind someone of the reasons why they don't want to relapse. They can help prevent an addict from relapsing by keeping his memory alive of what it was like when he was truly down and out and in the depths of his addiction. Other people's misery should remind you of yours.

Alcoholics Anonymous was the first twelve-step program. Other similar recovery groups, such as Narcotics Anonymous, have modeled themselves after AA. One can find local meetings for AA and NA by going to www.AA.org and www.NA.org respectively.

There is also Marijuana Anonymous (www.marijuana-anonymous.org). Anyone who thinks that marijuana is not addictive (because it is not addictive to them) should attend one of these meetings. Pot addiction is real. Just because you can't get addicted to pot does not mean that someone else can't.

References

[1] *Pass It On.*

[2] AA Fact File.

[3] "What is AA? Defining "Alcoholics Anonymous"" The General Service Board of Alcoholics Anonymous (Great Britain). Retrieved on 2006-11-27.

[4] AA General Service Office. "*A.A. Preamble.*" Retrieved on 2008-09-04.

[5] http://www.serenityfound.org/steps.html

[6] Morgenstern et al. "Affiliation with Alcoholics Anonymous after treatment: a study of its therapeutic effects and mechanism of action." Department of Psychiatry, Mount Sinai School of Medicine, New York, 1997 Oct; 65(5):768-7.

[7] Larimer, Mary E; Palmer, Rebekka S; Marlatt, G. Alan (1999). "Relapse prevention. An overview of Marlatt's cognitive-behavioral model". Alcohol research & health: the journal of the *National Institute on Alcohol Abuse and Alcoholism* 23(2): 151-160. ISSN 1535-7414. PMID 10890810. OCLC 42453373. http://findarticles.com/p/articles/mi_m0CXH/is_2_23/ai_59246580/pg_1

Chapter 15 Marijuana

I DECIDED TO COVER THIS subject because of the recent trend toward marijuana's medical use as well as debates about legalizing it for general consumption. State after state has legalized the medical use of marijuana, including my state of Washington. Washington and Colorado have recently legalized its recreational use as well. This probably has more to do with most people's own experiences with pot. Because most people have tried pot, and most found it not to be addictive for them, they believe that it can't be addictive for others either. However, although many people think that they got high on pot, they did not; most just became intoxicated by it. Let me explain.

Most people think they got high on pot, but most believe that it is not addictive for them. There is a problem with such sentiments; the two are contradictory. How can something that makes you high not be addictive? Either you got high on pot, and pot is addictive for you, or the reason why pot is not addictive for you is because it did not make you high. It means that most people's definition of high is wrong! Remember, the high is never sedating at first. Only a small percentage of people can get high on pot, and for them, it is addictive. My data on addiction overlap shows that, even among my opiate-addicted patients, only about 15% can actually get high on pot.

Because most people confuse their intoxicated state as the high, but know that it isn't addictive for them, they think that pot should be legalized for both medical and recreational uses. I believe that the proper use of medical marijuana probably has its merits. However, often pot is not being prescribed for any discernible medical use.

175

In many states that have legalized the medical use of marijuana, it has become an industry unto itself, and anyone who wants it for any reason can get it. There are no real criteria that outline who should or shouldn't qualify for it. Sure, there are guidelines, but they are so broad that anyone would qualify. In each state, only some doctors have signed up to prescribe it, and they often advertise their services on billboards and newspapers. It has become a highly lucrative business for some doctors. Often these doctors no longer practice medicine, but see patients for the sole purpose of dispensing medical marijuana licenses. Often, it is strictly on a cash-only basis.

I am not trying to paint all such doctors in a negative light. However, one must wonder whether this was what was intended when these states passed initiatives to legalize the medical use of marijuana. Some of these doctors never say no to anyone who walks in through their door asking for a prescription for pot with cash in hand. Most of us would not condone physicians who gave out prescriptions for opiate pain medication to anyone who asked for it.

Often, pot is being prescribed for pain. But does pot actually work for pain? There are a lot of very heated debates, but no good study proves this. We do have scientific data that shows it helps with nausea, appetite, and decreases the intraocular pressure in narrow-angle glaucoma patients. Other than that, not much else is proven.

No one is arguing that, for the terminally ill or cancer patients, pot shouldn't be used. For these patients, addiction is not the most pressing issue. However, the argument that pot should be used to treat any chronic pain or be legalized for general consumption needs to be reexamined.

For some, pot is addictive. How do I know? Because I have had patients who have told me they got highly euphoric on pot and ultimately got addicted to it. Until we understand what percentage of the public may truly be susceptible to getting addicted to pot, we should not legalize it for general consumption.

If we were to argue that because pot is not addictive to most that it should be legalized for general consumption, the same argument can be made for other drugs, including opiates and cocaine. In general, about 10% of the public is thought to be susceptible to opiate addiction.[1] Since most people are not susceptible, should we make opiates available over the counter like alcohol or tobacco? Of course, there are those who argue that pot is not as dangerous as these other drugs. They say it is not any more dangerous than alcohol and tobacco, which are available over the counter. They may be right, or they may be wrong. Until we know more about the positive aspects of marijuana use as well as its potential downfalls, I argue that we cannot unleash this on the general public.

I agree that we need to decriminalize marijuana use. Sending someone to jail for marijuana use (or any drug use, for that matter) just doesn't make any sense. It is a waste of taxpayer dollars as well as a loss of productivity to society. It is also destructive to the family structure. However, in my opinion, legalizing it will make matters worse, not better. The more people who are exposed to marijuana, inevitably the more will get addicted to it. Once the genie is out of the bottle, we may not be able to put it back in.

What is the difference between decriminalizing pot versus legalizing it? Decriminalizing it means that we will stop prosecuting someone for possession (for personal consumption) and use of pot. Legalizing it means that we make it available to anyone (above a certain age) and tax and regulate it like we do tobacco and alcohol. The difference is that with decriminalization, we are no longer going after the users, but the sale and distribution of pot are still illegal. Legalizing it means that we are regulating how it should be sold and distributed and collecting taxes. The real difference between the two is whether we explicitly condone its use and make it available to everyone (above a certain age, of course) or simply tolerate those who use it, while still prohibiting its sale and distribution. This may seem like a minute point, but the consequences are not.

Proponents of legalizing pot for general consumption argue that the taxes collected from legalizing it would generate a huge windfall for states. This movement is gaining momentum and is largely based on most people's perception that pot is not addictive. However, if you ask those who got hooked on pot, they will disagree that it is not addictive and is as benign as most people think it is. Eventually, the money spent on treating those who become addicted to it would outweigh any benefit from such a windfall. The taxes we collect on tobacco and alcohol are generally figured to cover only a fraction of the total societal cost we incur from their use.[2, 3]

Is Pot Safe?

According to a Gallup poll done in 2013, four out of ten Americans admitted to having tried pot at least once in their lifetime.[4] There is a scene in the movie *Romancing the Stone* with Kathleen Turner and Michael Douglas when Kathleen Turner's character is asked whether she has ever tried pot. She gleefully answers, "I went to college." Even Presidents Clinton and Obama have admitted to having tried it. For most, it is not addictive. But then, the same is true of all drugs. Some have said that pot gave them less of a buzz than cigarettes. It did for me!

My first experience with pot was in high school. I was with a few friends when someone lit a joint and started passing it around. When it came to my turn, I had a choice of either looking like a dork or trying to act cool. I imagine that's why most kids try it for the first time.

I took a couple of hits from the joint. What surprised me was that I felt nothing. I first attributed this to my fear. I thought that if my parents knew what I was doing, they would kill me! I thought that maybe I was too uptight to enjoy it.

My next experience with pot came in college and another time when I was in my 30s vacationing in Jamaica. Each time, some people I was sharing the joint with seemed to be enjoying it a lot more than I was. All it ever did for me was make me groggy and hungry.

There is empirical evidence that, over the last few decades, the potency of marijuana has increased.[5] I have been doing urine drug screens on my patients for a while, and I am seeing much higher levels of tetrahydrocannabinol

(THC) than I used to. THC is the active ingredient in pot. Other clinicians have reported this as well. Whether this is a pure sampling error or a true trend is the subject of fervent debates.

In the past, we have thought that smoking pot was relatively safe. Like chewing coca leaves, it probably was. However, over the last few years, this may have changed, especially when it is mixed with opiates.

When I am treating patients for opiate addiction with Suboxone, I usually overlook their use of pot. I will ask them, "How does pot make you feel?" If the answer is that it calms them down, I will overlook it. However, if the answer is that it makes them highly euphoric, they must agree to come off of it.

However, when I am treating patients for pain with opiates, I insist that they get off the pot or at least agree to curb its use. Why the disparity? It is because Suboxone is not a CNS depressant. The patient cannot overdose on Suboxone and pot. On the other hand, opiates are CNS depressants, and so is pot. Combining the two can have consequences.

In 2002, I had a 62-year-old patient with severe rheumatoid arthritis who overdosed on Vicodin and pot. Her Vicodin usage had not changed in years. She was taking six to eight Vicodin 5/500 a day.

The story goes something like this. She tells me that a friend gave her a pot brownie. She became unconscious with shallow breathing. Luckily, her daughter was in the house and called 911. She was given Narcan (naloxone) but this did not bring her out of her stupor. She was put on a ventilator to help her breathe until she was able to breathe on her own. Her Vicodin level was what you would expect with six to eight Vicodin a day. Her THC level was off the charts. It was greater than 500, the upper limit to which the THC level is measured.

In the past, we did not see levels above 500, but now, we routinely see numbers above the cutoff. If her overdose was mostly from the opiates, Narcan should have brought her out of it. The fact that she did not respond to Narcan points to pot as the culprit.

Her daughter told me (in confidence) that she thought her mother had been smoking pot for some time. Eating marijuana can result in much higher levels of THC. A person who is ingesting it may not realize how much he has ingested until it's too late. Unlike smoking it, ingesting it doesn't give that buzz right away, so you may ingest more. By the time the buzz starts to kick in, there may be more in your system. Unlike smoking, you can't just stop.

It was about this time that we started hearing about how pot had gotten stronger. Before this event, I didn't routinely test patients for pot. Now I do. Ever since then, I have had patients tell me their own experiences with pot also have changed. Most agree that the pot seems to have gotten much stronger. I had a patient, in his 30s, who told me that after smoking pot for the first time since college, he passed out.

In 2007, I had a patient who told me that he had a stroke while smoking pot. He did get extremely euphoric on pot, and he insisted he got hooked on it. He was also hooked on opiates, including methadone. He stated that he was increasing his pot usage daily until he had a stroke. He was 27 at the time. I was treating him for opiate addiction. As I have stated above, although I often overlook the use of pot when I am treating patients with Suboxone, in this patient, pot was also out. If you are trying to stay clean from one addiction, you can't be getting high on another drug. It doesn't work. You won't stay clean for very long.

What do I tell patients who have a medical marijuana prescription when they want opiate pain medications from me? I tell them they should go back and see the doctor who prescribed the medical marijuana for them. Theoretically, since pot was prescribed for their pain, the doctor shouldn't have any problem prescribing opiates for the pain as well. Invariably, doctors who prescribed medical marijuana for them will tell them that they don't treat pain and refuse to give them any opiate pain medications. Ironic!

If these doctors feel that mixing pot with opiate pain medications is safe, they shouldn't have any problems prescribing opiate pain medications to these same patients.

Most doctors who prescribe medical marijuana are family physicians who in the past probably had no problems prescribing opiate pain medications to their patients before they switched their practices to primarily prescribing pot.

Although there are increased reports of patients ending up in emergency rooms because of pot intoxication, there are heated debates as to why. Many proponents of legalizing pot will state that such statistics are false and skewed by the fact that there are often other drugs involved. I agree. More often than not, there are also opiates and sedatives involved. This should caution us about mixing pot with opiates, rather than strengthening the argument for their concomitant use. So far, there is no good data pointing out pot's danger when used alone. Many patients will use this as an argument that pot is safe.

When I am treating patients for pain with opiates, I insist that they stop (or significantly curb) their use of pot. If I knew that a patient was engaged in a potentially dangerous activity with the medications I was giving him, should I allow that patient to continue such behavior rather than point out to him the potential danger and try to stop such behavior?

As I have stated before, most of my pain patients have no problems stopping their pot use while on opiate pain medications when asked to do so. However, some would rather stay on pot and come off the pain pills. A few want both. Some of these patients think that I am being judgmental, but I just want to make sure that I am not harming them. Sure, if their THC level is low, I may overlook its use. However, usually, the THC level is off the charts.

If a patient were drinking heavily, I would also refuse to prescribe opiate pain medications unless the patient agreed to stop such behavior. I have had patients who consistently test positive for alcohol. Unless they agree to stop or curb their alcohol intake, I will discontinue prescribing opiate pain medications as well.

References

[1] http://www.pnas.org/content/95/16/9608.full

[2] http://www.health.state.mn.us/divs/hpcd/chp/cdrr/alcohol/pdf/final2004costfactshe et.pdf

[3] http://www.health.gov.on.ca/english/public/updates/archives/hu_04/tobacco/tobac co_revenue.html

[4] http://www.golocalprov.com/news/New-Gallup-Poll-Shows-38-of-Americans-Have-Tried-Marijuana-/

[5] abcnews.go.com/Health/wireStory?id=5051376

Chapter 16 Pain Management

SINCE I AM A PAIN specialist, I thought I should devote at least one chapter in this book to this subject. My goal here is not to cover the vast nuances of treating pain, but to provide some basic concepts about pain management. I will admit that this will barely scratch the surface on this topic, especially when it comes to chronic pain.

However, the reason why I felt it necessary to address this topic here is because so many of my addiction patients got hooked on pain pills that their doctors gave them years earlier. For them as well as others like them, I felt an obligation to address a basic fundamental understanding of pain management so that others won't get addicted to pain medications.

Unfortunately, when you are treating pain, you will inevitably run across addiction. Understanding and treating addiction is (or should be) an integral part of any pain management practice and vice versa.

What Is Pain?

Pain is defined as any unpleasant sensory or emotional experience. What a pain specialist treats is mainly the physical or the sensory component of the pain. We deal with both acute and chronic pain. Chronic pain is usually defined as any pain that lasts more than six months. Chronic pain is a different beast altogether from acute pain. Most acute pain heals on its own, no matter what we do—sometimes in spite of what we do. Often, too much interference from a health professional may actually hinder the healing process. The human body has amazing restorative and healing properties.

When it comes to most acute pain, as physicians, we should be providing TLC and reassurance that the pain will resolve over time, as well as educating our patients about the nature of their injury and giving guidance about what to expect, and what not to do, and teaching them when it is appropriate to gradually return to normal activities. As healers, sometimes letting nature take its course is the best plan we can follow.

Obviously, as astute physicians, we must sort out those problems that are less likely to resolve on their own and address them in a timely manner. For example, someone who comes in with low back pain, with pain shooting down his leg and a foot drop, should be managed differently than someone without any neurologic problems. Even though both may heal nicely with time, the person with a foot drop may develop permanent nerve damage unless the issue is addressed in a timely manner.

Without delving into the pathophysiology of pain, we will simply define pain as any unpleasant sensory experience arising from a physical injury.

Philosophy of Pain Management

The job of a physician is to help eradicate pain when possible and to help patients manage their pain the best they can when it is not possible to eradicate it. Especially when it comes to chronic pain, the goal of pain management is not necessarily the elimination of pain. The main goal of pain management is to improve quality of life and restore function to the best level we can.

The philosophy behind pain management follows the basic tenets of the Hippocratic Oath. As physicians, we take a solemn oath to provide aid and comfort to our patients, but more importantly to do no harm. The oath does not say anything about a cure, because a cure is not always possible. Even with all the advances in science and healthcare technologies today, we do not always have a cure for our patients' ailments.

Medicine is still more of an art than a science. It doesn't mean that medicine is not founded on science. It is. It's just that delivering medical care can't be taught just from a textbook. It takes years of face-to-face interaction with patients for most providers to fine-tune their skills. There is no cookie-cutter approach that will work for every patient, no matter how similar their problems.

Every patient brings with him his unique life experiences that affect how he deals with a given illness. This is even more important when it comes to pain. Often, when treating pain, a patient's emotional state as well as his own perception of the pain is more important than the actual cause of the pain itself. This is especially true when it comes to chronic pain.

However, given the arsenal of tools at our disposal, I tell my patients that we should be able to control their pain, even if we cannot get rid of it. A doctor who tells his patient that he just needs to learn to live with the pain should not be practicing pain management and needs to refer such patients to physicians who are willing to learn the art of pain management. At the same time, as physicians, we must not raise our patients' expectations too unrealistically.

Physicians who tell their patients that they can "fix" or "cure" what ails them with the next procedure or surgery often set their patients up for failure, and when this happens, patients' disappointment and anger are overshadowed only by the increased intensity of their pain. I tell patients that even chronic pain does have a way of resolving over time. Sometimes it comes about when a patient approaches his pain differently, through exercise, relaxation techniques, or dealing with anger or emotional pain that may have contributed to its longevity. However, even if the pain does not resolve, I reassure my patients that pain can be controlled. Of course, there are exceptions to every rule.

Methods of Pain Control or Elimination

While healing is taking place, a physician can help the patient control the pain by various means. This is usually done in a stepwise fashion, starting with the least aggressive or invasive means and adding stronger measures as needed. Pain control does not start with the use of strong opiate pain medications, but it often starts with behavior modification and over-the-counter (OTC) analgesics such as Tylenol (acetaminophen) and ibuprofen.

The following is a commonly used three-tiered approach to dealing with acute pain or injury. However, don't confuse the three-tier system to mean that one level must follow the previous one. They can be applied simultaneously. Think of the tier system as a measure of how severe the acute pain is, meaning the milder the pain/injury, the lower the tier of treatment; with higher levels of pain, as many levels as necessary are incorporated.

Tier 1 (Behavior Modification and Patient Education)

With any injury, patients must be made to understand to heed the pain as a warning sign that their body is trying to tell them what to avoid. Rest is essential for any healing to take place. This does not mean bed rest necessarily, but avoiding those activities that cause worsening of the injury. At the same time, modalities such as ice, heat, elevation, or splinting, or even assistive devices such as a cane or crutches, when appropriate, may be crucial in helping decrease the pain. We also use home exercise programs such as gentle stretching and self-directed home exercise at this stage.

Tier 2 (OTC Medications, Non-Opiate Pain Medications, and Therapeutic Modalities)

In the second tier of pain management, the OTC medications are used as mild analgesics. Tylenol and all non-steroidal anti-inflammatory drugs (NSAIDs) have analgesic properties. They are inexpensive and well tolerated for the most part. Often, a mild to moderate pain can be treated with these medications alone, along with the behavior modifications found in Tier 1. Although these medications are relatively safe (if used appropriately), there are a few things to know about them to prevent potentially serious side effects.

Tylenol (acetaminophen) can be hepatotoxic (meaning toxic to the liver) if ingested in a large quantity. The upper limit of Tylenol that can be safely taken in a 24-hour period for a healthy adult is four grams, or eight extra-strength Tylenol. A fatal dose of Tylenol for a healthy adult can be as low as six grams. This means there is very little room for error. You must keep in mind that many OTC cold medications have Tylenol in them. For patients with liver problems or for those who drink heavily, even a safe amount of Tylenol may be detrimental to their liver.

All NSAIDs (such as ibuprofen, Aleve, etc.) have potentially nephrotoxic (meaning toxic to the kidney) side effects, especially at high doses. Those patients with kidney problems should avoid NSAIDs until they have consulted with their physician. More commonly, all NSAIDs (except for Celebrex) have potential gastrointestinal side effects. Most of the time, the gastrointestinal side effects are minor and include upset stomach, nausea, heartburn, or abdominal cramping. However, sometime NSAIDs can cause ulcers.

Within the second tier, we also use non-narcotic medications such as Tricyclic Antidepressants (TCAs), serotonin uptake inhibitors, or even anti-seizure medications that can help with the pain as well as help patients sleep better.

Other interventions, such as physical therapy, modalities such as electric stimulation, myofascial release, ultrasounds, and chiropractic manipulations, massage therapy, acupuncture, trigger point injections, and homeopathic treatments, are often beneficial. As long as they are used judiciously, they can be a cost-effective way to treat most acute pain. However, aggressive physical therapy or strength training should be avoided until the pain has started to resolve.

Tier 3 (Opiate Pain Medications and Nonsurgical Interventions)

The third tier of pain management involves the use of opiate pain medications. Most opiate pain medications belong in the same class as heroin. All opiates have addiction potential (for some). Generally, the stronger the opiate, the more likely that someone can become addicted to it. Remember that most people are not susceptible to getting addicted to opiate pain medications, no matter how strong or how long they take the drugs.

The use of opiate pain medications has revolutionized the treatment of both acute and chronic pain. It has enabled physicians to help patients achieve a better quality of life and improve function when used appropriately. As a physician, I understand that some of my patients may get addicted to opiate pain medications. Although they start with good intentions, some patients may end up paying a high price if the treatment is not handled properly. Thus, physicians must be diligent about how these medications are used and help educate every patient about what addiction is and what the early warning signs are that he may be susceptible to getting addicted.

When used appropriately, this is probably the most cost-effective means of treating pain. For those who are not susceptible to getting addicted, opiate pain medications as a class, in many ways, are safer and more effective than any other modality. However, for those who are susceptible, these drugs can be quite addictive and dangerous.

A great fallacy that many physicians were taught is that when opiates are used to treat pain, patients do not get addicted. This couldn't be further from the truth. There is a grain of truth in this statement. It should instead say that when used appropriately, opiate pain medications are less likely to get patients addicted.

A key to understanding the above statement is that when you do not overpower the pain, even those who are genetically susceptible to getting addicted are less likely to get addicted. In other words, when pain medications are used to bring the pain down to a tolerable level but not to mask the pain, they should not cause addiction. However, when these medications are used to completely mask the pain for those who are genetically predisposed, opiates will cause euphoria and can lead to addiction.

The Right and Wrong Ways to Use Opiate Pain Medications

The patient must be made to understand that the pain is there for a reason. The pain is a message the body sends to the brain that there is an injury, and it is designed to prevent further injury from happening by preventing the patient from doing things that can further harm himself. One reason why a diabetic patient develops an infection or injury that goes unnoticed until it has wrecked havoc on the body is because diabetes often leads to peripheral neuropathy, nerve damage that eventually leads to an inability to feel pain.

Most of the time, pain can be brought under control with the use of opiate pain medications. These medications can be of great help in improving quality of life by helping manage pain. However, the wrong way of using opiates is to use them to block the pain so the patient can continue doing those activities that further harm himself. In other words, if you couldn't do something before you took the pain pills, you shouldn't be doing it after you take them. Pain medications should be taken so you can rest and recuperate rather than so you can continue to engage in activities that are detrimental to you.

Opiate pain medications can mask pain. They do not get rid of the underlying cause of pain. When taking opiate pain medications, one must understand that the cause of the pain is still there.

Side Effects of Opiate Pain Medications

All opiate pain medications can have side effects. The most common is constipation. As one increases the dosage or the potency of the medication, the constipation increases. Other side effects include nausea and vomiting, loss of appetite, itching, respiratory suppression, dry mouth, and urinary retention. Opiates also cause cough suppression, which can be a good thing for the right patient. Although most of the side effects tend to diminish over time, constipation and urinary retention do not. Early preventative measures such as using stool softeners, increased fiber intake, and good oral hydration can prevent constipation.

Although rare, urinary retention can be a serious side effect. Urinary retention refers to the inability to feel when the bladder is full, as well as an inability to fully empty the bladder. This may lead to urinary incontinence and leakage of urine without warning, which happens because of the spillage effect and can be quite embarrassing and annoying. It can also lead to urinary tract infections, as well as cystitis. This side effect is also dose-dependent and can be resolved by lowering the dose. However, if adequate dose reduction cannot be achieved without giving up adequate pain relief, some patients may find themselves having to catheterize themselves, where a small tube is inserted into the bladder to help empty it.

Itching, although uncommon, can be a quite annoying side effect of opiates. However, this should not be confused with a true allergic reaction. Luckily, this side effect often diminishes with time. Often, an antihistamine can be used to deal with the itching until it resolves on its own. With a true allergic reaction, the itching is accompanied by hives, a rash that is large, flat, and raised and is of uniform reddish discoloration. An allergic reaction does not subside over time but rather worsens with time. In a severe allergic reaction, called anaphylactic shock, one can get generalized swelling all over the body, including the throat, which can lead to suffocation and death. A true allergy to opiates is rare. However, if someone is truly allergic to an opiate pain medication, it means he is allergic to all opiates that belong in that class.

Although not a true side effect, one of the physical hallmarks of acute opiate intoxication is meiosis, a term used to describe an extreme pupil constriction when the pupils constrict to almost pinpoints. This usually happens with a moderate to high dose of opiates. Even in a patient who is opiate-tolerant, meiosis does not diminish over time, and, thus, it can be a useful sign that someone has recently used an opiate. In an emergency setting when a person is incoherent or unconscious, the presence of meiosis will indicate that the person is overdosing on opiates. On the other hand, as the patient goes into withdrawal from opiates, you will see pupils becoming fully dilated.

Dependence/Tolerance

Anyone taking opiate pain medications for an extended period of time will become physically dependent on them and will develop a tolerance to them. Please note: **Dependence and tolerance are not addiction**. Dependence describes the physical state that happens when exposed to these drugs on a long-term basis. This is manifested by the physical withdrawal that happens when opiates are taken away too quickly. Anyone who has been taking opiate pain medications for a long time will go through the physical withdrawal described below, but this does not necessarily mean they are addicted.

Tolerance is best described as the liver's ability to metabolize a substance better and faster once it has been exposed to that substance for a while. Patients taking oral opiate pain medication will notice that, after a while, it loses some of its effectiveness. However, the liver will not keep metabolizing the medication faster and faster over time. There is a break-even point where tolerance levels off, and there isn't any further loss of effectiveness unless the dosage or the strength is increased. Tolerance only happens with drugs that are taken orally. The transdermal and intravenous administration of drugs bypasses the liver, and therefore does not produce tolerance.

When treating chronic pain, it is important to make the patient understand that increasing the pain medication to achieve "no pain" eventually leads to the same level of pain relief as before. The reverse is also true. That is, a gradual decrease in the dosage of opiate pain medication can reverse this faster and faster metabolism. However, every time you decrease the medication, you may experience withdrawal symptoms and increase the pain for a while.

Withdrawal Symptoms

Withdrawal symptoms will vary in intensity depending on how quickly you are reducing the medication or how high a dose you are coming off of. These symptoms can range from flu-like symptoms to agitation, feelings of doom, elevated blood pressure, quickened heart rate, dilated pupils, diarrhea, runny nose, goose bumps, and abdominal cramps. Physical withdrawal symptoms usually last about a week.

As stated above, anyone who has been on opiate pain medication for a long time will go through withdrawal when coming off of it. This does not mean that he was addicted. Of course, anyone who is addicted will go through withdrawal when coming off of opiates too quickly, but this shared experience does not mean that everyone was addicted.

Although the withdrawal symptoms are similar among both those who got addicted to opiates and those who did not, one difference is the degree of pain the patients experience. A person who is not addicted to opiates will experience mild muscle aches and flu-like pain. However, a person who is hooked on opiates will experience severe pain with the withdrawal.

Importance of Sleep

For any healing to take place (especially for chronic pain), therapeutic sleep must be maintained or restored. Pain can be a great inhibitor of sleep, but lack of adequate sleep can greatly decrease a patient's ability to deal with pain, and the cycle spirals downward. Most of the time, adequate pain relief can be achieved to allow the patient to get a good night's sleep. When needed, other medications such as tricyclic antidepressants and even sleeping pills can be quite beneficial in helping the patient get the restful sleep he needs.

When it comes to sleep, it is not only the total amount of time spent sleeping that is important, but also the quality of sleep as well. Sleep that is interrupted many times may not provide the restorative healing properties needed. A healthy sleeping pattern means both adequate time spent sleeping as well as experiencing a deep sleep that allows one to reach the rapid eye movement (REM) sleep associated with dreaming. For reasons yet unknown, there is a restorative property to dreaming. Studies show that dreaming can help one cope with stresses in one's life by helping one come up with solutions to one's problems. It also seems to help us prepare for upcoming events by allowing one to play out different possible scenarios in our minds during our sleep. Studies show that, when a person is deprived of REM sleep, not only does his ability to deal with day-to-day stresses diminish over time, but his perception of pain also increases.

For those patients who are susceptible to becoming addicted to opiates, the pain medication acts as a stimulant. For the rest of us, it is a sedative. For most, it helps them sleep. However, for those who are susceptible to the opiate's allure, it has the unwanted consequence of keeping them awake at night much the same way that caffeine may keep someone from falling asleep. For them, the continued use of opiate pain medications, especially at night, may rob them of a good night's sleep. They may find themselves using sedatives like alcohol and benzos to help them sleep at night.

Michael Jackson's epic struggle with trying to get a good night's sleep is now familiar to most people, and most people know that he had a doctor administer a powerful intravenous anesthetic called Propofol (which ultimately killed him). Most people don't understand why this happened or why anyone would do such a foolish thing. However, my addiction patients relate to Michael Jackson's insomnia all too well.

For those chronic pain patients who are susceptible to opiate addiction, opiates are a double-edged sword. Although they give pain relief, they may deprive the patient of restful sleep. In reality, as long as the dose of the opiate pain medication is not too high relative to their pain, this should not be a problem. However, for most patients, this is something that takes trial and error to figure out, and often, this knowledge must be taught and is not intuitive.

Many can't figure out why a pain pill they took to help get some sleep is keeping them awake at night. They often think that it must be something else, such as stress or even pain. Thus, they may find themselves taking even more pain medications, which actually worsens the situation. Eventually, at a high enough dose, the somnolence finally kicks in, just as it does for an alcoholic after that seventh or eighth drink. However, this can be a dangerous game to play with opiates, because at a high enough dose, an overdose can occur. This is one sleep that you may pay for with your life.

Chronic Pain

When it comes to chronic pain, there are always multiple factors playing important roles in its continuation. It may seem like a force of nature to the patient suffering from it, so powerful that it seems like it cannot be controlled. Unlike acute pain, chronic pain is probably not likely to resolve on its own, at least not without some help.

As I have pointed out earlier, most acute pain, including back and neck pain, subsides on its own, sometimes in spite of what we do. Most acute pain subsides within six weeks. If someone wanted to make a lot of money treating acute pain, all they would have to do is tell their patients to show up at their office two or three times a week, have them go through an innocuous ritual and guarantee them that they will be better within six weeks, and they would be right 90% of the time. That's a damn good success rate. Some practitioners may even believe they are the reason for this incredible success.

Studies show that a little time spent educating patients about the natural course of their illnesses, encouraging them to rest and not to overly exert themselves, while not to become a couch potato, and handing out some mild analgesics would have done the same thing and is much more cost-effective than all the physical therapy, chiropractic care, massage therapy, and other things that we put our patients through.

However, for a small percentage of patients, the pain does not resolve over time. Sometimes it's because a more serious structural problem was overlooked. Other times, we just don't know why. Sometimes, there is no structural problem. Obviously, the best way to prevent chronic pain is to find the underlying cause of the pain others may have missed or overlooked and fix it. Even when you do this, sometimes, the pain does not always go away. It may improve, but may not necessarily go away.

Chronic pain is defined as any pain that has not subsided after six months. By the way, here we are talking about the same pain that has been there on a daily basis for more than six months. Some patients confuse pain they have had on and off for more than six months as chronic pain. Not so. A low back pain that flared up last year but went away for a few months and recurred is not chronic pain.

With some chronic pain, there is a structural etiology you can identify as the pain generator. But even when the pain generator is found and there are means to fix the pain generator (surgery, injections, or neurotomies), the pain doesn't always go away. It's as if the pain memory has been etched into the brain and cannot be erased, even when the cause of the initial pain is long gone.

Chronic pain, which is what most pain specialists deal with, is always multifaceted. By this time, the physical pain cannot be separated from the emotional state of the patient. With chronic pain, the pain cannot be separated from the brain and the environment or vice versa.

Progression of Pain over Time

Pain is the only sensation that does not diminish over time with continued exposure. We are all familiar with the term white noise, which describes how one blocks out background noise with prolonged exposure to such stimuli. This is a coping mechanism that most people have mastered to adapt to their environment. It's what allows us to tune out other noises when we are carrying on a conversation over dinner at a busy restaurant. However, when it comes to pain, this does not happen.

Not only does pain not diminish over time, it actually intensifies. Just like an annoying sensation that can become heightened over time the more you try to ignore it, the perception of pain will increase the longer it persists. What started as an annoying sensation can become all-consuming, debilitating pain!

Imagine someone scratching his nail on a chalkboard. Over time, does this become less annoying or more annoying? More annoying, of course. Chinese water torture explains this concept perfectly. A prisoner is strapped to a table or a bench. He is blindfolded and a single drop of water is dropped on his forehead repeatedly. Who hasn't had a drop of rain fall on his forehead at one time or another? However, in this case, the prisoner feels helpless to stop this. With the continued drip of water on his forehead, eventually the prisoner goes insane. How can such an innocuous sensation cause such a devastating effect?

There is probably an evolutionary advantage why a painful stimulus does not fade over time. A blacksmith working around a fire will learn to respect the fire and learn to avoid the fire with repeated exposure rather than become used to it. If he became used to the fire and tuned it out, it would increase his risk of greater injury.

I have learned that most electricians also develop a similar behavior. They develop a healthy respect for electricity. I do a test called a nerve conduction velocity study, where I stimulate a nerve in the body with a low electric current. Most patients tolerate this test as a mere nuisance. However, most electricians can't stand this test. Instinctively, they jerk their arms or legs out of the way from the source of the electricity. However, this so-called heightened awareness of the pain can become quite debilitating. What may have an evolutionary advantage can cost us quite dearly.

The Role of Stress, Anxiety, and Depression

Stress is a part of life. However, how one reacts to stress determines whether stress can have a detrimental impact on one's life or not. Others may find the same stressor to have a positive impact and can use it to their advantage. For example, a deadline to get a homework assignment or a project done may make someone finally get motivated to get the work done, while it can leave others feeling overwhelmed. For most of us, stress is not a problem unless it impacts us negatively.

When it comes to pain, any negative stress can increase the perception of the pain. Stress does not cause pain, but it can intensify it. It is amazing how a different level of stress in a patient's life can make the level of pain fluctuate overnight, both negatively as well as positively.

Anxiety comes about when a person feels that he has no control over what is going on around him. In his book *Feeling Good*, Dr. David Burns thinks that anxiety is a manifestation of an illogical thought that you cannot control. Anxiety is an emotion born out of a feeling of loss of control. In its extreme, this is one emotion that most of us would like to avoid. In a mild form, it is the rush of adrenaline associated with any mildly dangerous activity, both perceived and real. It is synonymous with fear and apprehension. In a mild form, it can help us focus on the task at hand and become more self-aware or aware of our surroundings. Physical responses to mild anxiety include increased heart rate, dilated pupils, and increased blood flow to the muscles, all of which can help us deal with the perceived danger around us.

However, as anxiety increases, both the psychological as well as the physical responses can turn negative. We lose the ability to focus and stay calm. Instead, we become easily distracted and jumpy. One may become overly focused on one thought or sensation and be unable to redirect one's focus elsewhere. Physical responses to high anxiety include heart palpitation, cold sweat, loss of bowel or bladder control, and even loss of consciousness. Obviously, such reactions would not be helpful in a real life-or-death situation.

In extreme cases, anxiety leads to feelings of doom and panic. It is a feeling of utter loss of control and a sense of imminent danger from which one feels unable to escape no matter what. For any living organism, there is no fear greater than believing that one is about to die and feeling utterly helpless to do anything about it. Such is the power of a panic/anxiety attack.

With chronic pain, anxiety is often the byproduct of the disease. Often, negative and irrational thoughts creep in and one feels unable to stop such feelings and thoughts from overpowering oneself. Just as the perception of pain can increase over time the longer the pain persists, the sense of anxiety can also grow and deepen over time.

Depression can set in when anxiety is not brought under control. Depression can present itself as both a deep sense of sadness and the inability to enjoy anything in life, as well as a lack of energy and a heightened sense of anxiety and dread from which the mind is unable to escape. Often, chronic pain can bring about deep depression in its victims. In such patients, you must treat both the pain as well as the depression because one disease can feed the other.

Faulty Belief System of Many Chronic Pain Patients

Chronic pain patients often suffer from faulty belief systems that seem to depress them because of their own negative thoughts. They may believe that their problem is much worse than it actually is. Some of these patients feel angry and see themselves as victims of some injustice. Often the anger at the perceived wrong done to them is blown out of proportion and is detrimental to the person's own recovery.

This may be the case when it comes to some work-man's compensation claims, motor vehicle accidents, mal-practice lawsuits, and other personal injury cases. They feel somehow they were wronged by the other party and may feel angry that they have suffered some grave injury by an act or negligence of others, and their anger some-times fuels their pain and can even prevent them from get-ting better.

Sometimes there is a perverse incentive for them not to get better, whether the patient is consciously aware of it or not. I am not suggesting that in all such cases there is fraud involved, but in some cases, even the patients suffer-ing from their perception of their role as a victim may not realize what is going on. In their minds, the perceived wrong is so great, they can't let it go, and the anger turns maladaptive. For some, the anger feeds their sense of vic-timization and heightens the pain.

Unfortunately, even after their cases are settled, these patients don't always get themselves out of this victim role, and their pain persists. Some patients do miraculously im-prove after they win a big settlement. However, others do not improve even when they win. It is as if they have con-vinced themselves of their own reason for their misery, and they can't stop feeling that way even when the incentive to stay angry and injured is gone. The only winners in these cases are the malpractice lawyers.

Some may even believe that somehow these patients deserve their pain. In this case, the emotion is that of guilt. Some chronic pain patients suffer from guilt and chronic low self-esteem. Guilt can be just as strong an emotion as anger. Often, guilt may be the byproduct of anger. Some-one who feels angry at his parents, spouse, or children of-ten feels guilty about his anger. They may resent a loved one, but feel guilty about their feelings and think that they must be a bad person for feeling that way. They can feel manipulated and trapped by their loved ones, but feel guilty for resenting them anyway. Some victims of domes-tic violence feel that they are responsible for their abuser's acts. Many victims of rape feel guilty that they somehow brought it on themselves. Such is the case with some chronic pain patients. For them, their pain is their cross to bear for their sins (metaphorically speaking).

Others suffer from the opposite but just as unrealistic belief that they should have no pain, not even the slightest amount of discomfort, and look upon any such sensation as an assault on their body. It is as if they have forgotten that they had ever experienced pain in the past. They may be suffering from sensitization to the pain, which we discussed earlier. However, from an observer's standpoint, they seem to magnify any little discomfort and suffer from a very low pain threshold. Often, they are labeled as malingerers and viewed as faking their illnesses.

Many chronic pain patients hold a deep belief that somehow everyone has just missed the actual cause of their pain and that the next doctor or the next test will find the cause, or the next surgery will finally fix their problem. For some this may be true, but for others, the reason why no one has found anything is that there isn't anything to find, at least not from a physical standpoint.

For them, I may suggest, subtly, that we may want to look elsewhere for the source of their pain. It may be psychological trauma or pain that is manifesting as physical pain. For some, it may be that they have developed hyperalgesia because they became addicted to pain pills. Such suggestions must be introduced just as a possibility and not thrust upon them as a statement of fact. If you tell a chronic pain patient, "Hey, since we can't find anything wrong with you, it must be all in your head," the patient's response would understandably be quite negative. He will be seeking help elsewhere and you have not helped anyone with such an approach.

However, when I raise the above possibility only as one of many possibilities we should look at, most patients are receptive. Once you help the patient understand that mind and body are intertwined and the psychological battle or stress that the patient may be fighting every day may be just as important as the physical cause of the pain, the patient may be open to this possibility.

For some, even a simple statement acknowledging that

they may be angry at their employers for their work-related injuries and that some patients may want to make their employers pay for their suffering by dragging out the workman's compensation claims may finally make them realize that the only people they are actually hurting are themselves. Such a realization can finally help them turn a corner in their recovery. For others, the reason for their pain is much more complex and can be directly related to some psychological trauma or pain they may be suffering from.

Some patients are ecstatic when someone actually puts a name on their suffering, even when it is fibromyalgia or chronic fatigue syndrome. Others may find solace when some other unrelated medical illnesses are diagnosed because they think it finally vindicates their suffering. Some will even go through surgery after surgery, even when earlier surgeries provided no benefit and may have even made their pain worse.

However, the most deadly of all faulty beliefs is that the pain will never go away and that they will just have to live with it. Unfortunately, many physicians are guilty of implanting or reinforcing this message. When I ask many of my chronic pain patients why they would believe such a thing, they tell me it's because all the other doctors told them that. When such a fatalistic attitude is deeply ingrained in the patient's psyche, it is an uphill battle to convince him to believe otherwise. When you take away the patient's hope, you have just doomed him to a life of chronic pain. When patients truly believe this, it becomes a self-fulfilling prophecy.

Many physicians, when frustrated, may tell the patient that they don't know what's wrong with him and he will just have to learn to live with it. Coming from a doctor, to a patient, this is like a life sentence to chronic pain. Even when the source of original pain is long gone, the pain sometimes persists as if it has been etched deep into their psyche. As physicians, our job is to aid and comfort our patients, even when we can't cure them. "I don't know what's wrong with you, so you should just learn to live with the pain" is not the message we should be giving our patients.

Instead, as physicians, we should be telling our chronic pain patients, "I may not have an answer to why you continue to have pain, but we should be able to help you manage your pain, and it is still likely that the pain will eventually resolve itself."

Anxiety and Depression

Anxiety and depression come about if a person feels that he is helpless in trying to control what is going on around him. Chronic pain not only seems to bring about anxiety and depression in some patients, but anxiety and depression also tend to magnify and prolong their pain. Any clinician will tell you that stress seems to magnify pain. Stress may not cause pain, but it sure makes it harder for someone to deal with his pain effectively. You cannot separate the mind from the body. One cannot treat the one without addressing the other. The way one feels about his environment and, in turn, himself has a direct impact on how he feels physically and how he functions and vice versa.

Psychological Pain

For some, chronic pain can be a byproduct of some deep psychologically traumatic event. Although it is true that all pain is technically in our heads, when it comes to some chronic pain, the source of the pain is the person's own psyche. For them, you truly cannot separate the mind from the body, and sometimes the pain from their psychological wound is much more intense and searing than any physical pain.

For these patients, psychological trauma often manifests itself as physical pain or illness. Psychosomatic illnesses and somatoform disorders are not myths. Deeply psychologically traumatic events *can* cause physical pain.

In mild forms, psychosomatic pain may cause headaches or even an ulcer. In severe cases, we are talking about a somatoform disorder where someone may develop hysterical blindness, loss of hearing or speech, or even paralysis.

I had a patient who became a paraplegic after a severe rollover motor vehicle accident. The patient was the driver of the vehicle and her fiancé, who was a passenger, was thrown from their vehicle and killed. At first, she was thought to have suffered a spinal cord injury. However, all the work-ups, including the MRI, CT-scan, and electrodiagnostic studies showed that the spinal cord was not damaged and the signals from her brain to her legs were working fine.

The patient was referred to me to help her with rehab. After consulting with a psychiatrist, we decided to give the patient a way out, an excuse to let go of the guilt that she felt about causing the accident, however misplaced it was.

We basically told her that we had figured out what was wrong with her legs. We told her that it was a temporary paralysis from the shock to the spinal cord that should resolve within six months from the time of injury. It was about six months from the motor vehicle accident when I first met her. We both reassured the patient that we expected her to make a miraculous recovery anytime soon. Sure enough, over the next week, the patient began to walk on her own. We both recommended that the patient see a counselor to help her with her grief (and guilt), but she did walk on her own. We never told her that this was a type of somatoform disorder.

When I first started my practice, one of the first patients I saw was an elderly woman in her late 60s who had suffered from chronic low back pain for at least two decades. All the usual work-ups for the low back pain came back negative. She suffered from other medical problems, including high blood pressure and heart disease. She was also extremely overweight. She came to my office in a wheelchair. She was on a low-dose opiate pain medication. She was referred to me by her neurosurgeon. Because of her incessant pain, even though there was no discernible pathology to operate on and although she was obviously a poor surgical candidate, he was considering surgery for her. However, he had asked me to evaluate her to see if there was something that he missed before he operated on her.

During our visit, I remember that I mostly just listened. I don't quite know what happened, but by the end of our thirty-minute visit, the patient told me something that she said she had kept a secret ever since she was a child. Apparently, her father had sexually molested her as a child, usually anally. She felt ashamed. For the longest time, she felt somehow she was responsible for his behavior. She kept this a secret from her late mother and other family members, even after her father had passed away. She also kept this a secret from her late husband and her children. She told me that she remembered the pain from her molestation vividly, and the low back pain reminded her of that pain. I don't know why she told me that story, nor do I remember what words of comfort I may have offered her when she did. I told her neurosurgeon not to operate and told him why.

Two weeks later, I got a call from one of her family members that she had passed away peacefully in her sleep. They also told me that she seemed quite happy and in much less pain and discomfort during the two weeks prior to her death. She never had that back surgery. To my knowledge, she did not reveal her secret to anyone else before she passed away. She affected me deeply. I can still visualize her demeanor clearly. She actually told me that she was infatuated with the handsome, young neurosurgeon who had sent her to me. She told me that, had she been 20 or 30 years younger, by gosh, she would have liked to have a crack at him. She knew he was married.

She and other patients like her have taught me over the years that when it comes to chronic pain, it's never simple. A psyche is just as important as the body, if not more. As a pain specialist, it is the psychological trauma or scars that are the most difficult to address and treat. Treating physical wounds, on the other hand, is a walk in the park.

Chapter 17 Addiction Overlap

MY DATA WILL SHOW THAT addiction to any drug has a genetic basis and every drug has its own genetic marker. However, it will also show there is an overlap between some addictions. This does not mean there is a direct one-to-one link, but it does mean that if you are susceptible to opiate addiction that you are a lot more susceptible to some other addictions compared to other members of the general public.

There is a saying in AA that "a drug is a drug is a drug." This means that if you can get hooked on one drug, then you can get hooked on any other drug. I vehemently disagree with this statement. It is based on false notions about addiction. There is a saying at the end of the Big Book that every alcoholic is an alcoholic because he/she is looking to fill a hole in his/her life. This may mean different things to different people, but it is generally accepted as meaning that every alcoholic is trying to self-medicate him/herself (with alcohol) to treat an underlying psychological or emotional trauma or need. It confuses abuse with addiction. If you believe that alcohol is being abused to self-medicate underlying depression, anxiety, or emotional pain, then you can understand why you would think that you could abuse any other drug to serve the same purpose.

However, I believe that addiction is not just abuse. Unless a drug makes you extremely euphoric early on, you cannot become addicted to it. I have known patients who may have gotten hooked on opiates, but alcohol held no allure for them, and vice versa.

Based on my observations, I realized that every drug must have a different genetic marker. For years, I have been asking my addiction patients about their experiences with different drugs. However, in the last three years, I finally started recording their answers. At first, I was sure that my data would confirm my belief that every addiction was independent, meaning that just because you are susceptible to one drug does not mean you are susceptible to other drugs as well. It wasn't until I had enough data that I could see a pattern emerging that was completely unexpected!

What I have been telling my patients is that every drug has a different genetic marker, which is true. However, I have also been telling my patients that just because you got hooked on one drug, it does not mean that you are more susceptible to getting hooked on any other drugs. I was dead wrong! My data shows that there is a link between some addictions, although not a one-to-one link.

Categories of Drugs

I categorized drugs into three groups: downers, uppers, and hallucinogens. Downers are opiates (regular opiates, methadone, and tramadol), alcohol, Ecstasy, pot, benzos, and muscle relaxants. Uppers are amphetamine, crystal meth, and cocaine. Hallucinogens are LSD and psychedelic mushrooms. In order to understand how these drugs affect those who are susceptible differently from those who are not, you need to understand how one group reacts versus the other.

Downers make those who are not susceptible to their allure tired, groggy, sedated, or intoxicated right off the bat. For those who are susceptible, these drugs do not sedate them, but stimulate them at first. As the dose is increased, the stimulation is accompanied by euphoria. However, at a high dose, both the feelings of stimulation and euphoria can be followed by feelings of sedation and intoxication. The aftermath of their high is sedation and intoxication.

Uppers make everyone stimulated. For those who are not susceptible to these drugs, that's all they do. They just stimulate or energize you. However, at a high dose, it makes those who are not susceptible feel too jittery or paranoid, which is not an enjoyable experience. However, for those who are susceptible to these drugs, they do not feel jittery at first, but extremely euphoric. The higher the dose, the higher the high. Only as their high fades do they feel jittery. The aftermath of their high is not intoxication, but jitteriness.

Hallucinogens cause everyone to hallucinate. However, some will describe their experience as a good trip, meaning an extremely enjoyable, orgasmic experience, while others will describe their experience as a bad trip, a nightmare from which they couldn't wait to wake up.

In order to understand whether you are susceptible to a given drug, you need to know which class the drug belongs to and whether your reaction to the drug was like that of someone who is susceptible to the drug or not. For example, although you may not like the aftermath of alcohol, if the first few drinks energize you, then you are susceptible to getting hooked on it. If the first few drinks calm you down, then you are not susceptible to its allure.

Another example is cocaine. If cocaine makes you wired, but there is no extreme euphoria, then you are not susceptible to becoming addicted to it. However, if cocaine gives you an orgasmic experience, then you are susceptible to getting hooked on it. The aftermath of coming down from a cocaine high is jitteriness. Even those who can get extremely high on cocaine hate this feeling.

There was a motor vehicle accident that happened on the east side of Seattle last year that ties the above concepts together. The driver was apparently going about 100 miles per hour, weaving in and out of traffic before he crashed into another car, killing the other driver. The local newspaper reported that a driver high on meth killed another driver. The article clearly showed that the driver who caused the crash was under the influence of something. He failed a field sobriety test and was booked for vehicular homicide. He tested positive for meth as well as pot. Because meth is a stronger drug, the newspaper as well as local news stations blamed meth for the accident. However, they were wrong. There are two things wrong with this story.

First of all, this man was not high at the time that he caused the crash. When someone is high, he is more awake and alert than before. As I have said before, the high produces the same chemical reaction in the brain as sex. It releases dopamine, the feel-good neurotransmitter. No one falls asleep having sex.

Secondly, meth is an upper, not a downer. Granted, he was probably high on meth earlier that day. A person coming down from the high from meth becomes wired and jittery, not intoxicated. So what caused the crash? It was pot.

Why would someone use an upper and a downer at the same time? To even himself out. He may love the high from meth, but he hates the jitteriness that follows, so he uses a downer like pot to calm himself down. But in this case, he overshot the mark. As the jitteriness faded, the pot became a lot more intoxicating and caused the crash.

I point out this story for two reasons: to illustrate what a true high is and to show the different aftermaths of different classes of drugs. Because the media doesn't understand addiction any better than most people, it portrays any altered state of mind as a high. Because most people hear of or read these depictions as the high, they too think that's what the high is—an altered state of mind. Anyone who is drunk out of his mind or is under the influence of any mind-altering drug is depicted as being high.

I go over how a drug affects those who are susceptible to it before I ask my patients about their experience with different drugs. Here are the results of my survey over the last three years. My only regret is that I did not start writing down my patients' answers earlier in my career.

The data came from 225 people who were all being treated for opiate addiction at the time. The survey was done over a three-year period, and each patient's responses were checked on at least two separate occasions during their treatment to ensure the accuracy of their responses.

The gray column (Y for "yes") represents those who got high on that drug and the white column (N for "no") represents those who did not. The data was entered chronologically. I grouped the drugs according to which class they belonged to: downers, uppers, and hallucinogens. Opiates were left out of the first group since the survey was being done on my opiate-addicted patients.

I was trying to see if there was a pattern. Is someone who can get high on one upper more likely to get high on other uppers, or vice versa? Unfortunately, I saw no such patterns, whether it was between classes of drugs or the potency of the drugs.

#	alcohol Y	alcohol N	pot Y	pot N	methadone Y	methadone N	Ultram Y	Ultram N	MDMA Y	MDMA N	benzos Y	benzos N	Soma Y	Soma N	cocaine Y	cocaine N	meth Y	meth N	amphetamine Y	amphetamine N	LSD Y	LSD N	mushroom Y	mushroom N
1	1									1			1			1		1		1	1		1	
2	1				1						1		1			1				1	1			1
3		1							1						1									
4		1													1									
5	1											1		1		1						1		1
6	1											1		1		1		1		1		1		
7		1										1		1		1				1				
8										1												1		
9	1															1								
10																								1
11		1				1		1	1			1		1		1		1		1		1	1	1
12		1							1			1		1	1	1	1	1						
13	1		1			1		1	1	1	1			1	1		1			1				1
14		1	1		1							1		1	1					1				
15		1	1		1	1			1	1						1				1		1		
16	1				1						1	1			1				1				1	1
17	1								1	1		1		1		1								
18	1					1				1	1	1			1		1	1				1		1
19		1								1		1		1		1	1	1		1				
20		1						1		1		1				1				1		1		1
21	1					1			1			1		1	1					1				1
22		1			1						1					1								
23		1				1		1	1			1			1									
24		1	1		1							1				1								
25		1				1						1				1								
26	1															1								1
27	1															1								
177	1								1			1		1		1				1				
178		1										1				1				1				
179		1										1		1		1				1				
180		1										1				1	1					1		1
181		1										1				1								
182		1			1		1			1		1		1		1	1							1
183		1			1	1				1		1				1							1	
184		1			1		1			1		1		1		1		1	1			1		
185		1				1		1			1				1			1			1	1	1	
186		1			1	1				1		1		1		1								1
187		1						1		1		1				1								
188	1			1	1	1						1		1		1				1	1	1		1
189												1				1				1	1			
190	1											1		1		1				1				

210

#	alcohol Y	alcohol N	pot Y	pot N	methadone Y	methadone N	Ultram Y	Ultram N	MDMA Y	MDMA N	benzos Y	benzos N	Soma Y	Soma N	cocaine Y	cocaine N	meth Y	meth N	amphetamine Y	amphetamine N	LSD Y	LSD N	mushroom Y	mushroom N
N	102	121	183	33	45	80	68	21	70	53	161	22	7	92	126	66	40	63	101	22	51	43	56	62
%	46%		15%		36%		23%		60%		12%		7%		34%		38%		18%		54%		47%	

Let me summarize the survey.

Alcohol
- 102 could get high
- 121 could not
- 46% susceptibility

Pot
- 33 could get high
- 183 could not
- 15% susceptibility

Methadone
- 45 could get high
- 80 could not
- 36% susceptibility

Ultram
- 21 could get high
- 68 could not
- 23% susceptibility

MDMA (Ecstasy)
- 70 could get high
- 53 could not
- 60% susceptibility

Benzodiazepines
- 22 could get high
- 161 could not
- 12% susceptibility

Soma (carisoprodol)
- 7 could get high
- 92 could not
- 7% susceptibility

Cocaine
- 66 could get high
- 126 could not

- 34% susceptibility

Crystal meth
- 40 could get high
- 64 could not
- 38% susceptibility

Amphetamine
- 22 could get high
- 101 could not
- 18% susceptibility

LSD
- 51 could get high
- 43 could not
- 54% susceptibility

Psychedelic mushrooms
- 56 could get high
- 62 could not
- 47% susceptibility

The above data shows that there doesn't seem to be susceptibility to a category of drugs, meaning that a person who
can get high on one downer does not necessarily get high
on all other downers, and vice versa. The same is also true
for uppers and hallucinogens. In fact, there is no pattern of
any sort that I could make out. This suggests that every
drug must have a different genetic basis. Although there
are a few patients who were susceptible to multiple drugs,
not one patient could get high on all drugs.

However, there does seem to be a link between some
addictions. Not a direct link, but an indirect one. Since the
above data was taken from my patients whom I was treating for opiate addiction, we can only generalize the findings to this group. At least among opiate-addicted patients,
a person is much more susceptible to drugs like alcohol,
MDMA, cocaine, meth, and hallucinogens.

Whether the reverse is true, I cannot say; do alcoholics
have a higher susceptibility to opiate addiction as well?

Almost a 50% susceptibility to alcohol addiction among the opiate-addicted patients would suggest that, but a survey needs to be carried out among alcohol-addicted patients to prove or disprove this theory.

Interesting Observations

Methadone and Ultram are both manmade opiates. The above data shows that about a third of my patients could get high on methadone. That number falls to a fourth for Ultram, not an insignificant number. Ultram is still considered a non-addictive drug and is not a controlled substance. This needs to change.

Soma is a muscle relaxant. It is classified as a non-addictive drug and is not a nationally controlled substance. However, in the state of Washington, it is classified as a controlled substance. Early in my career, I had a patient who overdosed on Soma. Luckily, she survived. When I asked her why she took more than the recommended dose, she told me that it made her feel good. I recently had another patient who overdosed on Soma. She was taking three to four at a time. The recommended dose is never more than one at a time.

Even among my opiate-addicted patients, only about 15% could get high on pot. These are the ones who can get extremely happy and energized on the pot and not feel dopey like the rest of us.

Although the susceptibility for crystal meth is 38%, the susceptibility for amphetamine is only 18%. Although the chemical structures of amphetamine and methamphetamine are very close, there is a huge difference in their addictive potentials.

Ecstasy (MDMA) is often mixed with other drugs. Therefore, true susceptibility to pure MDMA alone may not be as high as 60%.

For hallucinogens, the high susceptibility may be skewed by the fact that I recorded the patients' responses only if they had tried the drug more than once. I felt that one exposure to a drug would not give an accurate picture.

However, most people who tried a drug only once did not like their experience. Even for those who experienced extreme joy from the drug, most did have a bad trip once in a while. For those who are listed as not being susceptible, they always had a bad trip.

Case Studies

Case 1 – Rick A.

Rick was a 41-year-old male who I met in November 2004. Rick was a tall, lanky mechanic. He had been raised in the South, and although he didn't have a southern accent, he always addressed others with "Yes, Sir" and "Yes, Ma'am" politeness. Rick had injured his low back at work. He was working ten feet above the ground when a piece of equipment blew up and threw him 20 feet in the air, landing on his back. Rick was seen at a nearby emergency room with complaints of severe low back pain along with a broken nose. An MRI of the lumbar spine showed a herniated disc.

Rick's primary care physician referred him to me a month after his injury. Rick was on OxyContin 20 mg twice a day along with Percocet for the breakthrough pain. On the intake form, Rick admitted that he had a history of drug addiction as well as a family history of drug addiction. Upon further questioning, he told me that he had been hooked on heroin in the past. Rick had been clean and sober for years prior to our encounter.

Because Rick was in obvious pain from his injury, I chose to keep him on opiate pain medications. However, I decided to switch his baseline pain medication from OxyContin to MS Contin. Rick was agreeable to this. This was done in part because of the high abuse potential of OxyContin. Although patients can get addicted to MS Contin as well, it is less likely to be abused.

I went over the concept of addiction and why people get addicted. I explained to Rick that if he took the opiate pain medications below the level of his pain and tried not to mask the pain completely, he should not get addicted. Even though there was a chance that Rick may have become addicted to opiates again, I still had an ethical obligation to treat his pain as humanely as possible.

Rick went through a series of lumbar epidural steroid injections with me, along with physical therapy. However, when Rick failed to respond to the conservative treatment, he was referred to a neurosurgeon and underwent a lumbar laminectomy a short time later.

Following the surgery, Rick made some initial improvement. However, not too long after the surgery, Rick started having severe burning pain in his left leg. Physical examination showed that Rick had swelling and redness in his left leg with hypersensitivity to light touch. Doppler study ruled out a blood clot, and lab tests showed no evidence of an infection. A repeat MRI of the lumbar spine showed no evidence of recurrent disc herniation to explain the patient's worsening condition.

Rick's clinical presentation at the time was most consistent with reflex sympathetic dystrophy (RSD), also known as complex regional pain syndrome (CRPS) Type I, which is a rare condition where an extremity develops a severe burning sensation, swelling, and pain following an initial injury to the extremity or the nerve even after the initial injury has subsided. I started him on an anti-seizure medication called Neurontin to help control some of his symptoms, and I continued his opiate pain medications. I also had Rick undergo lumbar sympathetic nerve blocks.

Rick's symptoms started to subside. The swelling and redness in the left leg went away. Clinically, Rick seemed to be doing much better. However, Rick's subjective pain and the amount of his opiate pain medications did not change. I tried to gradually decrease his opiate pain medications without success.

After a few months of trying to wean him off the opiate pain medication, I suggested putting Rick on Suboxone to help him get off the opiate pain medication. I explained to Rick that, sometimes, pain might be perpetuated because the patient became addicted to the pain medication. Rick agreed to go on Suboxone. I told Rick that if his pain became worse I would put him back on his pain pills.

Suboxone has some analgesic effect. However, it is a fairly mild analgesic. When I switched Rick to Suboxone, he was taking the equivalent of 160 mg of morphine a day. Rick was taken off the opiate pain medication and put on Suboxone. Immediately afterward, Rick's low back and left leg pain got much better. Although Rick continued to have some pain, the pain was much more manageable.

A few months into the Suboxone treatment, I asked Rick whether he thought that he had gotten hooked on opiate pain medication while he was being treated for pain and whether he had any euphoric feelings early on. Rick told me the pain was real, but he admitted that he did have some highs and euphoric feelings from the pain medications early on. However, because he still had pain, he thought he was not becoming addicted to them at the time.

After months of being unable to wean him off the opiate pain medications, we were able to get Rick off the opiate pain medications by putting him on Suboxone. About six months later, I was able to wean Rick off Suboxone without any difficulty. His pain did not return.

I bring Rick up for many reasons. One, getting a detailed family and personal history of past opiate and other drug addiction is very important. Second, when appropriate, one must treat the patient's pain with opiate pain medications, even if there is a great risk that the patient may become addicted to it. But the most important lesson I want to share here is that, sometimes, ongoing pain may have more to do with the fact that the patient got hooked on the opiate pain medication than anything else.

Like Rick, the majority of my patients who took the Suboxone Challenge found their pain was much better on Suboxone than it ever was on their opiate pain medications. Eventually, we are able to wean them off Suboxone without their original pain coming back. Rick still refers other patients who he thinks are addicted to their pain pills to me. They say, "Rick says hi!"

Case 2 – Rich P.

Rich was a 48-year-old ex-Navy Seal who had intermittent low back pain ever since he injured his low back while he was in the military. He didn't fit the stereotype of a Navy Seal. He was a small-framed, skinny, mousy kind of guy. Rich had jumped out of an airplane and landed hard and sustained a disc injury in his low back. Rich was hospitalized for weeks and later received an honorable discharge for medical reasons. Ever since then, he has had low back pain. Over the years, it gradually became more persistent. During the last few years, the frequency and the intensity of his low back pain increased. He told me that he had been having flare-ups every few weeks.

The previous December, Rich was moving some furniture when he injured his back. The pain was so bad that he ended up going to an urgent care center. The pain was localized to the right side, with pain going down the right leg. Rich was taking ten Percocet 5/325 a day for pain. Rich had been on opiate pain medications more or less on a continuous basis for many years by the time I saw him. Physical examination showed that Rich was in severe discomfort. However, the rest of the examination was unremarkable.

Although Rich had been having low back pain for years, there hadn't been any imaging studies for at least six years. I ordered an MRI of the low back. Rich was given my article on pain management and addiction. We discussed the difference between physical dependence versus addiction.

I saw Rich after he got the MRI. Despite his disabling, chronic low back pain, the MRI came back fairly unremarkable. During this visit, I asked whether he had read my article on addiction. He said he had read it and understood it and reassured me that he was not addicted. I believed him. I promised to treat him, but, given the fact that there didn't seem to be any objective findings to justify the high level of opiate pain medications he was taking, I suggested that we try to get him into the best physical shape possible to see if we could gradually wean him off the opiate pain medications or at least bring his medication down to a lower level.

On our first visit, I did a urine drug screen. It came back positive for oxycodone (an ingredient in Percocet) and oxymorphone (its metabolite), but it also tested positive for Valium. He told me that he had taken one of his wife's Valium. He promised not to take any more controlled substances without first discussing it with me.

During our subsequent visits, Rich did not appear to be in any obvious discomfort, as he had during our first few visits. Over the next few months, I taught him exercises to strengthen his low back, and he seemed to be doing his exercises. During the subsequent visits, I performed a simple test to check the strength of his low back, and it showed an improvement in his strength. However, Rich's perception of his pain did not change.

During another of our subsequent visits, I repeated the urine drug screen. This time, it showed oxycodone as well as hydrocodone (an ingredient of Vicodin). I confronted him about this. He became angry and told me that I did not seem to believe he was in pain. Although I was giving him Percocet at the same dose he was on when I first started seeing him, he told me he needed more pain medication than I was giving him.

I told him I was willing to work with him, but I told him that he and I must agree on some guidelines and that he could not unilaterally increase his medications without discussing it with me first. Rich left my office angry and did not return.

Four months later, I got a call from Rich. He wanted to know whether I would take him back as a patient. I asked him why he wanted to come back and see me. Rich wanted to get off the opiate pain medications and go on Suboxone.

When Rich came back, he admitted that he had gotten hooked. He knew it years ago, but he could not bring himself to admit it. He also told me that, at times, he did have real pain, but other times, he was taking the pain pills not for pain, but because it made his life better (at least at first). He was tired of having to take pain pills. It did not give him the same euphoria it used to. Even after knowing that there was a way out, it took him months to decide to take the plunge and go on Suboxone.

I started him on Suboxone and got him off the pain pills. During our subsequent visits, I asked him about his pain. Rich admitted that the pain was actually much better. Any pain he had was now tolerable. Rich admitted that most of the time, the pain was never as bad as he had made it out to be. After all, he had to convince the doctors that he needed his pills.

During the course of our treatment, I got to know Rich much better. He was married when I first met him. Soon after he got on Suboxone, Rich went through a divorce. I asked him whether this had anything to do with his opiate addiction. The answer he gave me surprised me. It turned out that his wife was an alcoholic. As long as he was hooked on opiates, he was willing to tolerate her addiction to alcohol, and vice versa. However, when he became clean and sober, he could not tolerate her addiction and asked for a divorce. He could not understand why she couldn't stop drinking.

I asked him, "How did the alcohol make you feel?" He told me that it just mellowed him out and made him sedated. I asked him, "How did the alcohol seem to affect your wife?" He told me that she acted differently than him. She seemed to be having a lot more fun than he was. I asked him whether he thought his wife would have gotten hooked on alcohol if she had the same reaction to it as he did. He said probably not. He knew where I was going with this. Although the drug of choice may be different, the reason why someone gets hooked on it is the same; it makes that person feel really good. If one pursues that feeling, sooner or later, he will become hooked.

For various reasons, Rich never wanted to come off Suboxone. I had asked him to attend NA meetings to help him find another way to stay clean, but he couldn't see himself in the same light as those "addicts." Because he had gotten hooked on the pain pills that his doctors were giving him, he felt that his problem was different from those who got hooked because they were trying to get high.

I also offered my book for him to read, but he never took me up on it.

A year later, Rich started saying he didn't think that he got hooked on pain pills. Sure, he had a hard time coming off of them, but he said it was because he had pain. Not too long afterward, Rich developed prostatitis, an inflammation of the prostate. I had to take him off the Suboxone and put him back on the pain pills and an antibiotic. However, even after the prostatitis resolved, Rich kept complaining of severe pain. By now the prostate specific antigen (PSA) level came down to normal. I had no choice but to discontinue the pain pills. Rich reluctantly went back on Suboxone. Soon afterward, the pain went away.

I bring up Rich's case for this important reason. He, like most of my patients who got hooked on the pain pills their doctors were giving them, thought that his problem was somehow different from others who got hooked on opiates because they started out using them for a recreational purpose. Although I tried to explain that the reason why they got hooked was exactly the same as someone who got hooked on street drugs, namely because the drug made them extremely happy, it's not easy to make everyone understand. We need to help everyone let go of the old stereotypes in order to finally understand addiction.

Case 3 – May M.

May was a 28-year-old stay-at-home mom who was involved in a car accident the previous year. May was sweet, blond, a girl-next-door type. She was bright with a very likeable personality. She was a passenger in a vehicle that was rear-ended. She was seen at a nearby emergency room.

She was living in Canada at the time. She had moved down to the Seattle area about three weeks prior to our first visit. May had neck and low back pain since the injury. The neck pain was worse than the low back pain. She was complaining of numbness and tingling going down her right arm as well as her right leg. She complained of mild weakness as well.

On physical examination, May appeared to be in moderate pain. Otherwise, the rest of the examination was normal. Although her doctor in Canada had recommended an MRI, she was still on the waiting list to get the MRI when she moved back down to Seattle. I ordered an MRI.

She was being treated with OxyContin 80 mg twice a day for pain. May told me that 80 mg tablet was too strong at times, so that she was cutting the pills in half at times.

Because May stated that she was cutting the OxyContin in half because it was too strong, I decided to change the OxyContin to oxycodone 5 mg tablets. OxyContin is a long-acting formulation of oxycodone. However, when OxyContin is cut or crushed, the active ingredient will spill out all at once instead of being released gradually. I explained to her the danger of doing this.

We spent some time going over the concept of addiction. I gave her my article on addiction, and I also sent her home with a prescription for 5 mg oxycodone and asked her to keep a diary of how much she needed each day. Once we found how much she truly needed, I told her that we could put her on the right dose of a long-acting opiate pain medication, something other than OxyContin.

I got a phone call from May three days later. May had taken all the oxycodone that I had given her in a matter of a few days. I had given her enough oxycodone to last a week at the same dose that she was using the OxyContin. I had her come back and see me. May's urine drug screen from our first visit came back consistent with what she was taking.

I asked May what had happened. She told me that when she started taking as much oxycodone as she thought she needed to treat her pain, she found herself taking more and more oxycodone. May read my article on addiction, and told me she thought she was hooked. I spent some time making sure that she understood the difference between addiction and physical dependence. She told me she read the article many times and understood. She told me opiate pain medications always made her happy from the beginning. However, because she had pain, and because her doctors never told her that this was not a normal response, she thought everyone must feel that way with opiate pain medications.

By this time, the MRI of her neck came back and showed no significant pathology. There was no evidence of a pinched nerve or a spinal cord problem. After discussing different treatment options, we decided to take her off the opiate pain medications and put her on Suboxone. Afterward, her pain went away.

After May went on Suboxone, she told me about her experience with the opiate pain medications. She felt highly euphoric on them from the beginning. At a high dose, she did eventually feel intoxicated by them. After a while, she told her doctor that her pain was worse than it was to justify getting the pain medication. She felt somehow she had been betrayed by her own doctor, who kept giving her more and more pain medication without ever questioning her or discussing the possibility that she may be getting addicted. May felt that her previous doctor was too eager to just keep writing prescriptions. She was a young mother. Looking back on her experience, she was horrified as she now realized that she used to drive around while dopey from pain medications (as she was coming down from her high) with her young son in the car.

After she came off the opiate pain medications, May's family members told her they had noticed a change in her while she was on pain medications. They told her that she did not seem like her normal self. She was easily irritated and short with them. After she went on Suboxone, they told her they were glad to have her back. She asked them why they didn't say something earlier. They told her they didn't know what to say.

Months later, while she was still on Suboxone, May's father passed away. She was devastated. She told me that she came very close to relapsing. However, she was able to turn to her family, and they pulled her through it.

May often talked about how she felt betrayed by her own doctor. She told me family physicians should not be allowed to prescribe opiate pain medications, and that only those who specialized in pain and understood addiction should be allowed to prescribe them. I told her how few pain specialists there are and that such restrictions would mean that most patients with legitimate pain would not be getting the adequate pain relief they needed. I agreed that we needed to better educate both the medical community as well as the general public about what addiction is.

About a year into her treatment, May found out that her husband, Jack, was hooked on OxyContin as well. Apparently, he had been using it for a while, but he had kept it a secret from May. May brought him in to see me. He was a really nice guy. We discussed the concept of addiction and why some people are susceptible, whereas most are not. He admitted that OxyContin made him highly euphoric. He wanted to go on the Suboxone program.

About that time, May got pregnant. She was taken off Suboxone and put on Subutex (naloxone in Suboxone has been known to cause birth defects in mice). Because she became pregnant, I decided to keep her on the Suboxone/Subutex program until after her pregnancy was over. Going through withdrawal can cause a miscarriage. May did great. Nine months later, she delivered a healthy baby girl. The baby did not go through any withdrawal.

Many months later, I asked May and Jack, "What will you tell your kids about addiction when they are older?" Apparently, this was something they had been worried about and had discussed between themselves. Since they both had a genetic susceptibility to opiate addiction, the chance that their kids would be susceptible would be either 75% or 100%, depending on whether they were both heterogeneous or at least one of them was homogenous—not good odds either way.

Although they had been talking about it, they didn't know what they would say when the time came. For them, I offered the advice that I have laid out in the Prevention chapter. Instead of telling your kids that drugs are bad and how they can ruin your life, we should be giving them the tools to understand what addiction is, why some can get addicted to certain drugs whereas most don't, and what a true high is.

1. Most people are not susceptible to most drugs, but some people are susceptible to some drugs.
2. People can have night-and-day different reactions to the same drug.
3. The high is not what the media has been telling you. The high is not an altered state of mind, or a dopey, intoxicated, or out-of-control feeling. The high is anything that artificially makes you happy, sometimes extremely happy.
4. If you chase that happy feeling, eventually you will start having cravings for the drug and will become enslaved by the drug.

Case 4 – Cindy M.

Cindy was a 47-year-old nurse who had been suffering from low back pain for more than six months when I first met her. She had undergone a second neck surgery in March of that year. Cindy was a bit distant. She didn't voluntarily divulge anything about herself unless it was absolutely necessary. Cindy had the second neck surgery using a bone graft from her pelvis. Cindy initially thought that the pain was coming from the bone graft site, but the pain never subsided. The pain was worse with standing and also woke her up at night when she rolled over in bed.

The pain fluctuated greatly in intensity. Most of the time, the pain was mild, but sometimes it would become severe. Cindy continued to have some neck pain, but it was much better since her surgery. Cindy was taking about eight to ten oxycodone 5 mg a day to control her pain.

Cindy also had low back surgery five years earlier. She thought that her pain was similar to the pain that she had prior to her low back surgery. A subsequent MRI showed a herniated disc. I continued her on the opiate pain medications. We also did an epidural steroid injection.

A few weeks later, Cindy called me and told me that she had read my article on addiction and told met that she thought she was hooked on pain pills. Cindy wanted to get off the pain medications and go on Suboxone. I had her come in so we could discuss this.

At our next meeting, I made sure that Cindy understood what addiction was. Cindy told me that she had been hooked on pain pills for some time. Yes, she did have pain, but she had been taking pain pills for more than just pain for some time. By this point, Cindy realized that her addiction to pain pills was a bigger problem than the pain itself. At the same time, Cindy was ambivalent about what would happen once she came off the pain pills, whether her pain would become unbearable.

Because Cindy was still in a moderate amount of pain and had a legitimate reason for her pain, we decided to put her on methadone rather than Suboxone. Methadone is a much stronger pain medication than Suboxone. I explained to Cindy that most people who get high on other opiates usually do not get high on methadone. Cindy promised me that she would let me know if she did get high on methadone. After a few days of being on methadone, Cindy reassured me that she did not get any euphoria from methadone, and that the methadone seemed to be working for her pain.

A few months later, while we were still trying to get Cindy's pain under control, I got a call from Cindy's roommate that Cindy had been admitted to a hospital. Cindy had overdosed on opiates. I was crushed, thinking that I had contributed to yet another overdose. However, it turned out she had overdosed on Dilaudid, not methadone. I visited Cindy at the hospital. Cindy was ashamed about what had happened. Cindy had switched her methadone with Dilaudid with a friend and had overdosed on it.

When Cindy was discharged from the hospital, I put her on Suboxone. After going on Suboxone, Cindy told me she had battled with opiate addiction for years. It turned out that this wasn't the first time Cindy had overdosed on opiates. She had previously overdosed on oxycodone, but had chosen not to share this information with me before. I had Cindy get outpatient drug counseling as well as attend NA meetings.

After the dust settled, it turned out that Cindy's pain was not as unmanageable as we had thought. Cindy was actually able to return to work, and her pain was gone after she went on Suboxone. Since then, her low back pain has flared up at times. At one time, I had to take her off Suboxone and put her back on methadone (for a short period of time). However, by then, I had taught her how to manage her opiate pain medication so as to diminish the risk of her getting hooked on it again.

It has been over four years since Cindy first went on Suboxone. Cindy feels like her life is back on track. We have discussed getting her weaned off Suboxone, but Cindy is scared she will relapse if she comes off Suboxone. I reassured her that the craving would probably not be there when she comes off Suboxone. I told her the only thing that was going to prevent her from relapsing was how well she remembered the lessons she had learned.

I have not tried to force Cindy to come off Suboxone. I learned a long time ago that you cannot convince someone they are ready to come off Suboxone. When they are ready, they will let you know. She still attends meetings.

Case 5 – Kathy M.

Kathy was a 44-year-old female who was referred to me by her family physician. She had undergone a craniotomy for a brain tumor 16 years earlier. Ever since then, Kathy suffered from headaches. She was seeing a local neurologist who managed her headaches with a low-dose opiate pain medication until she moved to Nevada four years earlier. Recently, she had moved back to the Seattle area and was looking for a new pain doctor.

Kathy had been taking up to eight Norco 7.5/325 a day along with Fioricet with codeine. She admitted that she had been hooked on alcohol and cocaine in the past. Her addiction to alcohol was an ongoing battle; she told me that she had been clean for about six months when I first met her. She hadn't touched cocaine in years.

I did a urine drug screen test and it came back consistent with what she said she was taking and nothing else. After discussing different treatment options, I decided to have her try a new synthetic opiate that had just come on the market called Nucynta.

Although Nucynta is stronger than Norco 7.5/325, because it works on a different pain pathway than regular opiates, it was thought to be less addictive. It is in the same chemical family as Ultram (tramadol). I also gave Kathy my article on addiction.

On our next visit, Kathy told me that she got extremely high on Nucynta, and that she was taking up to four an hour. She realized she was getting hooked, and flushed the rest down the toilet. She was in withdrawal when I saw her again.

After discussing different treatment options, I offered her the Suboxone Challenge. Instead of going back on regular opiates, I suggested that she go on Suboxone. If the pain became intolerable, I promised to switch her back to her opiate pain medications. She agreed. I put her through the Suboxone induction and sent her home with instructions on how to increase the Suboxone gradually until she found the right dose.

On our next visit, Kathy told me she was doing great on Suboxone. The headache pain was not an issue. By then, she had read my article on addiction and told me that she had gotten hooked on the pain medications. She told me the reason why she thought she kept slipping back into her alcoholism was because the pain pills made her high. However, because a doctor was prescribing the pain pills and she did have pain, she did not think she would get hooked.

A few months into our treatment, she stopped going to AA meetings. I asked her why. She told me that she didn't need them anymore. She told me that the reason why she got hooked on alcohol and cocaine was because she was trying to mask the stresses in her life. I asked her how the alcohol and cocaine made her feel. She told me that they made her feel great at first, but later, all they did was help her mask her problems. I tried to explain to her that most people would never get any euphoria from these drugs. She did not believe me at first.

About a year into her treatment, Kathy brought in her daughter, who had gotten hooked on opiates. Until then, I couldn't get Kathy to read my book on addiction. After her daughter got hooked, she read the book. She told me that she finally got it. She now understood that addiction is genetic and that most people do not experience what she and her daughter had experienced from their drugs. She also went back to the AA meetings with her daughter. Soon thereafter, her daughter brought in her husband, who was also hooked on opiates, to go on the Suboxone program. Both she and her husband did great on Suboxone. However, when Kathy's daughter started doing great on Suboxone, Kathy stopped going to meetings again.

Because Suboxone helped with Kathy's headaches, we kept her on Suboxone even after she didn't need it anymore for her opiate addiction. She was on Suboxone for about three years when she slipped and fell and injured her tailbone. The x-ray showed no fracture, but the pain was bad enough that I ended up giving her a cortisone injection in the tailbone. I also took her off Suboxone and put her back on a low-dose opiate pain medication. I kept her on the pain pills for about two weeks. After she came off the pain pills, Kathy didn't see the need to go back on Suboxone. Her headache was still manageable.

A few weeks later, I got a call from Kathy. Kathy left a message on our answering machine, but her speech was so slurred my staff couldn't understand what she was saying. I listened to the message; Kathy was saying that she slipped up and had relapsed. She was asking me to call in the Suboxone for her. One of my staff members said, "I think she's high!" I told her that Kathy was coming down from her high, and that she was intoxicated when she called.

I called Kathy back. She was still slurring her speech when I spoke to her. She could hardly put two sentences together. I asked what she used. She wouldn't tell me. She just kept saying she was sorry and that she now realized she was an addict and that she would always be an addict and that she screwed up.

I told Kathy that I would call in the Subutex for her, but that she has to wait 24 hours from her last use before she took it. Otherwise, I told her Subutex would put her into full withdrawal. I told her that she could go back on the Suboxone the following day. I also had her daughter come over and spend a night with her. I told her daughter that if Kathy became a lot more incoherent to call 911.

Two days later, I got a call from Kathy thanking me for reminding her to wait 24 hours before taking the Subutex. I asked her to come in so we could talk. When she came in two weeks later, I asked what she used. She told me that she didn't use anything. She told me that her family physician had put her on a new antidepressant, and that it was the antidepressant that made her so loopy. I asked her why she wanted to go back on Suboxone. She couldn't answer that. I asked her whether she wanted to stay on the Suboxone. In a low voice, she said, "Yes."

I did not press the matter any further. I realized that she was too ashamed to admit to me face to face that she had relapsed. Although she was able to admit it on the phone, she couldn't do it in person; there was too much shame and guilt. Although she knew that she had problems with alcohol and cocaine, because she had gotten hooked on pain pills that her doctors were giving her, she had always thought that her problems with the pills were somehow different than her problems with alcohol and cocaine. This is not unusual.

Most of my patients who got hooked on pain pills think that their addiction is somehow different from someone hooked on heroin. Although I explain to them that most heroin addicts started out by getting hooked on the opiate pain medications that their doctors gave them, they see themselves as not being as "addicted" as a heroin addict is.

The fact that Kathy was so intoxicated and inebriated coming off her opiate high suggested that she had used something quite strong, possibly a high-dose oxycodone or even heroin. I knew that she wasn't coming off of a high from what I had given her after her fall. I asked her to go back to the meetings, and she agreed.

Case 6 – Monique L.

Monique was a 23-year-old model who had been hooked on opiates for many years. Monique had been using about ten OxyContin 80 mg a day (at $80 a pop, that's an $800 a day habit). Monique usually smoked it or snorted it. She had tried quitting on her own without success. Monique had gone through an inpatient detox the previous summer. As soon as she was discharged, she went back to using. Monique had recently gone through an outpatient drug rehab. Once again, as soon as she stopped the therapy, she went back to using.

Monique heard about Suboxone and was interested in going on it to help overcome her opiate addiction. She had gotten hold of some Suboxone through a friend and had been using it for a few days. Monique stated that this was the best she had felt in a long time. She felt normal, like her old self. She told me that she had no cravings while on Suboxone.

Monique was a child of mixed marriage as well as a single mother living with her grandmother while she tried to get her life back on track. Her grandmother had no idea what addiction was and couldn't understand why Monique would do this to herself as well as to her son. Monique got a new job and appeared to be straightening her life out. Over the next few months, she seemed to be doing great. All her urine drug screens came back clean.

A few months into her recovery, Monique ran into some legal problems arising from when she was using. Her ex-husband was also contesting her for custody of their child. At the first sign of trouble, Monique relapsed and tested positive for oxycodone. I had Monique start attending NA meetings as a condition for staying on the Suboxone program.

Over the next few visits, Monique continued to test positive for oxycodone intermittently. Her grandmother kicked her out of her house because she would get high in the house or have friends over to get high. She moved in with her boyfriend. She stopped attending meetings, and her urine drug screens continued to show opiates on multiple occasions.

I spent a great deal of time counseling Monique about why some people relapse. I pointed out that she must keep reminding herself of the reasons why she wanted to quit in the first place in order for her not to keep relapsing. She held a job, and felt that she was succeeding.

As a part of her court-ordered deal to maintain her probation status to stay out of jail, she was required to attend NA meetings and pass a random urine drug screen. Over the next few visits, we set up a program where she would go through random urine drug screens.

On one of these random urine drug screens, Monique tested negative for opiates, but she also tested negative for Suboxone as well. She had been getting Suboxone on a regular basis. I discussed the test result with Monique. She had a ready explanation. Monique stated that she had misplaced her Suboxone the previous week.

On the next random urine drug screen, Monique tested negative for opiates. This time, she tested positive for buprenorphine but negative for its metabolite, norbuprenorphine. One of the things that we look for in the urine drug screen is not just the presence of a drug, but also its metabolite. When the urine drug screen comes back positive for buprenorphine but negative for its metabolite, it indicates that the patient probably brought in someone else's urine and dissolved the Suboxone in it. Since the metabolite only shows up when the patient is taking the Suboxone, the lack of metabolite shows that it was dissolved in the urine.

I confronted Monique with this last urine drug screen result. The urine drug screen showed that Monique was not serious about staying clean. Monique had violated our agreement. I wanted to continue helping Monique, but I realized that she was not committed to her sobriety. I decided to discharge her from my care. I referred her to another Suboxone provider. I informed him of the problems I had had with her, and told him about the urine drug screen results.

I wished Monique well. I asked her to stay on Suboxone, but told her that she must commit to her recovery. I told her about the danger of relapsing. When someone tries to stay clean, when they relapse they are more likely to overdose. Monique thanked me. I gave her enough Suboxone until she could get in to see the other doctor.

The reason I discharged her was simple. She wasn't taking me seriously. She thought I was too soft. I kept giving her chance after chance. She thought she had figured out a way to beat the system. When that happens, I realize I can no longer help that patient. Forcing a patient to get help elsewhere can hopefully turn the patient around.

A few months later, I found out that Monique was in jail for a drug-related offense. After she came out of prison six months later, her grandmother came to visit me. She told me how hard Monique has been trying to quit since getting out of jail but was still relapsing. She begged me to take Monique back on the Suboxone program.

I had Monique as well as her grandmother come in to talk to me. I told them that I would take back Monique under the following conditions: that she show me that she was committed to her recovery by staying clean, that she agreed to random urine drug screens, and that she attended either weekly AA or NA meetings or get individual drug counseling. Monique agreed.

The next month, Monique did not show up for her monthly follow-up. My office called her three times asking her to come back and see me. On the third message, she was told that even if she had relapsed, I was willing to give her one more try as long as she was willing to follow through with her original agreement. She never came back.

Case 7 – Mark and Bill H.

Mark and Bill H. are fraternal twins. There are enough commonalities in their stories that I decided to share their stories together. They were 19 when I first met them. Their mother, who is a nurse, referred them to me. Apparently, I had treated a few patients from her clinic for addiction.

Both Mark and Bill had been hooked on opiates for a few years before I met them. Both had gone through several inpatient drug rehab programs, but they kept relapsing. Both were hooked on heroin, and both had been on the Suboxone program with another doctor, but because they both kept relapsing and failed multiple urine drug screens, they were discharged.

I saw Mark first. He would later point out that he was the older of the two. On our first visit, I asked Mark how opiates made him feel. He described the incredible joy he got early on. Mark told me that he also got high on Suboxone. Because this is pretty rare, I spent some time making sure that we were on the same page, that he wasn't confusing stimulation with extreme euphoria. It was apparent that he did get high on Suboxone. Of course, this meant that Suboxone was out of the question for him. I recommended that he go on the Vivitrol treatment. Vivitrol had recently won FDA approval for the treatment of opiate addiction. Mark did great on Vivitrol, at first.

I saw Bill a week later. He had just finished an inpatient drug rehab program. When I first saw Bill, I mistook him for Mark. I said, "Didn't I just see you?" He laughed and said, "No, I am Bill, Mark's twin brother." I did not know that Mark had a twin brother until then. Although they were fraternal twins, the resemblance was uncanny.

As I do with all of my new patients, I asked Bill how the opiates made him feel. He also told me that he got extreme joy from the opiates. I asked him how Suboxone made him feel. Unlike Mark, Bill did not get any euphoria from Suboxone. So, I kept Bill in the Suboxone program. But Bill kept relapsing. They were seeing a chemical dependency counselor, but Bill kept slipping up. After the third time, I gave Bill an ultimatum. Either he had to show me that he was serious about his recovery by staying clean or I would have to put him in the Vivitrol program with Mark.

Unlike Suboxone, once you get a shot of Vivitrol, you can't get high on opiates (or alcohol) for the next 30 days. This takes away the incentive to try to get high. Bill insisted that he would stay clean. On his very next urine drug screen, he failed. I ordered the Vivitrol and had Bill come in for the shot.

On his next visit, Bill brought his mother with him. I had not met her before. She was a very nice woman, but a little on the protective side. The reason why Bill had her come in with him was to have her explain to me why Bill couldn't get a shot in his butt. She told me that Bill was sexually molested as a child, and he couldn't let any man near his butt. She didn't tell me who the perpetrator was. I didn't ask.

I reluctantly agreed to keep Bill in the Suboxone program. However, after he failed two more drug screens, I had no choice but to insist that we change course. I talked to Bill's mother and expressed my concerns. Obviously, the Suboxone program was not working for Bill, and I could not, in good conscience, keep allowing him to do what he had been doing. By now, Bill wasn't taking me seriously. He thought that he could do whatever he wanted to do. I had lost my effectiveness as his doctor. She reluctantly agreed to talk to Bill and see if he would agree to go on the Vivitrol program. He finally gave in. I had his mother come in with him for the first injection to allay any fear of molestation. After Bill went on the Vivitrol program, he did great. He finally stayed clean (at first). His drug screens were finally clean.

About a year into their treatment, a tragic event happened. Apparently, the boys hadn't heard from their dad in a while. Their parents had divorced a long time ago. Bill went to check on his father and found him dead on the floor. His decomposing body was partly eaten by his starving dogs. The autopsy showed that he had died from a heroin overdose.

Understandably, Bill was inconsolable. I spoke with his mother and had him see a grief counselor. Although both Mark and Bill were about to finish the Vivitrol program, both their mother and I felt that it was best that we kept them in the program a little longer. Luckily, Bill did not relapse.

A few months later, Mark's girlfriend gave birth to their first child, a son. Mark was a proud father. He told me that he thought this would turn him around, that he would never relapse now that he had another human being to care of, and that he would never do to his child what his father had done to him and his brother, abandoning them because of his addiction.

About six months later, their father's estate was finalized. Both Bill and Mark came into a small fortune. Mark missed his next appointment. I called his mother and learned that Mark had gone on a binge. He left town with his inheritance, and she had learned that he was back on drugs. I gave her my deepest sympathy and told her that if she talked to Mark to let him know that I would take him back whenever he was ready.

Bill showed up to his next appointment. I asked him about Mark. Apparently, Mark had broken up with his girlfriend because of the drugs. Mark was devastated, but was not willing to go back on the Vivitrol program yet.

Bill did not show up for his next appointment. I learned from his mother that Bill had moved in with Mark, and that he too had relapsed.

Case 8 – Tony C.

Tony was a 72-year-old male who had low back pain on and off for years. Tony was a soft-spoken, nervous type. I had seen him in my office with his wife, whom I had treated in the past for her chronic low back pain, as well as with his grandson, whom I treated for OxyContin addiction.

When I first saw Tony, he told that he had been on oxycodone for the last one and a half years and thought that he was hooked on the pills. Tony had read my article on addiction that I had given his wife as well as his grandson. I give the article to all my patients. Tony had been trying to decrease the medication on his own without success.

Tony admitted he liked the way the pain pills made him feel at first. He did get excited and euphoric on the pain pills at first. Tony told me that he did have pain, but felt that the need for pain pills was greater than the pain itself. We put him on Suboxone, and Tony did great. The pain became a non-issue. We were able to wean him off Suboxone after six months. I treated his wife until she passed away a few years later.

Four years later, I saw Tony back in my office. He was living in New Mexico at the time. A few months earlier, he had injured his low back and his physician had put him on Vicodin. After a few weeks, his doctor became suspicious of Tony's behavior and cut him off the pain medications. At that point, Tony started going to Mexico to get his drugs. Tony knew that something was wrong, but he couldn't stop himself.

A few months into his relapse, Tony flew back up to Seattle to see me. Tony told me that he was in trouble, that he got hooked on opiate pain medications again. I asked Tony why he wanted to stop now versus a few months earlier. Tony admitted that he liked the way the opiate pain pills made him feel. It did more than alleviate his pain. It made him feel great at first. A few months into his relapse, he remembered why he wanted to quit years earlier. The drug that made him feel great at first was making him feel miserable again.

I put Tony back on Suboxone and asked him to find another Suboxone provider in New Mexico to help him stay on it for at least six months. I haven't heard back from Tony since.

Case 9 – Allen S.

Allen was a likeable 25-year-old young man who had been hooked on opiates for the previous four to five years. He got started on OxyContin while in college in the south. He stated that most of his friends were using. His parents put him through an inpatient detox twice, but each time, he relapsed. By the time I saw him, he was using OxyContin as well as heroin. His parents brought him up to the Seattle area to help get him away from his friends who were still using.

Allen stated that he had been trying to quit on his own unsuccessfully. He was able to get a hold of Suboxone from a friend, and he found that it helped him stay clean as long as he was able to get enough of it. However, as soon as he ran out of Suboxone, he went back to using. We put him on Suboxone, and he did great. I also asked him to attend meetings as a condition of going on the Suboxone program. Although he had agreed to go, he kept coming up with excuses why he hadn't.

About three months into his sobriety, I got a call from Allen. He left a message that he had lost his job. He felt that he couldn't afford to stay on the Suboxone. Each pill costs about $6. Most patients need two pills a day. He felt that he could get off the Suboxone without relapsing this time. Over the next three days, I tried to get in touch with Allen. I left him six messages asking him to call me back. I was planning to put him on the Subutex because it is cheaper than the Suboxone.

The following Monday, I got a call from his mother. Allen had overdosed and died over the weekend. He was at a party. One of his friends saw him do OxyContin, and Allen overdosed. The drug toxicology screen came back positive for Xanax and oxycodone, the active ingredient of OxyContin, but negative for Suboxone.

I felt devastated. I had begged all of my patients that if for some reason they did relapse, they must not go back to the same dose of the drug they used to use, because it could kill them. Unfortunately, Allen did not hear or remember my message. This time, Allen paid for his mistake with his life.

No one who has overdosed ever leaves a suicide note. They know it can happen, but they never think it could happen to them. No one is trying to kill themselves. It is an accident. They know about the possible danger, but the craving that keeps them coming back to the drug is stronger than any rational fear of overdose.

We mourn the death of celebrities when they accidentally overdose and die. They are only the tip of the iceberg. The true numbers of people who are addicted and pay the ultimate price for their addiction with their lives are much higher. Each death is just as tragic and just as pointless.

I try to instill in all my patients the seriousness of their disease, and how devastating its effects can be, not only in the number of lives that are ruined, but in the ultimate toll on lives that are taken as well. Yet, I keep losing patients to this disease.

Case 10 – Jan S.

Jan was a 21-year-old tall, blond female personal trainer who had low back pain on and off for a few years. She did not remember any specific injury that may have brought this on. Jan was in a car accident three years earlier, but she did not remember whether this made her low back pain worse or brought it on. Over the previous year, the pain had been coming on a daily basis.

Sports such as running and playing basketball did aggravate her low back pain. Her pain was also worse during her menstrual cycle. She saw a chiropractor and a physical therapist, but they did not help her pain.

A subsequent MRI of the lumbar spine showed a herniated disc. I did a lumbar ESI, which seemed to give her some pain relief. Jan was eventually put on Ultram, a drug that was originally marketed as a non-narcotic pain medication. A few years after Ultram was marketed, the FDA made the manufacturer change its designation from a non-narcotic to a narcotic pain medication. However, the DEA still has not classified it as a narcotic pain medication. General consensus is that Ultram is a very mild opiate pain medication. I chose Ultram because Jan had a family history of opiate addiction.

Jan was on the same dose of Ultram for about six months when she was admitted to the hospital for a seizure. The toxicology screen came back positive for Ultram but negative for anything else. A neurologist saw Jan. The EEG showed no epileptic foci. It was thought that she had suffered a seizure for an unknown reason. Jan was asked to have a follow-up EEG in six months and was told not to drive.

I met with Jan to go over what might have happened. I went over the concept of addiction. Jan denied that she was hooked. I continued to treat her over the next few months. Her urine drug screen came back clean for everything else except for Ultram.

A few months later, Jan was admitted to the hospital again. She had suffered another seizure. This time, Jan admitted that she had a problem. She was hooked on Ultram. She was buying Ultram on the Internet, and was taking a lot more Ultram than I was prescribing. Both times she suffered the seizures she had tried to stop Ultram on her own.

In the past, patients going through opiate withdrawal may suffer from severe physical withdrawal symptoms such as the shakes, muscle aches, and delirium, but not seizures. There were no documented cases of patients going through withdrawal from Ultram suffering seizure disorders, either. I reported Jan's case. Since then, other similar cases have been reported. We put Jan on Suboxone. She was also enrolled in an outpatient drug rehab program. She did well. After six months, we were able to wean her off Suboxone.

A few years later, I saw Jan again. She had apparently relapsed. She was buying Ultram on the Internet again. She had not suffered another seizure, but she was afraid that she might. I put her back on the Suboxone and had her go back to the meetings. She did great again. After about six months, we were able to wean her off the Suboxone.

By the way, Jan also got extremely excited and euphoric on other opiates. However, because Ultram was initially thought to be a non-narcotic pain killer, Jan had less apprehension about using it. Because of her family history of opiate addiction, Jan was leery about taking opiate painkillers, but Ultram had not registered such fear.

Case 11 – Mimi J.

Mimi was a 31-year-old female who had been hooked on opiates for the last one and a half years before I saw her. Her younger sister, whom I had previously treated for opiate addiction with Suboxone, referred her to me.

Mimi told me that she had dislocated her left shoulder the previous November. She was started on Vicodin, and she realized that she liked the way it made her feel. Although the pain finally went away, Mimi found it difficult to stop taking the Vicodin. Soon thereafter, she developed low back pain, and she had been on the Vicodin on a more or less continuous basis ever since.

She was taking a lot of Vicodin. Her physician prescribed her only 30 a week, but she was buying it on the Internet and was averaging 100 a week. Mimi had realized that she was hooked and had been trying to get off of it, but found it difficult to do it on her own. Mimi heard from her sister how well Suboxone had helped her.

I put Mimi on Suboxone, and she did great. However, about six months into her Suboxone treatment, Mimi started feeling ambivalent about whether she truly got addicted to the pain pills or not. Mimi admitted that she liked the way they made her feel, but she thought she had legitimate reasons for her opiate use. I had her re-read my article on addiction as well as the paper on which I had had her write down why she wanted to get off the opiates in the first place (something that I do with all my new addiction patients).

Since it had been six months into her Suboxone program, we decided to start weaning Mimi off the Suboxone. As soon as she got off the Suboxone, Mimi found herself back on the Vicodin, at ten a day. She was buying it on the Internet again. After that, she admitted that it was for more than just pain. Mimi told me that she had intense cravings for Vicodin as soon as she came off the Suboxone. We put her back on the Suboxone. Mimi was on it for another eight months before we weaned her off of it again. This time the cravings did not come back. The shoulder pain never returned.

It is not unusual for many to forget the initial trials and tribulations of their disease. Because there is such a negative stereotype of what addicts look like, most patients who get hooked on opiate pain medications can't see themselves in that light. As soon as their cravings go away, they may start thinking that it wasn't that big of a problem in the first place. Such is the danger of our faulty memory! We soon forget the bad things.

Case 12 – Jay H.

Jay was a 29-year-old man who had been hooked on opi-ates for two years when I first met him. He was using OxyContin 80 mg about four times a day. Jay swallowed OxyContin whole. About two months prior to our visit, Jay started treatment with another doctor and was put on Suboxone. Although this helped with his withdrawal symp-toms, he told me that it never got rid of the craving com-pletely. Jay was attending NA meetings.

Jay stated that he slipped up and used OxyContin the previous month. Jay was discharged from the other doc-tor's care for failing to follow through with his end of the contract. After Jay ran out of Suboxone, he went back to using OxyContin on a regular basis. But Jay was ready to quit. He found me through the Suboxone website.

Jay was interested in going back on Suboxone. He told me that he was committed to getting his addiction under control this time. I agreed to take him on as a patient. Over the next year, Jay did great. All of the urine drug screens, including the random urine drug screens, were clean. Jay continued to attend NA meetings. He told me that he felt great.

About the time we were planning to wean him off Suboxone, Jay injured his back. He was helping a friend move, and while lifting a heavy piece of furniture, he hurt his back. I saw him a few days later. He was in obvious pain. He was bent over and could barely walk. Physical ex-amination showed muscle spasms. After discussing differ-ent treatment options, I decided to take him off Suboxone and put him on methadone for pain management.

Over the next few weeks, Jay's pain seemed to get bet-ter. From a clinical standpoint, he did not appear to be in any significant pain. I tried to take him off methadone and put him back on Suboxone, but Jay kept insisting he was still in pain. After a few weeks, I did a random urine drug screen. It came back positive for oxycodone. It turned out that he had forged a prescription for OxyContin. I con-fronted him about this, but he insisted that he was taking OxyContin for his pain. Over this period, Jay's demeanor seemed to change. He had recently lost his job. Jay seemed to be getting more and more depressed.

I had spent a great deal of time over the previous year finding out more about Jay. He had a troubled childhood. His parents were killed in front of his twin sister and him when they were quite young. Apparently, his parents had been hooked on drugs. They were also dealing. One day, his parents were gunned down over a drug deal that went badly. Jay and his twin sister witnessed their parents being murdered in front of them.

Jay and his sister were raised by their older sister, who (along with her husband) routinely physically and psychologically abused them. On one of our visits, Jay told me, with tears in his eyes, that he had told his older sister and her husband that he forgave them. I asked whether he felt that saying that he forgave them made it easier for him to deal with it. He said no.

Jay had gone through years of counseling and psychiatric treatment, but he told me that it hadn't helped. He told me that he found solace in drugs. He told me that he did get highly euphoric on OxyContin early on, but the euphoria soon faded. It no longer made him euphoric, but it allowed him to dull his senses and allowed him to cope with his demons. He had perpetual insomnia, and drugs like OxyContin and Xanax allowed him to sleep and cope with his nightmares.

I told Jay that I could not justify prescribing opiates for him to help deal with his emotional pain and depression. By this time, I was able to enroll him in a free Suboxone assistance program for qualified patients. I can only have three patients on the program at any given time. Luckily for Jay, someone else was coming off the program after one year of allotted time. Jay was still off work and could not afford Suboxone otherwise.

After Jay went back on Suboxone, his demeanor improved. He was also less anxious and seemed less depressed. I once asked him to read a book by Dr. Elisabeth Kubler Ross on the five stages of grief. After reading it, he told me that he was still stuck in the second stage, anger.

I bring Jay up because some patients may abuse drugs not necessarily to get high, but to help them escape from their reality. Some of these patients will get hooked because the drug makes them highly euphoric, but others will not. For those who are not addicted, once you treat their underlying psychological problems, their "addiction" goes away. However, for those who get hooked, you must treat both the addiction as well as the underlying psychological ills. Otherwise, you will never get their addiction under control. These are the most challenging patients.

The fact that Jay did get highly euphoric early on indicates that he did get hooked. However, the reason why he had such a difficult time coming off of the drug probably had more to do with the fact that he was abusing the drug to help him deal with the emotional pain and scars of his childhood.

Because Jay had no insurance at the time and because his experience with counselors and psychiatrists had not been positive, I had him read Dr. David Burns' book *Feeling Good*. I had him use the worksheet from the book to help categorize his negative thoughts and beliefs to help him come up with a better way to help him deal with his demons. This actually worked. Eventually, we were able to get Jay off the opiates and the sedatives and go back on the Suboxone program. He still struggled with nightmares from time to time, but they seemed more manageable.

I believe that emotional pains are real. In fact, some chronic pains are probably second to psychological traumas. Sometimes, psychological pain can be much worse than any physical pain. There is a definite link between the mind and the body. We cannot separate one from the other. Yes, when a patient tells me that he is in pain, I believe him. The question I try to ask is what is the source of the pain.

Case 13 – Ben R.

Ben was a 44-year-old attorney who had been hooked on opiates for a year prior to our first meeting. He had been using OxyContin 80 mg twice a day. Ben usually crushed OxyContin and ingested it orally. He had heard about Suboxone and was interested in going on Suboxone to help him get off his opiate addiction.

Ben was married. He had a private practice. Ben admitted that he had some stresses in his life, but they were mostly because of his addiction. He had kept his addiction hidden from his wife. He suspected that she knew something was up, but did not believe that she knew about his addiction. Ben admitted that he did not get started on opiates because of pain, but out of curiosity. He started with Percocet, and then soon moved on to OxyContin. What was fun at first soon led to uncontrollable urges.

Ben's initial urine drug screen came back positive for oxycodone as well as Xanax and methamphetamine. I told Ben that although Suboxone would help with his opiate addiction, it would not help with the methamphetamine addiction. I asked Ben to attend NA meetings or enroll in a drug counseling program. Ben agreed.

Ben once told me that the high he got from methamphetamine was as good as any high he had from OxyContin. This is not true of all patients who get hooked on opiates. Most find no euphoria from methamphetamine. Most just find that it makes them jittery and paranoid.

Over the next few months, Ben kept testing positive for methamphetamine, but negative for opiates. Ben also failed to follow through on his commitment to attend NA meetings or get counseling. After his third consecutive dirty urine drug screen, I discharged him. I wished him well. I gave him enough Suboxone for 30 days and the names of other physicians in the area who treated addiction.

I bring Ben up because his case illustrates that some patients do have multiple chemical dependencies. Although Suboxone helps with opiate addiction, it does not help with methamphetamine addiction. Methamphetamine, commonly known as crystal meth, is a psychostimulant. Although it is highly addictive for some, the exact mechanism as to why someone gets addicted to it is not well understood. We do know that it triggers a release of dopamine, norepinephrine, and serotonin. Thus, it stimulates the mesolimbic reward pathway, causing euphoria. However, Suboxone does not block cravings created by methamphetamine addiction. Ben wasn't the only one I have treated who did not respond to Suboxone when they were hooked on methamphetamine.

I saw Ben about two years later. He asked me to take him back on the Suboxone program. He was back to using OxyContin as well as methamphetamine. This time, he told me that he was serious about his recovery. I took him back after he agreed to get help by attending NA meetings or getting individual drug counseling. Over the next few months, he kept testing positive for methamphetamine again, although he tested negative for opiates. He also never followed through with his promise to attend meetings or get counseling. I found it necessary to discharge him from the Suboxone program again.

Case 14 - Andy D.

Andy was a successful 47-year-old businessman who had been hooked on opiates for the previous eight years. Andy initially broke his right ankle and was started on pain medication to ease the pain. Andy found that he liked the way the pills made him feel, and before he realized it, he was taking much more than he was supposed to. Eventually, he was getting pain medications from two different doctors as well as buying them on the street.

Andy was a recovering alcoholic. He told me that he used to attend AA meetings regularly, even when he was first getting addicted to opiates. Andy told me that, at first, he did not think that getting addicted to pain pills was the same as being addicted to alcohol. However, once things started getting out of control, he realized that an addiction was an addiction, but by then it was too late. He felt hopeless. He stopped attending meetings.

Over the last few years, Andy had been averaging 80-120 mg of OxyContin a day, along with 12 Vicodin and ten Ultram a day. He told me he did all this while keeping it a secret from his wife and continuing to work. Andy told me that he had tried stopping many times without success.

A month earlier, Andy had admitted himself into an inpatient detox unit. He was put through a quick detox. Andy was discharged home on Suboxone 8 mg twice a day. He was scheduled to start an outpatient drug rehab program. The only problem was that his outpatient drug rehabilitation program did not want him on Suboxone. They were insisting that Andy come off the Suboxone.

I spoke with the administrator of his outpatient drug rehab facility and explained to him that Suboxone is not addictive, that we were not switching one addiction for another. However, the administrator explained to me the facility's policy. I spoke with the medical director of the facility. He regretted his facility's policy, but informed me that he could not convince the board of directors that they should allow the patient to remain on Suboxone.

I informed Andy about his outpatient drug rehab program's policy on Suboxone. Andy felt he had no choice but to come off Suboxone. However, after coming off Suboxone and noticing how strong his cravings were, Andy chose to go back on Suboxone. He also chose to stay with his outpatient drug rehabilitation program because he had already financially committed to it. However, he chose not to reveal that he was still on Suboxone. They did routine urine drug screens, but since Suboxone is not a true opiate, it does not test positive on a urine drug screen unless you are specifically looking for it. Andy finished his outpatient drug rehab program. Since going on Suboxone, Andy has been clean and sober. I encouraged him to go back to his AA meetings.

About a year later, Andy's son overdosed on opiates. Although he survived, the hypoxia caused brain damage and left him in a vegetative state. I once asked Andy whether he had ever discussed addiction with his son. He muttered, "No."

Case 15 – Vivian A.

Vivian was a 52-year-old pharmacy technician who had upper back pain for quite some time. She was from New Jersey. Vivian was a very high-strung person. She complained of the stress from work as well as from that of her own making. Vivian was one of those perfectionists who always felt that she had to give 110%, but felt that it was never enough.

All the work-ups, including CT of the chest and MRIs of her neck and upper back, were normal. Vivian was taking four Vicodin ES a day. She apparently had been on the same dose for quite some time. I agreed to take over her pain management. I went over the concept of addiction versus physical dependence and gave her my article on addiction. Her urine drug screen came back consistent with what she was taking.

Over the course of the next year, I helped manage her pain and her pain medications. I taught her a home exercise program to help strengthen her upper back. We maintained her pain medication at the same dose. Vivian never lost a prescription or called in for early refills. She seemed like an ideal patient.

A year into our treatment, Vivian came in to see me. She told me that she didn't know how to tell me that she had gotten hooked on pain pills. She felt so ashamed. After reading my article on addiction, she knew she was hooked. However, it took a year for her to get up the courage to admit this to herself. Vivian told me that she did get highly euphoric on the pain medication. It also energized her; it would keep her up at night if she took it right before bed. Vivian was taking a lot more than I was giving her. She was buying it on the street.

She told me that her pain was real, but the addiction had become a bigger problem than the pain itself. I went over the concept of addiction versus physical dependence and made sure that she understood the difference. She did. We got Vivian off the opiate pain medication and on Suboxone. Soon after going on Suboxone, her pain went away. Even her stress improved. Vivian, apparently, was more stressed about her addiction than anything else.

I see a lot of patients like Vivian. Many chronic pain patients for whom we really can't find the cause of their pain could be hooked on their pain medications. Yet, we believe them when they say they are in pain. Unless there are obvious signs they are hooked or are abusing pain medications, we feel compelled to treat their pain. Because we never ask them, "How did it make you feel?", we never distinguish those who may be getting hooked versus those who are not. They are usually put on a chronic pain medication regimen. Some will show obvious signs of getting addicted over time. Others don't. I find that the only way I can help these patients is by educating them about what addiction is and why some people get addicted. Only then will they allow me to help them.

Case 16 – Bob A.

Bob was a 28-year-old male who was involved in a car accident on the job a week before I saw him. He was stopped at a light when he was rear-ended.

Bob had neck and low back pain ever since the injury. The pain was localized to the neck as well as the low back. After examining him, the ER physician diagnosed Bob with a whiplash injury to his neck and low back and discharged him on Vicodin and ibuprofen.

His primary care physician referred the patient to see me. Bob was taking a lot more pain medication than his physician felt comfortable with. When I first examined Bob, he seemed to be in moderate pain. There was evidence of some soft tissue injury, but nothing serious.

I explained to Bob the proper use of opiate pain medications as well as the concept of addiction and why anyone gets addicted. Because Bob was in obvious pain, I agreed to help manage his pain. I put him on eight Vicodin a day, but gave him only a week's supply at a time.

After a few weeks, it was obvious that Bob was getting better. He appeared to be in less pain. His range of motion improved and the tenderness subsided. However, his use of pain medication did not decrease. In fact, on one occasion, Bob told me that this was the best he had felt in years, and he did not see why he would ever want to stop the pain pills. I told Bob that this was a trap. What made him feel good at first would eventually turn on him and would become a necessity to just feel normal. I told Bob that he needed to decrease his pain medication so as not to get hooked.

Shortly afterward, Bob was discharged from my care. I had tried to wean him off the pain medication without success. I talked to him on numerous occasions about the proper use of the opiate pain medication and the danger of chasing the euphoric feeling. I told him we could put him on Suboxone to help get him off opiate pain medications. Bob didn't think that he had a problem. I wished him well and discontinued his pain medications.

A few months later, Bob came back to see me. He told me that things were out of control. He was seeing another physician who kept prescribing him more and more pain medications. However, Bob was also buying as much opiates on the street as he could get a hold of. His wife was about to leave him because of his addiction. Bob thought about the drugs all the time. It made him high and he liked it, at first. He now realized that I had been right. He did not like being hooked, although he liked getting hooked. He wanted out.

I helped Bob go on Suboxone, and he did great. By the time he came back to see me, his pain was not an issue. He remained on Suboxone for about six months. We got him off Suboxone without a problem.

A year later, Bob called me. He recently had a kidney stone, and because of this, he was put back on opiate pain medications. He hadn't told his current doctor about his past problem with opiates because he was afraid that his doctor would not give him any pain medication. Again, he liked it. He didn't stop after his kidney stone passed. He kept telling his doctor that he was in pain, and his doctor kept giving him pain pills. Soon afterward, Bob was buying it on the street again. When Bob was back down in the dumps, he called me to get back on Suboxone.

I told Bob that I would put him back on Suboxone on one condition. This time, he must attend NA meetings on a weekly basis as part of his Suboxone program. I also had him read my book. After another six months of Suboxone and meetings, I was able to wean him off Suboxone. I have not heard back from Bob since.

Case 17 – Tina A.

Tina was a 32-year-old stay-at-home mom who had been hooked on opiates for one and a half years before I met her. She was started on Vicodin after her c-section. Tina liked the way it made her feel. After a month, Tina was taken off of the pain pills. However, she found herself buying them on the Internet. Tina initially thought that she could stop any time. However, it soon became clear that she couldn't stop. She had been taking 10–15 Norco 10/325 a day for a few months. She had been trying to quit on her own without success.

Tina heard and read about Suboxone and was interested in going on Suboxone to help get over her opiate addiction. She found me on the www.Suboxone.com website. I went over the concept of addiction versus physical dependence. Tina was hooked. I put her on Suboxone, and she did great.

I bring Tine up because it was really difficult to convince Tina that after one and a half years of being on Suboxone that she should be able to come off it. Tina felt that her life was back on track and everything was going so well. She was afraid that if she came off Suboxone, she would fall right back into her addiction.

Tina never told her husband or her family about getting hooked on pain pills because she was ashamed. I explained to her that she only got hooked on pain pills because it made her feel good, not because there was some intrinsic character flaw in her.

She was the epitome of the girl-next-door, a soccer mom. She was sweet, kind, and personable. She was great with her infant son. If she could get hooked on pain pills, anyone can (if they are genetically susceptible). I gave her my article on addiction and asked her to share it with her husband. I am not sure if she ever did. I also asked her to attend at least one NA meeting. She told me that she would feel awkward. She felt that people who get hooked on drugs are the "low-lifes," the junkies portrayed on TV. She couldn't bear to put herself in the same light. I explained to Tina that that was not the case.

I told Tina that anyone could get addicted if they were genetically susceptible. I told her the only reason why some people get addicted is because of the way the drug makes them feel. Most will never get hooked on anything, but those who are susceptible will get hooked if the brain is stimulated strongly enough. Once hooked, it is difficult to quit on one's own will-power alone.

Case 18 – Betty R.

When I first met her, Betty was an 18-year-old female who got hooked on opiates when she was 13. Betty's boyfriend introduced her to OxyContin and got hooked. Her parents put her through two inpatient drug rehab programs, and she relapsed both times.

By the time I saw her, she was using black tar heroin. Betty was using it intravenously. She had tried to get herself off the opiate many times without success. About two months before she saw me, one of her friends gave her Suboxone, and Betty realized that she was able to stop for the first time. However, when she ran out of Suboxone, she found herself back on heroin.

Betty was living with her parents. She was a sweet, innocent-looking, beautiful blond girl. She could have passed as a poster child for a Sunday School teacher. Her demeanor was not that of someone beaten down by addiction.

She did great on Suboxone until she relapsed a few months later. I bring Betty up to show why Suboxone alone is not the answer. Unfortunately, although Suboxone helps with cravings, unless the patient is ready to get off the drug, it will never prevent that person from relapsing. Sometimes, Suboxone makes it too easy for some patients to quit. They feel great on Suboxone, and soon they forget what it was like to be hooked. They forget the reasons why they wanted out in the first place.

Human memory being what it is, one often forgets the bad things, but remembers the good things. When an addict forgets what it was about being addicted that made her want out, she will relapse because the allure of getting high is still there.

Unfortunately, young people are often victims of this mindset. Although I insist that they write down the reasons why they wanted to quit in the first place and attend weekly NA meetings, they often relapse. Although Betty agreed to attend meetings, she never did. I did not discharge Betty, but after a few failed urine drug screens, Betty stopped showing up for her appointments.

I saw Betty a few years later. Her brother, who had recently gone through an inpatient drug rehab program at their parents' insistence, had overdosed and died. He, apparently, had gone right back to using as soon as he was discharged, and it killed him this time.

Betty was devastated. She had relapsed herself and was using when she came back to see me. She wanted to go back on Suboxone and wanted to stay clean forever this time. I put her back on Suboxone and had her attend meetings. This time, she went. It has been a little over a year since she has gone back on Suboxone. She still attends NA meetings and sees a drug counselor. I recently asked whether she felt that she was ready to come off Suboxone. She told me that she was not. I promised to keep her on Suboxone until she felt she was ready.

Case 19 – Diane A.

Diane was a 35-year-old female who was referred to me by her family physician. Diane has had neck pain on and off for quite some time. She told me that she initially injured her neck from a motorcycle accident seven years earlier. She was thrown from a motorcycle and broke her leg. At first, Diane did not notice any significant neck pain. However, the neck pain came on gradually and never completely went away. The pain was localized to both sides, with some numbness going down her right arm. Diane also complained of headaches associated with her neck pain.

Diane had been taking opiate pain medications for her neck pain for quite some time. She told me that what worked the best for her was the Vicoprofen 7.5 mg tablets and that she usually took about four a day. However, her insurance would not cover Vicoprofen. She told me that Vicodin upset her stomach because of the Tylenol.

The MRI of the cervical spine done in March of that year did not show any significant pathology, including any herniated disc or foraminal stenosis. Diane had gone through months of physical therapy, chiropractic treatment, and massage therapy. She had no family history of drug dependence.

My examination did not show any neurologic deficit. It showed decreased range of motion in the cervical spine along with tight neck muscles and some tenderness on palpation.

The fact that a patient was taking four Vicoprofen 7.5 mg a day, even if it was for quite some time, was not alarming. I agreed to take over her pain management. I went over the concept of addiction versus physical dependence. I gave her my article on addiction. I started her on some simple cervical stretching exercises. She was discharged home with a prescription for one-week supply of her pain medication. I also did a urine drug screen.

Diane called me about a half hour after she left my office. She was calling from her car on her cell phone. She told me that she had started reading my article on addiction and found herself crying. She had pulled over and finished the article. Diane was crying when she told me that everything she had told me earlier in my office was a lie.

She had been hooked on opiate pain pills for some time. She had been getting pain medications from multiple doctors. She was averaging 10–15 Vicoprofen a day—not four. She wanted out, but she was afraid to tell her doctors. She thought that if they found out, they would cut her off without offering any alternative. Diane felt so relieved when she read my article and found out that there might be a way to get her life back. I asked her to come back and see me.

After we put her on Suboxone, Diane did great. She was on Suboxone for about six months and we were able to wean her off Suboxone without a problem. I kept her primary care physician abreast of her confession to me (with her consent). At first she was reluctant, but I explained to her that it was just as important for her to understand what addiction is and why she got hooked as it was for her doctors to understand it.

I bring Diane up to show that many patients are going from doctor to doctor to get pain medication because they are hooked. They don't know that there is a solution to their problem. So they go from doctor to doctor telling lies to get their drugs. When a doctor becomes suspicious that there may be more going on, they move on to another doctor.

This wasn't the first time a patient stood up after belaboring me with a story of how much pain he has and why, when after I explained to him what addiction is, why some people get hooked, and that there are ways to treat this, he then turned around and told me that everything he had told me earlier was a lie and that he would rather go on Suboxone than continue with his drugs.

By this, I am not saying that every chronic pain patient is hooked. I am just saying that many are. By educating our patients about what addiction is, by not being judgmental, and by offering them a way out, one can help those who are addicted get the help they need rather than perpetuating their problems.

Case 20 – Danny E.

Danny was a patient who I first met when he was 38-years-old. Danny had sustained a very serious injury the previous December. He fell in his bathtub and developed a large bleed in his back. Danny had a very complicated hospital course, including liver, kidney, and respiratory failure. He had to undergo emergency evacuation of a blood clot. Danny made a remarkable recovery after being in a coma for almost two weeks. It was a miracle that he survived. Danny was discharged home the following January.

He was walking with a walker and was complaining of weakness in his left leg when I first saw him. The weakness had been attributed to his prolonged bed rest and illness. On our first visit, I picked up motor weakness not only in his left leg but also in both arms. Danny also had increased reflexes in both arms and legs as well as a clonus in both ankles. These are what we call upper motor neuron signs, meaning that he had a spinal cord compression in his neck. I scheduled him for an emergency MRI of his cervical spine, which showed a severe spinal stenosis and a spinal cord injury in his neck. Danny underwent emergency cervical spine surgery to take the pressure off his spinal cord. After the surgery, Danny made a remarkable recovery. Over the next year, he regained his strength and was able to walk without any assistive device.

I saw Danny intermittently over the next eight years. He was always grateful for what I had done for him. He always had a smile on his face. He went through a divorce. He lost his business, retired, and moved to San Juan Island. Danny was being treated by his family physician on the island. He was on a low dose opiate pain medication.

I saw him again in 2005. Danny wanted me to help manage his pain. He was taking eight Vicodin a day. His family physician, who had been managing his pain medications for years, was retiring. Danny wanted me to take over his pain management. I agreed.

The next day, I got a call from Danny's fiancée. She was concerned about his opiate use. After listening to her concerns, I asked her to come in and see me along with

266

Danny. She reluctantly agreed. By then, Danny's urine drug screen results came back. It tested positive for hydrocodone, an ingredient of Vicodin, as well as for cocaine.

It turned out that Danny had been hooked on opiates as well as cocaine for years. Danny admitted that the fall that he had eight years earlier was caused by his opiate use. His last marriage had broken up because of his addiction. He had lost his business due to his addiction.

Danny agreed to go on Suboxone. A month into his sobriety, Danny told me that he had run into his old drug dealer. He told me that he was able to smile and walk away. Danny was on Suboxone for three years. After a year on Suboxone, I suggested trying to wean him off Suboxone, but Danny was too afraid. He felt that Suboxone had given him his life back and was afraid to come off of it. He attended NA meetings at my insistence. After three years, I finally convinced Danny to come off Suboxone. His cravings did not come back.

Conclusion

MY JOURNEY IN TRYING TO understand addiction has not been without missteps. I have learned about addiction only after terrible things happened to my patients or to those around me. I learned how ill-prepared I was to recognize it or deal with it. The more I learned, the more I realized how little I had known.

Everything I have learned about addiction came from observing, listening to my patients, and reading as much as I could about it. Over the years, I learned that most people, including the medical community, do not fully understand this problem. When I've given my article on addiction to my addiction patients, their responses have been overwhelmingly positive. They tell me that everything I have written about addiction is true, that it puts everything in perspective, and it helps them understand their own problem. Over the years, many have asked me to publish my knowledge and insights about addiction, so more people can be helped.

The Current Definition of Addiction

Currently, addiction is defined as "a continued behavior in spite of knowing that such continued behavior will harm oneself." It is characterized by "the lack of self-control and feeling of helplessness in spite of such knowledge." Unfortunately, although this describes the behavior that we call addiction, it does not explain why it happens.

A Better Definition of Addiction

Addiction is a disease of the brain that happens:
- when a person who is genetically susceptible to a drug gets exposed to that drug,
- the drug elicits such a highly enjoyable experience, the true high, that will make the person want to chase such a feeling,
- when such overstimulation of the pleasure spot is repeated over and over, the brain becomes rewired, and over time a craving for the drug sets in,
- then the behavior that we now call addiction follows, and what we see makes sense.

We have failed to understand addiction because we saw it simply as a set of behaviors rather than what was going on inside the brain. No one asked the right question! **How did the drug make you feel?**

To summarize, addiction is a disease, an illness. There is a genetic basis for addiction. This genetic variation makes drugs affect people differently. The reason why anyone gets addicted is because the drug makes the person highly euphoric (at first). Addiction happens when you chase that euphoric feeling. With repeated excitation of that pleasure spot in your brain, you get hooked. The brain of someone who is addicted to a drug changes over time; an increased number of dopamine receptors in the brain explains the craving. Then the craving, which is the hallmark of any addiction, sets in.

This craving is stronger than the desire for life itself and cannot be reasoned with. It brings about the destructive behavior that we call addiction. It is not a lack of willpower that prevents Johnny from stopping his destructive behavior. Some will say it takes a life-altering event or for an addict to hit rock bottom for him to finally want to get off that ride. The hold the craving creates is that strong.

The reason addicts finally want to quit is because once they are truly hooked, they feel more misery than joy. The drug that made the person happy eventually takes away that happiness. Not only it is harder and harder to achieve the same high, one loses the ability to feel happy with everyday activities that used to give one joy. A person who is truly addicted is not a happy person because he cannot find any joy outside of the drug. Once addiction takes hold, one's personality changes because of the unhappiness. However, even when the addict finally wants to get off the roller coaster ride of the highs and lows the addiction brings, the craving makes it difficult for him to stop.

However, with advances in science and with medications such as Suboxone and Vivitrol, we can finally offer hope. Suboxone and Vivitrol can help squelch the craving so it is easier to quit. However, these medications are not enough. If you make it easier for someone to quit without making that person understand and remember the reasons why he wanted to quit in the first place, he is likely to relapse.

Once an addict actually gets the demons to go away and gets his life back, the only thing that will prevent him from relapsing is how strong his memory is about what it was like when he was at the mercy of his addiction. Bad memories often fade, whereas good memories linger. However, if one forgets the bad memories, the price of relapse is too high. The only way to keep the bad memories alive is by revisiting them on a regular basis.

"Don't judge someone unless you have walked a mile in his shoes."- Anonymous

We need to treat addiction with compassion and understanding. Unless you know what it was like for an addict, you shouldn't judge them. We need to educate people so we can help those who are just starting out on their journey down the path of addiction to stop before it's too late, or to help those who are already addicted find a way out of their addiction.

We need to stop criminalizing addiction and offer treatment instead. In order to do this, we need to get past our Hollywood stereotypes of what an addict is and understand that addiction crosses all ages, races, sexes, and socioeconomic barriers. It is not only more humane to treat nonviolent drug offenders in a drug rehab program rather than incarcerating them, but it is also more cost-effective. It makes no sense to subject these people to the three-strikes laws that have overcrowded our courts and prisons.

Hopefully, by shedding light on what addiction is, we can have more intelligent discourse about our drug policy, the war on drugs, and drug prevention. Instead of telling people to "Just Say No," we can explain to them that, although most people will not get addicted to drugs, some can. And the reason why anyone gets addicted is because of the way the drug makes him feel extremely good at first, but such euphoria will eventually lead to sheer despair.

Prevention

There is a lag time between when the brain is first aroused to when the craving finally sets in, and with proper education, we can teach people not to chase such a feeling. For example, if a young person understands that if he feels like a million bucks after a few drinks, this means he is genetically susceptible to becoming addicted to alcohol, he can stop before it's too late. Such knowledge can help him understand that, if he continues on this course, he will become his alcoholic parent(s). Knowing this, he can stop before addiction takes hold.

The best way to prevent someone from getting addicted in the first place is not with scare tactics, but with knowledge of what addiction is and what a true high is. When it comes to talking about addiction, we have made the mistake of telling people that anyone can get hooked on drugs and that everybody's response to drugs is the same. The image of a frying egg in a skillet and an actor saying, "This is your brain on drugs!" conveys such false messages.

But the worst thing we have done wrong is we have misrepresented the high. The high is always portrayed as an altered state of mind where someone feels dopey, intoxicated, and out of control. Nothing could be further from the truth. The true high is anything that artificially makes you happy, sometimes extremely happy! With any high, there is a heightened sense of awareness at first. With certain drugs (downers), a state of intoxication can follow the high, but it is never what an addict is chasing.

Because of this misconception, someone who smokes pot and gets dopey thinks he is high. Because of that, when he finds another drug extremely pleasurable, he does not realize he is getting high. He just thinks, "Hey, I feel great! Why would I ever want to stop?" It's only when the craving sets in does he realize there is a problem. Had he known that the dopey feeling was not the high, but that happy feeling was, he could have had the foresight not to chase that feeling.

Key points to teach everyone about addiction:
1. Most people can't get hooked on most drugs, but some can become hooked on some drugs.
2. People can have a night-and-day different reaction to the same drug.
3. The high is not what the media has been telling you. The high is not an altered state of mind or a dopey, intoxicated, or out-of-control feeling. The high is anything that artificially makes you happy, sometimes extremely happy.
4. The high produces the same chemical reaction in your brain as sex. It releases dopamine, the feel-good neurotransmitter. The drugs just do it much quicker and more intensely than sex. As with sex, the high produces excitement and extreme joy, not sedation.
5. If you chase that happy feeling, the drug will eventually rewire your brain and you will start having cravings for that drug and will become enslaved by the drug.
6. Because there is a time lag between your first exposure to a drug (and after repeated stimulation of that pleasure spot) and when the craving finally sets in, one can prevent oneself from getting hooked by not chasing that high.

Most people who got hooked on drugs did not realize that

they were getting hooked early on because they did not realize that they were getting high; they equated the high
with that dopey feeling. Had they known that the extreme
joy was the high, I believe most would not have chased it.

Unfortunately, there is a lot of misinformation out there
about addiction. In this book, I have attempted to bring
together what I consider to be the underlying truth beneath many myths about addiction and to sort out the
truth from the half-truths and misunderstandings.

Since I have never suffered from addiction myself, I
had to learn about it from others. At first, this was out of
guilt after a patient I was treating for pain overdosed and
died on the pain pills I was giving him. Guilt is a powerful
motivator. The drive to learn as much as I could about this
disease came out of a feeling of necessity and desperation
to help my patients. In the end, they were the ones who
taught me. Being an outside observer and listening to my
patients, I began to understand their problems with a
clearer picture. Sometimes it takes an outsider to look at
something from a different perspective to help make out
the forest for the trees.

This book is an attempt to clarify the muddy discussions surrounding this often-misunderstood subject. The
most popular current theory on addiction is that it is a
maladjusted coping mechanism to deal with one's underlying stress or ills. In no way am I suggesting that what I
have written here is the whole truth. The truth does not
change, but our understanding of it invariably does.

I apologize to those patients (and their families) whom
I have failed from getting addicted, and to those who have
died as a result of their addiction. I hope this book will help
others avoid the pitfalls of addiction as well as help give
physicians the tools they need to help those patients who
are addicted. There are many lost souls out there looking
for someone to lend them a helping hand in conquering
their demons. I have looked deep down into the depth of
the despair they have dug for themselves and have helped

some find their way out of the abyss. When this happens, the joy is truly great, and a life can be saved.

Our journey in understanding this disease is not done. Even though I have laid out what addiction is and why it happens, there are a lot of unanswered questions. It is my hope that this book will offer new insights for some, but more importantly, I hope that it will stimulate heated discussions about this subject that will help bring this subject to a greater public awareness that in the end will help all of us understand it better.

With empathy, caring, and better understanding, I do believe we can make a difference in the lives of many people who are addicted or are on their way to becoming addicted. But most importantly, when we truly understand addiction, we can help others understand it so that they don't fall victim to this devastating illness.

Yes, knowledge gives you power. With true understanding about addiction, we can finally win the war on drugs! It can't be done by trying to cut off the supply, but only by drying up the demand. It can't be accomplished with scare tactics or telling people that "drugs are bad!" It can only be done by teaching everyone the truth about addiction and what the true high looks like. Only through education can we accomplish this! Let's change the world for the better!

Kyle Oh, M.D.

Definitions

Agonist

An agonist, in our context, refers to a chemical that binds to the receptor and stimulates or releases the neurotransmitter, thus enhancing its natural effects. All naturally occurring and synthetic opiates can be deemed opioid agonists.

Addiction

A continued behavior in spite of knowing that the continued behavior will harm oneself. It is defined by a lack of self-control and feelings of helplessness in the face of such continued behavior.

Amphetamine

Commonly referred to as "Speed," amphetamine is a stimulant. It was once widely used as an appetite suppressant to promote weight loss. Its medical use has since been relegated to the treatment of ADD/ADHD, attention deficit disorders, and narcolepsy. Among ADD/ADHD patients, amphetamine seems to have an opposite effect than in most people. Instead of making them hyper, it seems to calm them down and allow them to become more focused. It is strictly regulated, and its recreational use as well as its use for weight reduction is banned.

Antagonist

A substance that binds to the receptor site, but blocks the release of the neurotransmitter. Opioid antagonists, naloxone and naltrexone, bind to the opioid receptors and effectively block the receptor and prevent them from binding to opiates and endorphins.

Barbiturates
Central nervous system (CNS) depressants derived from barbituric acid are used as anesthetics and sedatives. They are commonly referred as "downers" and "acids." Their use in a clinical setting has been mostly replaced by benzodiazepines due to safety profiles. The most commonly known barbiturates are Phenobarbital (which is still used to treat seizure disorders), Pentothal, and Quaalude.

Benzodiazepines
Often just called "benzos," these are a class of medications known as hypnotics or sedatives and tranquilizers. They exhibit sedating and calming effects on a person. Most commonly used benzos include Xanax (alprazolam), Valium (diazepam), Ativan (lorazepam), Klonopin (clonazepam), Restoril (temazepam), and Librium (chlordiazepoxide).

Cocaine
Cocaine (benzoylmethyl ecgonine) is an extract from the leaves of a coca plant.[1] It is a CNS stimulant that acts as a dopamine re-uptake inhibitor. In other words, it prevents the reabsorption of dopamine once it is released. Whereas opiates release dopamine, cocaine prevents dopamine from being re-absorbed. Although the mechanism of action is different, the effect that opiates and cocaine produce can be similar; they both produce increased levels of dopamine in the brain. Although cocaine is not an opiate, the two are often lumped together as narcotics.

Dopamine
The feel-good neurotransmitter in our brains. It is responsible for making us content, happy, and euphoric (at different levels). It is responsible for rewarding those behaviors that are usually good for us. Very high levels are associated with schizophrenia, whereas very low levels are associated with Parkinson's disease, where there is a lack of emotion.

278

Delirium Tremens (DTs)

A symptom of withdrawal from alcohol, benzodiazepines, or barbiturates. DTs can be fatal, usually as a result of seizure disorders. The major difference between opiate withdrawal and DTs is that DTs can involve hallucinations, both tactile and visual. Otherwise, a person going through DTs will experience a lot of the same physical symptoms, such as the shakes, tachycardia, and elevated blood pressure, as seen with opiate withdrawal.

Ecstasy (MDMA)

A street name for MDMA (3,4-Methylenedioxymethamphetamine) and a "date rape" drug. It is a derivative of methamphetamine. It is a stimulant as well as a mild hallucinogenic. It is thought to enhance feelings of intimacy and reduce inhibition, fear, and anxiety. It was first used in couples' counseling. It has since been banned by all UN nations.

Endorphins

Naturally occurring opioids that your brain produces. The brain has natural chemicals that help alleviate pain as well as produce a sense of well-being and euphoria. One of the ways acupuncture has been shown to provide pain relief is by releasing these natural endorphins in the brain. This was accidentally discovered when patients who received pain relief from acupuncture treatments had these effects reversed by being given naloxone, an opiate antagonist.

Heroin

Heroin is an opiate synthesized from morphine. When used intravenously, it crosses the blood-brain barrier much more quickly than morphine because of its acetyl group. Heroin binds strongly to the mu-opiate receptors. It breaks down into morphine, which also binds highly to the mu-opiate receptors. When someone is using heroin, what we see in the urine drug screen is the morphine, not heroin. There is also no metabolite of morphine, hydromorphone, evident in the urine drug screen. When someone is using morphine, the urine drug screen shows both morphine and its metabolite, hydromorphone.

Hyperalgesia

Unlike tolerance, hyperalgesia describes a state when prolonged exposure to opiate pain medications actually seems to increase the intensity of pain in some patients. Often, it also becomes generalized and spreads. It is a controversial topic, and one that is often used to describe why some people's pain is never adequately controlled once they go on opiate pain medications. The basis of hyperalgesia is thought to be an increase in the number of opiate receptors in the brains of those patients who become addicted.

Methamphetamine

A psychoactive stimulant, commonly referred to as "meth" or "crystal meth." As the name suggests, its molecular structure is very similar to that of amphetamine and so they share common properties. The only current medically licensed use of methamphetamine is a Schedule II drug called Desoxyn used for treatment of ADHD and exogenous obesity.

Mesolimbic (dopaminergic) pathway

One of the neural pathways in the brain, which is thought to be responsible for pleasurable feelings associated with rewarding those behaviors that are usually good, such as eating and sex. It is one of the four major pathways where dopamine is found. All addictions are believed to involve hyper-stimulation of this pathway.

Morphine

One of the naturally occurring opiates found in the opium plant. It is the most abundant opiate found in the plant. It strongly binds to the mu-opiate receptors. It is the drug that all other opiates are compared to. Unless the substance, regardless of its similarity in chemical structure to other opiates, creates similar effects on the CNS as those of morphine, it is not classified as an opiate.

Naloxone and Naltrexone

Both are opioid antagonists. Naloxone (Narcan) is a short-acting opioid antagonist and is used in emergencies to reverse the effects that opiate overdose has on respiratory and CNS depression. Naloxone strongly binds to the μ- opioid receptor and weakly to the κ- and δ-opioid receptors. It also blocks the effects of endorphins. Naltrexone is a long-acting opioid antagonist. It binds strongly at μ- and κ-opioid receptors and, to a lesser extent, to δ-opioid receptors.

Narcotics

Although narcotics and opiates are often referred to interchangeably, they are not the same thing. All opiates are narcotics, and all opiates are derivatives (natural or synthetic) of opium. These include morphine, codeine, hydrocodone, oxycodone, oxymorphone, hydromorphone, and fentanyl. The US Drug Enforcement Agency often refers to all illicit drugs under the Controlled Substance Act as narcotics. However, although cocaine, pot, and methamphetamines are often classified as narcotics, they are not opiates.

Opioids and Opiates

Often referred to interchangeably. They both refer to chemical substances that have a morphine-like action on the brain.

Overdose

This occurs as a result of CNS and respiratory suppression. At high enough doses, opiates can cause extreme sedation and suppress breathing to the point where the body is not getting enough oxygen, and death ensues. Narcan (naloxone) can reverse these side effects.

Benzodiazepines, barbiturates, and pot (also CNS suppressants) can also cause respiratory failure, but Narcan does not work in these cases. Only manual or mechanical respirator aid such as with a ventilator can help the person until the level of the drug falls below the point that he starts to breathe on his own.

Overdoses on stimulants like cocaine, amphetamine, and crystal meth result in extremely high blood pressure that can cause stroke or heart attack.

Physical Dependence
Characterized by withdrawal symptoms when a substance is suddenly discontinued or decreased. Anyone who has been on opiates for a prolonged period will be physically dependent. The same can be said for prolonged exposure to caffeine or sleeping pills. However, because a person develops physical dependence on a drug does not necessarily mean that the person is addicted to it. Addiction is psychological, not physical.

Pseudoaddiction
Exhibition of all signs of addiction but no addiction is present. A patient with pseudoaddiction may hoard medications, call for early refills, shop around for doctors, etc. Pseudoaddiction occurs when the patient's doctor is not adequately managing the patient's pain, usually because there is a lack of trust between the patient and the doctor. It is iatrogenic. The patient's "addiction" disappears once the patient's pain is adequately managed.

How do we know that these patients are not addicted? Because once their pain is properly managed, the addiction behaviors go away. One difference between a person who is addicted versus one is exhibiting pseudoaddiction is that in those who are addicted, escalating pain medications usually does not make the above behaviors go away. Rather, it may increase such behaviors.

Tolerance
Characterized by decreased effectiveness of a drug over time. It only happens with oral medication when one's liver learns to break down the ingested medication faster. A good example of this is chronic alcohol use. Those who are just starting to drink may get drunk after one or two beers, but after some time and repeated use, it may take a six-

pack to get drunk. Reduction in effectiveness stabilizes over time and does not usually continue to decline unless the dosage is increased.

Although the CNS effects of orally ingested opiates occur over time, tolerance to its most common side effects, mainly constipation, does not occur. Constipation is directly dependent on the dosage and the strength of the opiate. When opiates are taken non-orally (i.e., intravenously or transdermally), constipation is much less common or severe.

Withdrawal symptoms

Categorized as physical and psychological. Everyone who has taken drugs for an extended period experiences physical symptoms, whereas the psychological symptoms occur only in those who become addicted.

Physical

Consists of flu-like symptoms, agitation, feelings of doom, elevated blood pressure, increased pulse, dilated pupils, diarrhea, runny nose, goose bumps, and pain (the degree of which may vary according to whether the patient is addicted or not).

Psychological

For those who are hooked on opiates, the physical withdrawal symptoms are followed by psychological withdrawal symptoms. These consist of lethargy and somnolence. One with such symptoms has no energy and can't get up in the morning. The drug was giving him the kick he needed to get up and get going.

---

[1] Aggrawal, Anil. *Narcotic Drugs*. National Book Trust, India (1995), p. 52-3. ISBN 81-237-1383-5

Addiction Handout

This is a handout that I give to my patients.

Addiction is defined as "a continued behavior in spite of knowing that the continued course will harm oneself." It is characterized by "the lack of self-control and feeling of helplessness in the face of such continued behavior." While this describes addiction after it has taken hold, it does not explain why it happens.

There are many misconceptions about addiction. We have moralized it by saying that drugs are bad and that we should "Just Say No" to drugs. We have equated the behavior with the disease. We confuse abuse with addiction. We have also misled people. For example, when an actor shows a frying egg in a skillet and says, "This is your brain on drugs," besides trying to scare you, the message it sends is that anyone can get hooked on drugs and that everyone's reaction to drugs is the same, which is false. Only about 10–15% of the population is thought to be susceptible to opiate addiction. The rest of us are immune. And every drug addiction has a different genetic basis.

The worst thing that we have done wrong when it comes to discussing addiction is the way the high has been

285

portrayed. What does an image of someone who is high look like on screen? He looks "stoned" with a glazed look in his eyes, dopey, intoxicated, and passing out. Even the term *dope* is synonymous with illicit drugs because most people think that's what these drugs do—make you dopey. Because kids think that anything that alters their mind gets them high, they think they are high when they smoke pot. However, most people do not get high on pot. Most just get intoxicated. So when a drug makes someone feel really good, he doesn't realize he is high. Dopey is not high. Happy is!

The high produces the same chemical reaction in your brain that sex does. It just does it much more quickly and more intensely. It releases a chemical in your brain called dopamine, the feel-good neurotransmitter. That's why one wants to chase that feeling. It's only when such a euphoric feeling is chased and repeated that the craving sets in over time and addiction takes hold.

If you have ever seen the movie *When a Man Loves a Woman* with Meg Ryan and Andy Garcia, there is a scene when Meg Ryan's character, an alcoholic at the end of her addiction, stands up in her first AA meeting and describes her initial reaction to alcohol that tells us why anyone becomes addicted to anything. She stands up and says, "When I was 15, I had my first beer and I liked it. So, I had another and another." Most of us do not remember our first drinking experience because it was not very memorable. Alcohol, for most of us, is an acquired taste. However, for those who are susceptible to becoming addicted to alcohol, the first taste of alcohol produced such a highly euphoric and enjoyable feeling that they remember it vividly years later.

The reason why some people don't understand why others get addicted is because they do not have the same response to these substances. They say, "Gee, all it does for me is makes me groggy and nauseous." They think that others must have the same experience as they do. Why can't Johnny just quit? Of course, if Johnny had the same experience as they did, he wouldn't have gotten hooked. On the other hand, if they felt the same way that Johnny did, they might have gotten hooked as well.

Because addiction is based on genetic predisposition, we should treat addiction as a medical illness rather than a character flaw. It is not a weak mind or a lack of moral compass that leads some people to fall victim to addiction, but rather a medical illness that brings about the behavior that we call addiction. Addiction crosses all ages, races, sexes, and socioeconomic lines. For those who are genetically predisposed, it is a lifelong condition; one does not become immune to it with age.

Once you become addicted, you are no longer in control of it; it controls you. What an addict wants most is usually to get off the roller coaster ride of "highs" and "lows" that addiction brings. However, he feels helpless and is often unable to stop the escalating pattern of addiction despite knowing what is happening.

Early on, before a person becomes addicted and loses control, he may not want to stop because he feels good. I often hear early on from a patient who is getting addicted, "Why should I stop when it makes me feel so good?" Later on, after addiction has taken full control and the patient feels powerless, I hear "I don't want it anymore, but give me more."

If something makes you feel that good, what's wrong with continuing it as long as you can get a steady supply of it? The problem is that when the brain is overstimulated too often, the number of dopamine receptors in the brain will increase over time. This is thought to be the reason behind cravings, as well as the reason why normal things that used to give one pleasure no longer do. An addict no longer finds pleasure in the simple things in life, like eating or sex. It changes the person. Family members often notice that their loved one is no longer himself.

Unlike others who have gotten addicted to street drugs after experimenting with them, a patient who gets addicted to opiate pain medication may not realize he is getting addicted early on. Because he thinks that dopey feeling is the high, when the drug makes him feel good, he doesn't realize he is getting high until it's too late. Only when he starts having cravings for the drug does he realize that something is wrong.

If one understands addiction and its early warning signs, one can avoid getting addicted by decreasing or stopping the opiate medication. If you take pain medications below the level of your pain, the chance that you will get addicted is much lower.

However, for those who get hooked on opiate pain medications, once they are hooked, their pain never goes away. In fact, the more pain medications you take, the worse the pain seems to get. It's only when addiction is brought under control that the pain settles down. This concept is called hyperalgesia.

Common early signs that you may be at risk for opiate addiction
(Mnemonic is SIG)

- Does a low dose of opiate **stimulate** or energize you rather than sedate you? Do you act like the Energizer bunny when you take it?
- Does it cause **insomnia**? Are you cleaning the house in the middle of the night after you took a pill that you thought would help you sleep?
- Did these medications make you feel real "**good**," euphoric, or high (at first)?
- Do you think that this is the best thing that God put on this green earth?
- Does it make you feel younger?
- Is it better than sex? Or does it make sex better (at first)?
- Does it promise you the moon?
- Does it make you feel better than you should, even if there was no pain?

Unless something makes you feel good (I mean, really good), why would anyone get addicted?

Normal vs. Abnormal Responses

Remember that some drugs, such as alcohol, opiates, and pot, are downers, whereas other drugs, such as cocaine, amphetamine, and crystal meth, are uppers. For those who are not susceptible to these drugs, the downers act as sedatives right off the bat. They intoxicate us or calm us down. For those who are susceptible to these drugs, they act as stimulants and make them feel euphoric. Even for those who can get high on these drugs, eventually sedation may overtake them as the euphoria fades, but sedation is not the initial response.

For drugs that are uppers, those who are not susceptible to these drugs become stimulated and energized by them, but these drugs do not produce any euphoria. In fact, at high doses, most feel wired and jittery and may find the experience very unpleasant. However, for those who are susceptible to these drugs, they can produce extreme euphoria. For them, jitteriness only follows their high. Those who are coming down from their high from an upper do not become intoxicated but jittery and wired.

Suboxone/Subutex (buprenorphine HCl)

Are you are hooked? For those patients who are hooked on opiates (whether prescription medications or street drugs), now we have an effective treatment option. Before Suboxone and Subutex came on the market, the only medication available to treat opiate addiction was methadone. However, methadone was a dismal failure, because when the patient stops methadone, the craving comes back.

With Suboxone and Subutex, we can finally treat withdrawal symptoms as well as cravings. The therapeutic ingredient in both Suboxone and Subutex is buprenorphine. Buprenorphine is a partial opiate agonist, which means that it binds to the opiate receptors without triggering them. Thus, it eliminates the craving the brain has for opiates without triggering the release of chemicals that gives rise to the feeling of euphoria and high. When treating withdrawal symptoms, patients can be weaned off Suboxone/Subutex in a matter of weeks. When treating addiction, patients need them for 6–12 months.

If you have been off opiates for more than one month, and you decide to go back to using them for whatever reason, please do not go back to the same dose that you were using when you stopped—IT CAN KILL YOU! The tolerance that you developed over time is now gone. That 80 mg of OxyContin that you used to smoke on a regular basis can now kill you. Unfortunately, many of my patients learned this the hard way.

By the way, now there is a monthly injectable treatment for alcoholism and opiate addiction. It is called Vivitrol. It is a monthly injection of medication called naltrexone. The naltrexone gets the craving under control for both alcohol and opiates.

Relapse Prevention

Why do some people relapse? If you have a monkey on your back that tells you that you must get high, it's not a choice. No matter how strong your willpower, you may fail. All it takes is one dose to send you down the spiraling path of addiction. However, when you wake up and there is no craving, then whether you decide to get high or not is a choice; a bad choice, but still a choice. Suboxone gives patients a second chance. It gets rid of the craving. Why, then, would anyone go back?

The reason why many addicts relapse is because they forget how bad it was when they were truly hooked. They remember how good it felt getting high, but forget the misery of being addicted. For most things, it is better to forget and move on. However, for addiction, the price you pay for forgetting can be too high. Often, an addict who relapses pays for his mistake with his life. Those who attend Narcotics Anonymous (NA) or Alcoholics Anonymous (AA) meetings do better because the meetings remind them of how bad addiction truly was. You can find local meetings by going to the www.AA.org or www.NA.org websites.

Useful Links

http://www.aa.org/	Alcoholics Anonymous
http://www.na.org/	Narcotics Anonymous
http://www.asam.org/	American Society of Addiction Medicine
http://www.samhsa.gov/	Substance Abuse and Mental Health Service Administration
http://www.aapmr.org/	American Academy of Physical Medicine and Rehabilitation
http://www.pain.com/	Pain.com
http://www.ampainsoc.org/	American Pain Society
http://www.aapainmanage.org/	American Academy of Pain Management
http://www.spine-health.com/	Spine health site
http://www.spine.org/	North American Spine Society
http://www.suboxone.com/	Suboxone web site
http://www.painmed.org	American Academy of Pain Medicine
http://www.theacpa.org	American Chronic Pain Association
http://www.painfoundation.org	American Pain Foundation
http://www.painconnection.org	The National Pain Foundation
http://www.rsdsa.org	RSD/CRPS Association
http://www.KirklandSpinecare.com	my website

291

Index

CPSIA information can be obtained
at www.ICGtesting.com
Printed in the USA
LVOW04s1508291015

460297LV00024B/1142/P

9 781497 446083